RELIGION AND SOCIETY

RELIGIOUS EDUCATION

PERSPECTIVES, TEACHING STRATEGIES AND CHALLENGES

RELIGION AND SOCIETY

Additional books and e-books in this series can be found on Nova's website under the Series tab.

RELIGION AND SOCIETY

RELIGIOUS EDUCATION

PERSPECTIVES, TEACHING STRATEGIES AND CHALLENGES

RICHARD COUDERT
EDITOR

Copyright © 2019 by Nova Science Publishers, Inc.

All rights reserved. No part of this book may be reproduced, stored in a retrieval system or transmitted in any form or by any means: electronic, electrostatic, magnetic, tape, mechanical photocopying, recording or otherwise without the written permission of the Publisher.

We have partnered with Copyright Clearance Center to make it easy for you to obtain permissions to reuse content from this publication. Simply navigate to this publication's page on Nova's website and locate the "Get Permission" button below the title description. This button is linked directly to the title's permission page on copyright.com. Alternatively, you can visit copyright.com and search by title, ISBN, or ISSN.

For further questions about using the service on copyright.com, please contact:
Copyright Clearance Center
Phone: +1-(978) 750-8400   Fax: +1-(978) 750-4470   E-mail: info@copyright.com.

NOTICE TO THE READER

The Publisher has taken reasonable care in the preparation of this book, but makes no expressed or implied warranty of any kind and assumes no responsibility for any errors or omissions. No liability is assumed for incidental or consequential damages in connection with or arising out of information contained in this book. The Publisher shall not be liable for any special, consequential, or exemplary damages resulting, in whole or in part, from the readers' use of, or reliance upon, this material. Any parts of this book based on government reports are so indicated and copyright is claimed for those parts to the extent applicable to compilations of such works.

Independent verification should be sought for any data, advice or recommendations contained in this book. In addition, no responsibility is assumed by the Publisher for any injury and/or damage to persons or property arising from any methods, products, instructions, ideas or otherwise contained in this publication.

This publication is designed to provide accurate and authoritative information with regard to the subject matter covered herein. It is sold with the clear understanding that the Publisher is not engaged in rendering legal or any other professional services. If legal or any other expert assistance is required, the services of a competent person should be sought. FROM A DECLARATION OF PARTICIPANTS JOINTLY ADOPTED BY A COMMITTEE OF THE AMERICAN BAR ASSOCIATION AND A COMMITTEE OF PUBLISHERS.

Additional color graphics may be available in the e-book version of this book.

Library of Congress Cataloging-in-Publication Data

ISBN: 978-1-53615-832-8

Published by Nova Science Publishers, Inc. † New York

CONTENTS

Preface		vii
Chapter 1	The Tacit Dimension in Religious Education *Deborah Court*	1
Chapter 2	An Ecological Model for the Encounter of Identities in the Religious State Kindergarten in Israel *Orna Schneider*	19
Chapter 3	Sharing Christian Spirituality at Secular Universities *Nuria Toledano*	55
Bibliography		77
Related Nova Publications		271
Index		275

PREFACE

Religious Education: Perspectives, Teaching Strategies and Challenges attempts to conceptualize the depth and complexity of religious education through Michael Polanyi's notions of personal knowledge and the tacit dimension of knowledge.

In Israel, some non-religious Jewish families enroll their children in kindergartens of the state religious education system, even though they do not belong to the mainstream religious community. The authors offer an ethnographic study of the sociological-educational processes taking place in these kindergartens.

The closing chapter discusses the possibilities for learning from Christian spirituality in the framework of a post-modern European university.

Chapter 1 - Arguably more than any other field of education, religious education involves and addresses the whole person. Knowledge, skills, attitudes, belief and feeling are interwoven; hearts, minds and souls are called upon to engage. Much of religious education happens in the moment, in interaction between teacher, student and text. This chapter attempts to conceptualize this depth and complexity through Michael Polanyi's notions of personal knowledge and the tacit dimension of knowledge. Polanyi intended these ideas to encompass much more than factual and procedural knowledge. His ideas offer a way in to unpacking religious education. Since

Polanyi's work was published in the late 1950's and early 1960's, scholars in many fields, notably teacher education, have built on and expanded Polanyi's concepts and applied them to their own fields. This chapter follows in this tradition. In the first section Polanyi's work is reviewed. The second section briefly examines how educationists have applied Polanyi's work to teachers' professional knowledge, developing the concept of teachers' personal practical knowledge. The third section builds on the first two and presents a conception of the tacit dimension in religious education, the dimension where knowledge, faith and spiritual striving are intertwined. Finally, suggestions are offered as to how this conception might be applied to religious education in teaching, teacher preparation and curriculum development.

Chapter 2 - One influence on the shaping of community identity is the presence of the 'other'. In Israel some non-religious (secular) Jewish families enroll their children in kindergartens of the state religious education system (SRES), even though they do not belong to the mainstream religious, the Modern Orthodox (M.O), community. This chapter offers an ethnographic study, using ecological systems theory, of the sociological-educational processes taking place in these kindergartens. Findings point to the creation of three diverse educational patterns that reflect a wide variance, to the point of creating contradictory patterns: the pattern of religious hegemonies- glorification of the Modern Orthodox identity and exclusion of the secular identity; the pattern of respect - preserving the categories of religious identity while applying strategies of respect to the secular appropriation of religious spaces; and an illusory multi-identity pattern in which glorification of secular identity and exclusion of religious identity takes place. The variety of patterns established in which identities are pushed out occurs due to administrative and pedagogical autonomy in the kindergartens in Israel. On the one hand, the varied and even opposing patterns point to a pluralistic educational system that allows new members to integrate into the community without posing a threat; on the other hand, the differences constitute a disadvantage to the educational system. Placing the teachers in a position of power has led to a rupture in the religious boundaries of the SRES kindergarten, leading to a creation of patterns of identity formation that are at variance with the core religious identity of the MO education system to which the kindergartens belong.

Chapter 3 - This chapter discusses the possibilities opened up for learning from Christian spirituality in the framework of a post-modern European university. On the one hand, the study is framed within the current debates around the purpose and meaning of the public – secular – University. On the other hand, it deals with the challenges that modern universities are facing for attending students' religious needs. The insights come from an initiative undertaken by a Spanish university with the aim of enlivening the commitments of the youth with the nature and demands of ultimate questions. The study suggests that introducing religious insights in the context of a secular education is an area that is by no means easy to approach, but where there are opportunities to draw bridges between reason and religious spirituality.

In: Religious Education
Editor: Richard Coudert

ISBN: 978-1-53615-832-8
© 2019 Nova Science Publishers, Inc.

Chapter 1

THE TACIT DIMENSION IN RELIGIOUS EDUCATION

Deborah Court[*]
Bar-Ilan University, Ramat-Gan, Israel

ABSTRACT

Arguably more than any other field of education, religious education involves and addresses the whole person. Knowledge, skills, attitudes, belief and feeling are interwoven; hearts, minds and souls are called upon to engage. Much of religious education happens in the moment, in interaction between teacher, student and text. This chapter attempts to conceptualize this depth and complexity through Michael Polanyi's notions of personal knowledge and the tacit dimension of knowledge. Polanyi intended these ideas to encompass much more than factual and procedural knowledge. His ideas offer a way in to unpacking religious education. Since Polanyi's work was published in the late 1950's and early 1960's, scholars in many fields, notably teacher education, have built on and expanded Polanyi's concepts and applied them to their own fields. This chapter follows in this tradition. In the first section Polanyi's work is reviewed. The second section briefly examines how educationists have

---

[*] Corresponding Author's E-mail: deborah.court@biu.ac.il.

applied Polanyi's work to teachers' professional knowledge, developing the concept of teachers' personal practical knowledge. The third section builds on the first two and presents a conception of the tacit dimension in religious education, the dimension where knowledge, faith and spiritual striving are intertwined. Finally, suggestions are offered as to how this conception might be applied to religious education in teaching, teacher preparation and curriculum development.

Keywords: knowledge, Polanyi, religious, spiritual, tacit, teaching

INTRODUCTION

Many religious educators know how hard it can be to engage young people in religious instruction. Adolescents especially may be a hard group to teach, careening as they are through stages of identity formation, physical changes and sexual maturity, swings between altruism and cynicism, and underneath it all an earnest seeking for meaning in a confusing world. Considerable faith-based literature exists on what to teach and what values to espouse. There is research on the relation of religious education to government policy and social justice, and on how religious education is undertaken in various countries. There are some studies of young people's relationship to prayer; these studies are often survey-based (Robbins and Francis 2005) and lack richness. Qualitative studies (Collins-Mayo 2008) portray more of individuals' experience of prayer. Yet overall, we have little understanding of how young people experience religious education, how they understand, feel and evaluate their religious instruction, and whether and how it reaches them on a meaningful level. Our lack of research knowledge is, "to some degree, a simple lack of interest and attention among sociologists. But the problem also stems from failing to put useful religion questions on many good surveys of youth, which typically understand and measure religion in narrow and deficient terms" (Smith, Faris, Denton and Regnerus 2003, 113-114). This narrow research approach stems in turn from inadequate conceptualization of the area to be researched. Some studies link religion and spirituality, and these may come closer to a rich conceptualization. Perhaps because of the sensitivity and fluidity of children's spirituality, such studies are often conducted with older students (for example, Locum at el 2016, who studied the intersection between religion, spirituality and education among university students). Studies of younger children face particular ethical and methodological challenges; nonetheless, we need such studies.

What kind of research could help us understand the inner religious world of a young person, in order to engage with it in our teaching? What kinds of curriculum and teaching could engage young people's souls? We ourselves, researchers, curriculum developers and teachers, are seekers after religious depth and meaning. This is a lifelong quest; researchers and religious educators may (or may not) be a little farther out in the choppy sea, but we are in the same boat as the young people we wish to teach and inspire. And while this existential condition of our humanity will ever remain thus, we can perhaps steer into calmer, deeper waters if we can go some way toward conceptualizing the goal that we all seek. Conceptualization of this complex, sensitive, inner world could guide both research and teaching. That is the purpose of this chapter.

POLANYI'S CONCEPTION OF PERSONAL KNOWLEDGE AND THE TACIT DIMENSION OF KNOWLEDGE

What is a conception? A *concept* is usually defined as a general understanding of something - an object, idea or notion. Conceptions are richer, more complex, have a normative element, and may be more personal; one's personal possession, as it were, of a concept, that person's understanding of it. Without getting too lost in philosophical distinctions, it is worth noting that the concept-conception distinction is a matter of some philosophical debate. For instance: "The concept-conception distinction underwrites the *possession-mastery* [of a concept] distinction. One can possess a concept without having an appropriate conception, without mastering it…causal powers involved in *inferential* processes that explain *systemacity* and *productivity* of thoughts are linked solely to *concept-*

possession, whilst causal powers that are involved in judging what sort of entities fall under a concept are linked to having a *conception*" (Ezcurdia 1998, 190-191) [all italics in original].

According to Polanyi "All our conceptions are heuristic…A problem… is a conception of something we are striving for. It is an intellectual desire for crossing a logical gap on the other side of which lies the unknown, fully marked out by our conception of it, though as yet never seen in itself" (Polanyi 1958, 128). Conceptualization in the present context will require not only "thinking otherwise" (Penn 2018) about religious education, but accessing an inner world of feeling, soul, knowledge, instinct, memory and yearning and attempting to capture this world, however inadequately, in words. But not only in words: in practical human interaction between student, teacher and text as well. This will require exceptional teachers and also willing students. The assumption here is that most students are willing, and indeed, hungry, to access that inner world. Our overt messages will always leave "something behind that we could not tell, and its reception must rely on it that the person addressed will discover that which we have not been able to communicate" (Polanyi 1966, 6).

Polanyi's search for a new conception of knowledge led him to "a novel idea of human knowledge from which a harmonious view of thought and existence, rooted in the universe" emerged. He began his quest to "reconsider human knowledge by starting from the fact that we can know more than we can tell" (Polanyi 1966, 4). Before we begin the quest in this chapter to conceptualize that which quite profoundly cannot be told – the human soul, mind and purpose, as contained in the body of a child or adolescent – let us look very briefly at where Polanyi's quest to conceptualize knowledge, led him.

As a scientist, Polanyi strived for a richer conception of knowledge than the accepted positivist claim of absolute, objective truth. He rejected the idea of scientific detachment. People do not "know" in some purely objective way, said Polanyi; they are moral beings, each with his or her own store of experiential knowledge and ways of thinking. The individual knower builds from his or her own personal knowledge in the process of perceiving external evidence. Knowing is, in effect, always personal. Scientific rules may guide scientific enquiry, but discoveries may also contradict rules and be reached through intuition and inference. It is impossible for a person to explain exactly how he or she knows, anymore than that person can explain exactly how s/he recognizes a face, or balances while riding a bicycle. The complex of personal knowledge held by an individual is tacit, in that it cannot be fully explained. Thus, we know more than we can tell.

APPLICATION OF POLANY'S CONCEPTION TO EDUCATION: TEACHERS' PERSONAL PRACTICAL KNOWLEDGE

Teacher education provides an instructive example of how the idea of a tacit knowledge dimension can broaden and enrich research and practice in a particular field. Building on earlier work in practical knowledge, Freema Elbaz brought discussion of teachers' practical knowledge to the fore in 1981. She did not, of course, coin the term practical knowledge. Different than Plato, who valued rationality above all, Aristotle defined three kinds of knowledge, theoretical, practical and productive. Practical knowledge for Aristotle is "knowledge of contingencies. What are the local circumstances that need to be addressed if one was to work effectively or act intelligently with respect to a particular state of affairs" (Eisner 2008, 4)? According to Eisner (2008) Aristotle's view is close to the kind of thinking and analysis that entered the social sciences in the 1960's, partly in response to the positivist tradition (a legacy from Plato, among others) that dominated philosophy, science and social science in the first half of the 20th century. Polanyi himself expressly stated that his work was aimed at offering an epistemological alternative to the positivist notion of scientific detachment and objective, provable knowing as the only valid knowledge; rather, there is "personal participation of the knower in all acts of understanding. But this does not make our understanding *subjective*. Comprehension is neither an arbitrary act nor a passive experience, but a responsible act claiming universal validity. Such knowing is indeed *objective* in the sense of establishing contact with a hidden reality; a contact that is defined as the condition for anticipating an indeterminate range of yet unknown (and perhaps yet inconceivable) true implications. It seems reasonable to describe this fusion of the personal and the objective as Personal Knowledge" (Polanyi 1958, vii-viii). So we have *practical knowledge*, the situational knowledge of what to do, and *personal knowledge*, the fusion of one's *tacit knowledge* with external conditions. Elbaz began to combine these three ideas into a richer conception of teachers' knowledge than that which had for decades dominated research and teacher training.

Elbaz said that teachers hold much more than explicit, objective knowledge of child development, classroom management and content knowledge of the particular subjects they teach. Rather, they hold what she defined as situational, personal, social, experiential and theoretical knowledge, as well as values, and that these are combined in a personal mix that is both explicit and implicit, or tacit, and is profoundly practical in that it is expressed in the act of teaching. After Elbaz many other researchers built on this conception, notably Clandinin (1986) and Connelly and Clandinin (1985), who spoke of teachers' *"personal practical knowledge."* These writers and those that followed them credited Polanyi's notion of tacit knowledge as essential to understanding teachers' knowledge. This body of work, which continues to this day, has changed the ways teacher education is conducted and the ways teacher knowledge, teacher development and teaching practice, are conducted (see, among numerous examples, Oss 2018). In addition to the fields of teaching and teacher education, tacit knowledge is a recognized component of professional knowledge in fields as diverse as nursing (Herbig, Bussing & Ewert 2001) and management (Armstrong & Mahmud 2008).

As we move to the main topic of this chapter, religious education, we must be clear that religious education is not just about knowledge, explicit or tacit. But it is *personal*, it should be *practical* in that it guides one's life, and the parts that mean the most to a person – the spiritual connectness, if you will, are *tacit,* in that they could only be explained in an approximate fashion to someone else.

THE TACIT DIMENSION IN RELIGIOUS EDUCATION

It is reasonable to assume that one of the main goals of religious education is to bring students to what William James called a "religious attitude in the soul" (James 1902, 53), an internal religious make-up that permeates one's life. But how is this to be achieved? It almost certainly involves the learning of texts and rituals, which are the bedrock of every organized religion, but is that enough? Does knowledge of religious texts and practices imbue us with religious attitude, or do we need in some way to connect with, as James calls it, the "unseen order" through direct experience? The great psychological and religious thinker Carl Jung writes that when a person does not relate well to institutionalized religions' "dogmatic assumptions" the Church (Jung wrote from a Christian context) "recommends more faith, as if this gift of grace depended on man's good will and pleasure. The seat of faith, however, is not consciousness but spontaneous religious experience, which brings the individual's faith into immediate relation with God" (Jung 1957, 2006, 85). C.S. Lewis (1955) famously described spontaneous religious experience as being "surprised by joy." Religious literacy is important, as is living a decent, moral life guided by religious principles. Being educated into a religion means being part of a community of tradition, practice and faith. All of these are important. But what about individual spiritual experience and connection? Religious experience is ineffable and is certainly not teachable; yet surely enabling such experience is or should be an aim of religious education. It should be stated here that "religious" and "spiritual" are not necessarily interchangeable terms, though they are often conflated. Spirituality and spiritual experience may of course be unconnected to any organized religion. While a religion is definable by its creed, its history, texts and practices, spirituality is "an intractably diffuse and deeply personal concept" (Harlos 2000, 614). Spirituality, like religious experience, is not definable. I will use the terms spirituality and spiritual experience here in a religious context, and will mean personal connection with God, a deep and perhaps sudden sense of meaning, understanding and joy, achieved through, concurrent with or enabled by religious study or practice.

I submit that this personal, perhaps sudden sense of meaning, understanding and joy *is a kind of knowledge;* knowledge that is ineffable and indescribable; when we have such experience, we know more than we can tell. This fits well with Polanyi's notion of tacit knowledge. Polanyi wrote as a scientist. We can extrapolate for the religious context from his description of the scientific intuition that leads scientists to sudden insight and new discoveries. This scientific intuition arises from a basis of rational knowledge, experimentation and computation; it reveals suddenly, in a flash of insight, a solution to a problem, a solution which must then be tested and proven. Regarding the work of mathematicians, Polanyi writes that "the mathematician works his way towards discovery, by shifting his confidence from intuition to computation and back again from computation to intuition, while never releasing his hold on either of the two...The alternation between the intuitive and the formal depends on tacit affirmations, both at the beginning and at the end of each chain of formal reasoning" (Polanyi 1958, 1962, 131). This is at the very least a useful metaphor for the interaction between religious experience and religious learning. There may be some self-taught mathematicians who "see" solutions, but their ability to prove and formalize them is necessarily limited. Systematic work and high-level knowledge of mathematics deepens the intuitive insight and enables the formal contribution. In the context of religious education, religious knowledge takes the place of mathematical knowledge, and insight into God replaces insight into mathematical solutions. Clearly persons completely unattached to and not knowledgeable in any religious tradition can have spiritual experiences - through music, nature, etc. – but I postulate that formal religious knowledge and personal religious experience, in interaction, can bring about a deep, multi-faceted "religious attitude" that will positively guide and permeate a person's life. Spiritual experience without religion is valuable but limited. Religious knowledge without religious experience misses the actual *person*, the soul within, and may lead to the abandonment of religion. I have written elsewhere that,

> In religious education, the curriculum, the teachers, the tests and the routine, often conspire to make mastery of textual material too dry to

awaken a memory of the young child's untroubled knowledge of God, too distant from adolescents' search for meaning to help them find it in religion, too intellectual to spark real spiritual connection. Text study and knowledge are important, but should spiritual connection not also be a goal of religious education? Could spiritual experience be the missing link between religious knowledge and internalization of "the religious attitude in the soul?" If so, how can we do better at connecting mastery of knowledge with hearing the precious, quiet voice of the soul and sensing the unseen order that underlies all things (Court 2013, 252)?

This "place" of connection, where knowledge and direct experience meet, is the tacit dimension that religious educators must grasp, nurture and strive towards.

What would curriculum for this kind of religious education look like? It should certainly detail religious texts and practices to be learned. These learning goals can be expressed in quite a structured way. Evaluation of student learning flows logically from such structure. Then, while we cannot teach, promise, evaluate or verify religious experience, we must include it as a revealed and valued aim. And while learners might not know to express it as such, surely it is their aim as well: finding *meaning*, what young people (and not just young people) yearn for.

As we drew on Polanyi's scientific intuition and insight as a metaphor for religious experience, so we can draw on the work of Elliot Eisner for help with curriculum aims. Eisner brought his knowledge as a painter to the business of curriculum and educational research, writing about artistry in education and about expressive outcomes, as opposed to behavioral objectives. According to Eisner, artistry is that unquantifiable element of education that "courts surprise, it plays at the edge of possibility, it trades in ambiguities, it addresses dilemmas, and it provides a certain kind of delight, if one can take some risks" (Eisner 2005, 2). We can intend expressive outcomes, hopefully we can to some extent enable them, but we cannot plan and structure them. As we cannot teach scientific intuition or artistic sensibility, we cannot teach spiritual connection and experience. But we can express these as aims in our written curriculum, we can discuss ways that all religious learners (teachers and curriculum planners included) might be graced with such experience through, or in companion with, structured learning and practice. And we can acknowledge that such experience can never be evaluated. Regarding evaluation of art, Eisner says,

> Given the absence of a formula or an algorithm, how are judgments about rightness made? I believe they depend upon somatic knowledge, the sense of closure that the good gestalt engenders in embodied experience; the composition *feels* right. Work in the arts cultivates the modes of thinking and feeling that I have described; one cannot succeed in the arts without such cognitive abilities. Such forms of thought integrate feeling and thinking in ways that make them inseparable. One knows one is right because one feels the relationships. One modifies one's work and feels the results. The sensibilities come into play and in the process become refined. Another way of putting it is that as we learn in and through the arts we become more qualitatively intelligent (Eisner 2004, 5).

Parallel to Polanyi's discussion of the interaction between scientific insight and intuition, and scientific structure and rationality, Eisner describes the interaction between an indescribable artistic "rightness" and the cognitive rules and abilities that allow one to "feel the relationships." One is incomplete without the other; they complement, enrich and enable each other, in science and in art. The argument in this chapter is that this is so also in religious education. Religious learning in some way enables religious experience, if learning conditions are conducive (flexible, joyful, serious but never punitive, rich with humor, inviting questions); religious experience deepens and enriches religious learning.

It is inescapable that the central factor in conducting religious education that marries learning of texts and practices with personal spiritual experience, is the teacher. We need, first and foremost, teachers who are themselves seekers, who can share the journey in an authentic way. These teachers are patient, lively and flexible, they really see and hear their students as individuals, they are knowledgeable but do not claim to know everything, they are not afraid to express their own doubts and certainties. They are both humble and inspired. They listen, ask and engage.

Pedagogy should involve reflection, exploration of the conceptual spaces between and within the words of texts and prayers, and respectful exploration of students' questions of meaning... Pedagogically, in religious classrooms, this can include an approach as simple as slowing down prayer, so that there is space between the words for reflection. Talking about the words of prayers can make them personal and connect them to each student's experience. Text study should never be just an intellectual exercise, nor should it be used for a kind of closed, authoritative moralizing. Rather, it should be connected to meaning in students' lives. Teachers should fill their classrooms not only with intellectual rigor but with debate, and with humor, zest for life, creativity and fun. They can include song to lift the heart and story to engage the imagination. Imagination frees the mind from the bonds of cognition. Teachers should issue a pedagogical invitation to students to imagine (Court 2013, 259).

Teachers who can do this are working from their own personal practical knowledge of teaching, of teaching religion, and, at least among those who have been graced with such experience, of spiritual experience.

What of research? Research into all aspects of education is important. Research insights can improve curriculum, teacher preparation and practice, administration and leadership of schools, and understanding into learning styles and learning development. What might research that acknowledges the tacit dimension in religious education, look like?

First, we need research into the teaching of religion. We can learn here from the example of teachers' personal practical knowledge. That conception enriched research into teaching in the following ways. In a classic 1997 article, Connelly, Clandinin and Fang He sketched the history of research into teaching and stressed the major contribution of research into teachers' knowledge, which was born in the 1980's, in changing the paradigm of research into teaching.

Traditionally, it was assumed that teacher characteristics (e.g., warmth, firmness, punctuality) and teaching/learning methods and processes (e.g., lecture, laboratory, seat work, drill) were the main teaching areas of importance to student learning. In contrast to the concern for teacher characteristics and teaching/learning methods, the assumption in teacher knowledge research is that the most important area is what teachers know and how their knowing is expressed in teaching. On this assumption, teacher knowledge and knowing affects every aspect of the teaching act. It affects teachers' relationships with students; teachers' interpretations of subject matter and its importance in students' lives; teachers' treatment of ideas whether as fixed textbook givens or as matters of inquiry and reflection; teachers' curriculum planning and evaluation (Connelly, Clandinin and Fang He 1997, 666).

Previous to this kind of work, research was done *on* teachers, but not *with* them. Researching teachers' personal practical knowledge means making them partners on a journey of discovery, working "directly with teachers in all aspects of the lives in classrooms, outside classrooms and in their personal lives. Ideally this is done collaboratively in such a way that teachers become research participants: teachers help define the purposes of the research, suggest interpretations, and comment on the final results...such research results have a strongly authentic, insider, feel to them" (Connelly, Clandinin and Fang He 1997, 666-667). In the case of teachers of religion, this means acknowledging both their expertise and their personal, ongoing journey of religious discovery. Such research reveals new insights for the participants as well as for the larger academic community that will read the published results. Such work will probably involve narrative, participant observation and other collaborative qualitative research approaches. Clearly the researchers themselves need to be focused on learning with and from the teachers; partners working together to explore teachers' tacit knowledge as well as their revealed values, beliefs and strategies.

We will also need to investigate students' experiences, not through surveys but through conversations with children, invitations to older students to write about their experiences, doubts, hopes and searching, and participant observation in classrooms. The goals will be twofold. First, to contribute both theoretical and operational knowledge of how to conduct effective religious education. Second, and no less important, to enhance students' learning experiences vis a vis both growth of knowledge and personal sense of connectedness and meaning, through involving them in study of these areas. There are many ethical and methodological issues involved in research with young children, including access, informed consent and researcher effect, that are beyond the scope of this chapter. Because of the complexities of working with younger children, most studies of young people's spiritual experiences are conducted with high school and university students. But this should not deter researchers from attempting to understand the experiences of the whole age-range of learners. Freeman and Mathison (2008) discuss use of conversations, play, drawings and writing as ways of accessing children's experiences. In addition, they present the possibility of partnering with young people in a kind of action research where, like teachers working with researchers to access and articulate their own personal practical knowledge, children become active participants in study of their own learning. Such collaboration must involve "authentic relationships in which partners learn about each other's worlds in the process of working together on shared interests" (Freeman and Mathison 2008, 170-171). In researching religious education, collaborative action research between teachers and students holds great potential for enhancing the cognitive, emotional and spiritual dimensions of everyone's experience - students, teachers and researchers. Tacit knowledge cannot be perfectly articulated, and that is not the point. Self-reflection on such knowledge, and sharing with others, can enrich experience and give a sense of religious community.

CONCLUSION

Polanyi contributed immeasurably to enriching the idea of scientific knowledge by debunking the belief that only measurable, rational, provable, systematic thinking comes from and leads to scientific knowledge. He added intuition, personal knowledge and the understanding that all these different kinds of knowledge – the rational, and the intuitive and personal – exist in interaction in what he called the tacit dimension, and that given this, we know more than we can tell. Elbaz, Clandinin, Connelly and others built on these ideas in the field of teaching and teacher education, giving us the conception of teachers' personal practical knowledge that has changed our understanding of how teachers learn and how they draw on their personal practical knowledge as they teach. Eisner contributed new conceptual understanding of education and educational evaluation when he introduced the idea of education as artistry, bringing artistic sensibilities to the practice of education. The present conception of the tacit dimension in religious education intends to follow in this tradition.

The central argument of this chapter has been that religious knowledge acquired through religious education coexists with private, personal, spiritual experience, each enriching the other. Spiritual experience is ineffable and indescribable; it is a kind of tacit knowledge. Study of religious texts, rituals and prayers, the revealed materials that can be planned for, taught and evaluated, is the basis of religious education. Spiritual experience and revelation are gifts of grace, and though we cannot plan for, explicitly teach or evaluate them, we must acknowledge them as aims and try, through good teaching on the part of teachers who are themselves seekers, to enable students to experience God beyond the level of cognition. Religious learning deepens spiritual experience; spiritual experience gives life and meaning to religious learning. These two aspects interact in the tacit dimension of religious education.

REFERENCES

Armstrong, Stephen and Mahmud Anis. 2008. "Experiential Learning and the Acquisition of Managerial Tacit Knowledge. *Academy of Management Learning & Education* 7, no. 2: 189-208. https://doi.org/10.5465/amle.2008.32712617.

Clandinin, D. Jean. 1986. *Classroom Practice*. London: Falmer.

Clandinin, D. Jean and F. Michael Connelly. 1985. "Personal Practical Knowledge and the Modes of Knowing, In *Learning and Teaching the Ways of Knowing*, edited by Elliot W. Eisner, 174-98. Chicago: University of Chicago Press.

Connelly, F. Michael, D. Jean Clandinin, and Ming Fang He. 1997. "Teachers Personal Practical Knowledge on the Professional

Knowledge Landscape. *Teaching and Teacher Education* 13, no. 2: 665-74.

Collins-Mayo, S. 2008. "Young People's Spirituality and the Meaning of Prayer." In *Religion and the Individual: Belief, Practice, Identity*, edited by Abby Day, 33-46. London & New York: Routledge.

Court, Deborah. 2013. "Religious Experience as an Aim of Religious Education. *British Journal of Religious Education* 35, no. 3: 251-263. https://doi.org/10.1080/01416200.2012.750596.

Eisner, Elliot W. 2008. "Art and Knowledge." In *Handbook of the Arts in Qualitative Research*, edited by J. Gary Knowles and Arda L. Cole, 3-11. Thousand Oaks, CA: Sage.

Eisner, Elliot W. 2005. *Reimagining Schools: The Selected Works of Elliot W. Eisner*. NY: Routledge.

Eisner, Elliot W. 2004. "What can Education Learn from the Arts about the Practice of Education?" *International Journal of Education & the Arts* 5, no. 4: 1-13. http://ijea.asu.edu/v5n4/.

Elbaz, Freema. 1981. "The Teacher's "Practical Knowledge": Report of a Case Study. *Curriculum Inquiry* 11: 43-71.

Ezcurdia, Maite. 1998. "The Concept-Conception Distinction. *Philosophical Issues* 9: 187-192.

Freeman, Melissa and Sandra Mathison. 2008. *Researching Children's Experiences*. NY: The Guildford Press.

Harlos, Karen. P. 2000. "Toward a Spiritual Pedagogy: Meaning, Practice, and Applications in Management Education." *Journal of Management Education* 24, no.5: 612–627.

Herbig, Britta, Andre Bussing and Thomas Ewert. 2001. "The Role of Tacit Knowledge in the Work Context of Nursing. *Journal of Advanced Nursing* 34, no.5: 687-695. https://doi.org/10.1046/j.1365-2648.2001.01798.x.

James, William. 1902. "Lecture III, The reality of the unseen." In *The Varieties of Religious Experience: A Study in Human Nature*. Gifford lectures on natural religion, Edinburgh, 1901–1902: 53-76. NY: Longmans, Green & Co.

Jung, Carl. 1957, 2006. *The Undiscovered Self*. NY, NY: Penguin.

Lewis, Clive Staples. 1955. *Surprised by Joy: The Shape of My Early Life.* Orlando, FL: Harcourt, Brace and Company.

Locum, Russel G., Susan Densmore-James, Laura A. Staal, Elyse C. Pinkie and Dana A. E. Yokum 2016. "Exploring Spiritual Needs in the Classroom: Implications for Educators." *Forum on Public Policy On-Line* 1: 1-18.

Oss, Debora. I. B. 2018. "The Relevance of Teachers' Practical Knowledge in the Development of Teacher Education Programs." *Profile: Issues in Teachers' Professional Development* 20(1): 167-178. https://doi.org/10.15446/profile.v20n1.62327.

Penn, David S. 2018. "Against the Generation Gap: Thinking "otherwise" about adolescence." *Religious Education* 113(1): 61-72.

Polanyi, Michael. (1966, 2009). *The Tacit Dimension.* Chicago: University of Chicago Press.

Polanyi, Michael. (1966, 2009). "The Logic of Tacit Inference." *Philosophy* 41(155): 1-18. https://doi.org/10.1017/S0031819100066110.

Polanyi, Michael. (1958, 1962). *Personal Knowledge.* Chicago: University of Chicago Press.

Robbins, Mandy and Leslie J. Francis. 2005. "Purpose in Life and Prayer among Catholic and Protestant Adolescents in Northern Ireland." *Journal of Research on Christian Education* 14(1): 73-93. https://doi.org/10.1080/10656210509484981.

Smith, Christian, Robert Faris, Melinda L. Denton and Mark Regnerus. 2003. "Mapping American Adolescent Subjective Religiosity and Attitudes of Alienation towards Religion: A Research Report." *Sociology of Religion* 64:(1): 111-133.

BIOGRAPHICAL SKETCH

Deborah Court

Affiliation: Bar-Ilan University, Israel

Education: EdD, University of British Columbia, Canada

Research and Professional Experience:

Deborah Court is Professor of Education at Bar-Ilan University in Israel. Her research centers on school culture, religious education, the nature of teachers' knowledge, and qualitative research methodologies. A Canadian who has lived in Israel for more than twenty years, she is keenly aware of the importance of interfaith and intercultural education.

Publications from the Last 3 Years:

- Court, Deborah. 2018. *Qualitative Research and Intercultural Understanding*. London: Routledge/Taylor and Francis.
- Amit Alon, Nili and Deborah Court. 2018. Contemporary Israeli Theory and Philosophy of Education: Pressing Issues, Major Trends and Practical Implications in the Multicultural Construction of Israeli Education. *Curriculum and Teaching* 33(2) (In press).
- Schnieder, Orna and Deborah Court. 2017. The Pedagogy of 'Community as law'. *Studies in Education* 18/19: 2-36. (In Hebrew).
- Court, Deborah. 2016. The Dawning of our Knowledge. *Religious Education* 111(3): 244-249.
- Shashoua, Ayella and Deborah Court. 2016. Analysis of Classroom Discourse in 'Personal Education' Classes in Light of the Theories of Dewey, Piaget and Vygotsky. *Curriculum and Teaching* 31(1): 67-87.
- Abbas, Randa and Deborah Court. 2015. Two Ethnographers Embark on a Narrative Journey. *The Qualitative Report* 20(9): 1448-1457.
- Court, Deborah and Jack Seymour. 2015. What Might Meaningful Interfaith Education Look Like? Exploring Politics, Principles and Pedagogy. *Religious Education* 110(5): 517-533.

- Court, Deborah and Randa Abbas. 2015. Future Orientation in a Traditional Society: Higher Education and the Israeli Druze. *Religion and Spirituality in Society* 5(3): 9-17.
- Burstein, Alissa B. and Deborah Court. 2015. A New Model of the Parent Volunteer. *Education and Society* 33(1): 51-75.
- Court, Deborah. 2015. A Jewish Core Curriculum to Live By. *Religious Education* 110(1): 5-9.

In: Religious Education
Editor: Richard Coudert

ISBN: 978-1-53615-832-8
© 2019 Nova Science Publishers, Inc.

Chapter 2

AN ECOLOGICAL MODEL FOR THE ENCOUNTER OF IDENTITIES IN THE RELIGIOUS STATE KINDERGARTEN IN ISRAEL

Orna Schneider[*]
Department of Early Childhood Education, Shaanan College,
Haifa, Israel

ABSTRACT

One influence on the shaping of community identity is the presence of the 'other'. In Israel some non-religious (secular) Jewish families enroll their children in kindergartens of the state religious education system (SRES), even though they do not belong to the mainstream religious, the Modern Orthodox (M.O), community. This chapter offers an ethnographic study, using ecological systems theory, of the sociological-educational processes taking place in these kindergartens.

Findings point to the creation of three diverse educational patterns that reflect a wide variance, to the point of creating contradictory patterns: the

[*] Corresponding Author's E-mail: ornash66@gmail.com.

pattern of religious hegemonies- glorification of the Modern Orthodox identity and exclusion of the secular identity; the pattern of respect - preserving the categories of religious identity while applying strategies of respect to the secular appropriation of religious spaces; and an illusory multi-identity pattern in which glorification of secular identity and exclusion of religious identity takes place. The variety of patterns established in which identities are pushed out occurs due to administrative and pedagogical autonomy in the kindergartens in Israel. On the one hand, the varied and even opposing patterns point to a pluralistic educational system that allows new members to integrate into the community without posing a threat; on the other hand, the differences constitute a disadvantage to the educational system. Placing the teachers in a position of power has led to a rupture in the religious boundaries of the SRES kindergarten, leading to a creation of patterns of identity formation that are at variance with the core religious identity of the MO education system to which the kindergartens belong.

Keywords: Religious State School Education System (RSES), kindergarten, ecological edge, community identity, religious hegemony

INTRODUCTION[1]

Identity in the Religious Community

Possibly the most outstanding trait shaping the identity of the Modern Orthodox community is its members' adherence to religious beliefs. This belief system creates the homogenous character of the community and holds it together (Garred 2013; Sagi 2006; Sagi 2017; Schwartz 2003). Over much of their history, Jews have tended to emphasize the religious aspect of their communal identity, and indeed, for centuries, Jewish identity was anchored in religious observance which led the individual members of the community to identify with the communal identity of their environment (Ben-Rafael and Ben-Haim 2006; Shavit, Sasson-Levy, and Guy Ben-Porat 2012)

---

[1] This article is based on part of the doctoral dissertation written at the School of Education of Bar-Ilan University, under the guidance of Prof. Deborah Court.
The research was partially sponsored by the Lockstein Center for Jewish Education in the Diaspora, and the Institute for the Research and Advancement of Jewish Education.

Jewish beliefs are anchored in the world of Jewish Religious Law (Halachah), and so, the attitude toward Halachah determines the boundaries of the religious community and the level of orthodoxy of its members (Leon 2009). Its theological interpretations establish the community's religious identity and determine the way ritual is observed, Jewish Festivals are celebrated, the form prayer takes, which books on religious issues they study, the way they interpret the commandments, and even the way they relate to their religious leadership. It also extends to the place of ritual artifacts and sacred music, an adherence to a certain dress code for men and women, and they may even speak a certain language variation which identifies them as a separate group (Ben-Rafael and Ben-Haim 2006; El-Or 2006; Sagi 2017). Therefore, an examination of the existence of these rites and rituals and their meaning, makes it possible to signify the quality of the individual's commitment to the community, while at the same time marking the unique boundaries of religious observance within the community. Doing so will also mark non-members of the community as "other", those who do not belong to it (Ben-Rafael 2006: Sagi 2017).

The influence of the "other" is one of the components which affects the formation of communal identity. In other words, certain characteristics of outsider communities (the outgroup) may slowly infiltrate the fabric of the central community (the ingroup) (Gilchrist, Bowles and Wetherell 2010). The periphery of the community where the identity of the outsider culture can take hold may be defined as the ecological edge culture. This area is the frontier which joins the outgroup to the more centralized ingroup, and manifests core characteristics of the ingroup placed side by side with the unique aspects resulting from the intrusion of the outsider culture (Barak and Gidron 2009; Ben-Rafael and Ben-Haim 2006; Strayer et al. 2003). The edge is flexible, open to change and inter-cultural encounters, and is in a constant state of flux so that the relationship between the two groups is helpful to the self-definition of the ingroup. Nevertheless, considering that the edge is part of the community, the intrusions of the outgroup on this part of the community also serve to evolve the identity of the community as a whole (Breakwell 2010; Clemence and Lorenzi-Cioldi 2014; Shavit, Sasson-Levy, and Ben-Porat 2012; Wenger 1998). However, the advantage of this openness lies in the fact that it allows fast-paced change, and alongside this also enables new members of the community to be absorbed into the community without posing a threat (Cohen 2006; Augoustinos and Donahue 2014; Turner, Davidson-Hunt and Flaherty 2003).

The State-Religious School System

In Israel, the meeting between communities with different identities takes place in the religious state-school education system (RSES). The establishment of this K-12 educational system was made possible by the work of the Religious Zionist movement and the realities of coalition government. The RSES is a separate branch of the Ministry of Education, known as the religious education subdivision (Keel 1977), was awarded legal standing through legislation, and is in charge of the RSES (Dagan 2006; Gross 2011). "The religious state education law defines the RSES as a public-school education, but its institutions' curricula, teachers and inspectors reflect the observant[2] way of life" (the religious state education law 1953). This law affords equal standing to both public school systems, secular state education and religious state education, thus enabling each sector to realize its objectives (Bar-Lev 1986; Bar-Levi 2011) while at the same time laying the groundwork for the internal educational autonomy of the RSES (Keel 1977).

Under the law of religious state education, the RSES has always been obligated to accept any pupil whose parents are interested in a religious education for their child, even though the RSES is overtly religious in its outlook. As a result, the enrollment is characterized by a wide variety of pupils from families with varying levels of religious observance. Furthermore, pupils from so-called traditional Jewish families or those whose homes are not in the least observant and may be classified as secular

---

[2] The use of "observant" rather than "religious" seemed more in keeping with the spirit of the article, and is also more commonly used to denote the orthodox Jew. At times I used the term "Modern Orthodox" as this stream of Judasim is the one that sends its children to the religious state schools.

Jews can also enroll in the RSES (Dombrowski 2010). The term 'traditional' is a loose one (Goodman and Yona 2004) and relates to families who may be 'celebrant-but-not-observant' and who feel at liberty to choose their relationship with Judaism and the identity which it forges (Arian and Ceasar-Sugarman 2009; Yadgar 2012). In contrast, secular Jews are defined as a group manifesting dichotomous identity categories compared to the categories of identity in the religious community (Buzaglo 2005, 2008; Yadgar 2010).

The RSES saw its mission as bringing its enrollment closer to Jewish values, and to serve as a bridge between the various factions of the country's citizens and Jewish religious issues. This endeavor has turned the RSES into a heterogenous educational system, both in terms of religious observance within its walls, and socially (Dagan 2006; Keel, 1987; Lipschitz, 2011). Accordingly, pupils from traditional and secular Jewish families comprise some 25% of the RSES enrollment (Dagan 2008). There are those who view the integration of pupils from these types of homes as an advantage for the RSES, as its framework may strengthen these pupils' feeling of Jewish identity which may have been marginalized through the family's desire to belong to the secular part of society (Dagan 2008; Gross 2011; Keel 1987; Lipschitz 2011). Others see this reality as a disadvantage because of the conflict between the communal identity, the ideology of the pupil's environment, and the school's ideology and its religious (observant) educational identity (Zahavi 2011).

The long-term integration of secular Jews within the RSES brings about a cultural meeting between communities whose identities are not only different, but where the secular identity may even be opposed to what the religiously observant community represents (Bar-Levi 2011; Carriere 2013; Cohen, 2006). This situation poses a complicated social challenge for the RSES (Dagan 2006; Dombrowski 2010). This is especially true for the kindergartens within the RSES (Schneider 2015, 2016). In Israel, all kindergartens are independently managed units, both in terms of physical structure and curriculum.

The educational unit is managed by one autonomous early-education teacher who is the only person in charge of what happens in the classroom, both in terms of management and pedagogy (Frish 2012; Nir-Yaniv 1984; Oplatka and Stundi 2011; Sverdlov et al. 2010). In the case of the RSES kindergarten teacher, the autonomy is even broader because there is no structured, state-wide curriculum to teach religious values under the auspices of the RSES administration. Therefore, the kindergarten teacher is empowered to write lesson plans which deal with teaching topics connected to the world of religious values (Achituv 2012; Odesser 2007; Schneider 2015).

The meeting within the RSES, between communities manifesting a Modern Orthodox identity and those who do not, takes place in an autonomous educational reality, and leads to the following research question: how does the RSES kindergarten cope with the intrusion of those whose identity is secular?

Ecological Systems Theory

In order to examine the sociological-educational processes, the Ecological Systems' Theory model was used (Bronfenbrenner and Morris 1998; Cicchetti and Valentino 2006; Pianta and Stuhalman 2003). This model bases itself on the developmental inter-cultural approach as it examines the student-teacher relationship within an advanced, broad, dynamic fabric, as well as the interaction of individuals within the surrounding social circles in which they live. The following is a presentation of the ecological circles which characterize the Ecological Systems Theory (Bronfenbrenner 1979, 1986), and the way they may be adapted to this research: the Microsystem: the immediate environment the individual comes into daily contact with, which in this research means the relationship between the kindergarten teacher, the children and their parents, and the way they find expression in a variety of practices and discussions initiated by the teacher.

The Mesosystem: this circle relates to the ties between two microsystems, which here means the cross fertilization between the kindergarten teacher and the RSES inspectorate. The Exosystem: the external circle with which the individual does not have direct contact, but which affects him or her in various ways. In this study it relates to RSES policies as they are set forth in an official document known as the "RSES Position Paper" (Dagan 2008), where guidelines for the manner in which the RSES is supposed to function are presented.

Cicchetti and Valentino (2006) added two dimensions to the Bronfenbrenner model which add a transactional perspective to the ecological circles and relate to the quality of the influences which may impede the process, as opposed to those which inspire and promote it, and the time dimension which aids in differentiating between transient causes which have a short time span, and those which are long-term. The quality and time dimensions aid in examining which actions taken by the educational environment succeed in achieving the objectives of religious observance and the building of a religious community identity, and which impede it.

METHODS

The study used the ethnographic approach, which outlines the culture of an environment or location by means of observations, interviews, and the collection of cultural documentation (Atkinson and Hammersley 2000; Grbich 2007, 2012; Spradley 2016). Three different tools were used to allow triangulation to validate the findings (Denzin 1978; Guba and Lincoln 2005; Lewis, 2015; Sluski and Alpert, 2007). In addition, a multiple case study was used to allow each case study (the kindergarten) to narrate its own unique story, while at the same time it helped to understand the different events by comparing and contrasting them (Stake 2006; Stake 2013; Yin, 2009). The data was collected over a period of two school years and focused on the many administrative areas under the kindergarten teacher's responsibility.

Research Tools

- Observations: Once every six weeks, observations were carried out in the kindergarten. These included participant observations of the teachers' pedagogical work. Each observation lasted about three hours, and also included the organization of the educational environment which supplied non-verbal data concerning the identity of the kindergarten (Diamant 2005, 2007; Handelman 2004). The physical environment was photographed as well as filmed. In total, 17 observations took place in each kindergarten and hundreds of photographs were taken. In addition, observations of cultural events where parents participated took place in each and every kindergarten. In total, 75 observations took place.
- Interviews: Before and after each observation, the kindergarten teacher was interviewed. In total, 150 interviews took place. In addition, members of the parents- committee of the kindergarten were interviewed, as well as the entire chain of command over the RSES kindergarten.
- Cultural documentation study: Documents written by the kindergarten teachers were studied, including their lesson plans which they had submitted to the inspectorate, as well as communications they sent to the parents. In addition, emails (cultural documentation) sent off by the RSES administration to its employees were also studied.

Analytical Methods

All the date compiled was entered into the Narralizer program, a software which aids the scholar in realizing his or her intuitive abilities, so essential to qualitative research, while at the same time maintaining the analytical principle which reinforces the appropriate use of language and the choice of words in their natural setting, exactly the way they were collected (Shkedi 2011). The Narralizer program uses "data encoding and retrieval"

(Grbich 2007, 2012) which allows using the data in a variety of merging and classification techniques, and to construct theory.

The analysis was carried out by means of a multidimensional approach which combined textual content analysis and textual form analysis.

- The dimension of content- in accordance with the model suggested by Kasen and Kromer-Nevo (2010), and based on Strauss and Corbin's "grounded theory model" (Glaser & Strauss 2017; Strauss and Corbin 1997). Theories were constructed on the basis of understanding and interpreting events taking place in the research field, on the one hand, providing a framework of thought to anchor the study, while on the other hand offering the flexibility necessary for the inductive process which includes a number of analytical stages.
- The dimension of form- based on critical discourse analysis (CDA) which deals with the discourse-power relationships invested in spoken and written text of community identities (Blommaert 2005; Fairclough 1993, 2013; Gee 2004; Schiffrin, Tannen and Hamilton 2001). This method is based on the belief that in order to expose phenomena of social inequality (Van Dijk 2001, 2015) one must examine the construction of interaction between the participants, among others, by the discursive position of the speaker vis-à-vis the interlocutor (Hart and Cap 2014; Kupferberg 2010).

Participants

The sample consisted of five kindergartens selected by means of non-probability sampling from the category of purposive sampling. This method yields rich data which serve the study's objectives: In three RSES kindergartens the population was affiliated with Religious Zionism, (Moses 2009) while in the remaining two, although they belonged to the RSES branch of the educational system, the children came from secular communities not affiliated with Religious Zionism, and thus constituted the cultural-ecological edge (Barak and Gidron 2009; Ben-Rafael and Ben-Haim 2006; Strayer et al. 2003). In addition, representatives of the kindergartens' parent-committees also took part in the study, as well as regional and national inspectors of the RSES.

FINDINGS

The encounter between the observant (Modern Orthodox) identity and the secular one occurred when communities lacking religious identity moved to the cultural ecological edge of the RSES kindergartens, resulting in the formation of different identity patterns in the RSES kindergarten environment. These include characteristics from the central community's core, Religious Zionism, side by side with the characteristics of the secular identity of the outgroup communities[3] (Barak and Gidron 2009; Ben-Rafael and Ben-Haim 2006; Strayer et al. 2003). The interaction between the ingroup and the outgroup brought about a change (Breakwell 2010; Wenger 1998) in the RSES kindergarten and added new shades of identity. An analysis of events when religious (observant) and secular identities meet within the kindergartens uncovered three different identity patterns, all of which can be linked to one of the ecological circles: the mesosytem, triggered by the teachers, resulted in three different differential identity patterns, whereas the mesosystem, triggered by the inspectorate, and the exosystem, triggered by the RSES position paper, resulted in one pattern only.

The Religious Hegemony Pattern

The religious hegemony pattern is located on one extreme of the spectrum, and exists only in the microsystem circle which is activated by the

---

[3] The findings of this study did not show differences between kindergartens with a secular populations and those with 'celebrant-but-not-observant' ones. Therefore, this article uses the term "secular" throughout to denote the two populations.

kindergarten teacher exclusively. The approach which promotes religious hegemony is based on the belief that it is important to maintain the religious character of the kindergarten, and therefore, it is important to keep out behaviors not in the spirit of Judaism and Halachah. The teacher's desire to maintain the kindergarten's hegemonic religious identity leads her to negate certain practices by children and their parents in two ways:

Secular Identity Delegitimization Pedagogy

The religious hegemony labors to delegitimize the secular identity because it violates the implementation of religious codes. Secular persons' lifestyles and the way they experience their day of rest, the Shabbath, contradict Jewish religious law, Halachah, and is therefore delegitimized. An example of this delegitimization is Yael's report of her reaction to the story by one of the children from a secular household of his family outing on the Shabbath: "Yaniv, for example, comes from a secular home and tells me that on the Shabbath his parents took him on a road trip; I say to him: But you are not supposed to travel on the Shabbath" (Yael, ingroup kindergarten, Religious Zionism). For the sake of religious hegemony, which supports one absolute truth, the truth of Halachah- the lifestyle of this boy and his parents is delegitimized.

Aside from the kindergarten teacher's delegitimization of the boy's outing on the Shabbath, findings showed that the parents' committee of the kindergarten also act the same way. A group of observant parents opened an email distribution group where decisions concerning the management of the kindergarten were made. The group included only email addresses of the observant parents and so the secular parents' voice was not heard. In fact, their right to have an opinion was essentially denied. The representative of the parents' committee explained why secular parents could not be part of this email distribution list. "When we send important announcements concerning the kindergarten, they [the secular parents] are not interested in participating in discussions about what kind of kindergarten they would like to see" (Irit, representative of the parents' committee, ingroup, Religious Zionism).

Exclusion is not confined to the kindergarten but is encroaching upon the secular household as well, and the pattern of religious hegemony is, in fact, escalating. Children from observant households may be discouraged from visiting those from secular homes, as their parents may fear that their children's observant lifestyle may be negatively affected by this contact. "It is a little problematic to invite [friends]. A mother of a secular child would like to invite playmates, but the children from religious homes do not come. "Their parents are raising them according to a specific lifestyle, such as not having television, and there [in the secular household] it is different" (Irit, kindergarten teacher ingroup, Religious Zionist).

Implementing Monolithic Religious Codes

Parallel to not allowing children from secular homes to express their identity, the educational environment enforces certain religious practices intended to fill the vacuum where these children find themselves as the result of excluding their secular identity.

Dress Code

The kindergarten teachers are in charge of the codes of behavior and dress which mark the kindergarten as a religious environment. However, the teachers believe that their responsibility does not end at the gate. For example, the kindergarten teacher expects boys to wear a skullcap, which is a distinct symbol of the observant Jew: "I tell the boy: 'you have to wear your skullcap when you go home. You should put it on your head as soon as you wake up'." (Yonit, ingroup kindergarten, Religious Zionism). Laws concerning dress-code extends to females as well, both mothers and girls: "I tell the mothers to dress modestly when they come to the kindergarten, no low-cut neckline or short skirts" (Yael, ingroup kindergarten, Religious Zionism).

Keeping Kosher- Monolithic Jewish Law (Halachah)

Jewish law governing kosher food is an issue with clearly defined, and strictly enforced, rules. When parents bring birthday cakes to the kindergarten, for example, they are expected to buy only those with the strictest kosher certification "To us it is important they bring products with strict certification [...] when it comes to the parents, I prefer to be stricter and ask for BADATZ[4] certification, because I do not want to make mistakes" (Yael, ingroup kindergarten, Religious Zionism).- The BADATZ certification is considered more stringent and therefore Yael prefers, in deference to the Halachah, to demand uniformity in the level of kosher certification for all the products parents bring into the kindergarten, even if the latter are not that stringent in their own home.

In Summary

The pattern of religious hegemony, situated at the edge of the continuum, exists only in the microsystem circle. In other words, this pattern is triggered by the kindergarten teachers only. They fear "social pollution" (Douglas 2004) which may result from the entry of outgroups into the kindergarten (Morrison 2008). Social pollution threatens the religious identity of the community in the RSES framework (LeBaron and Abu-Nimer 2003), and from this stems the kindergarten teachers' monolithic attitude which results in the glorification of the religious identity category and the exclusion of the secular one. The voice of one ideal 'silences' dissenting ones, the 'others', based on the precepts of Jewish religious law, the Halachah. In the name of religious hegemony, which holds with one single absolute truth, that of the Halachah, the secular lifestyle is excluded not only from the kindergarten space, but this exclusion is expanding outside its fence as well, into the home of the secular family. Side by side with invalidating expressions of secular identity, monolithic religious codes are implemented whose objective is to fill the void created as a result of the exclusion of the secular identity.

---

[4] The acronym BADATZ means court of justice and is an ultra-orthodox body granting certificates to permitted foods.

The Pattern of Respect

The pattern of respect is located in the middle of the continuum. It protects the religious identity category while at the same time using strategies to appropriate the secular identity into the realm of religious observance. "When I educate children from the secular households, I must respect them and their parents" (Yona, ingroup kindergarten Religious Zionism). However, this happens not by excluding the secular identity, but rather by ignoring it. This pattern is the only one in which three ecological circles exist - the microsystem, the mesosystem, and the exosystem.

The Microsystem Circle

The kindergarten teacher allows for the slow acclimatization of the secular child into the religious identity circles and religious observation. It is important to note that in the educational discourse a much-repeated term is 'respect' in all its forms, and emphasis is laid on the need for sensitivity, both toward the child, and the family. In the field, the kindergarten teacher's wish to respect secular children and their parents is translated into two pedagogical practices which seem mutually exclusive. The first is the 'turning-a-blind-eye pedagogy' which is used when the secular child relates family events that contradict Jewish religious law:

> "I do not want children to have disagreements with their parents; after all, I know the households they come from. Even if they say to me: 'This past Shabbath we took a trip to the beach', I turn a blind eye and ignore it. I simply move on to a new topic [...] I won't say: 'what do you mean, trip to the beach on the Shabbath?' Seriously, this is a population that chose my kindergarten and they want a religious environment [...]. So, I turn a blind eye. I simply ignore the implications of what the child told me and move on" (Miri, ingroup kindergarten, Religious Zionism).

The kindergarten teacher opted for turning-a-blind-eye pedagogy, a respectable solution which on the one hand does not negate the secular children's experiences, and on the other hand does not open them up for discussion. In this manner the kindergarten teacher respects the secular child while reducing the religious children's exposure to phenomena that are inappropriate in terms of the spirit of Jewish religious law. The second pattern is the 'baby-steps' pedagogy which help the child to adjust to the religious environment. For example, the kindergarten teachers related that teaching Jewish religious practices, so foreign to the children from secular homes, takes time. For example, the fact that the Halachah requires boys to wear a skullcap:

> "They wear the skullcap when they are inside the kindergarten, but when playing in the yard, they find this uncomfortable. They are not used to having something on their heads, and they have no idea why they need it […]. The need for a skullcap is not something they bring from their home environment" (Avia, outgroup kindergarten, Religious Zionism).

The children who are not used to wearing a skullcap undergo a slow process of acclimatization which allows them to get used to this symbol of the religious Jew.

In one of the kindergartens, it was found that time, as a factor in internalizing Modern Orthodox practices, depends on the secular parents' responses to this process. For example, according to Halachah, one is supposed to say an appropriate blessing before eating anything:

> "The issue of having to say a blessing when eating a specific kind of food was something I introduced very slowly. This is not something you can expect to happen all at once. I let myself feel the children's reaction and took baby steps, also with the parents. I saw how I slowly made some progress in the right direction" (Miri, ingroup kindergarten, Religious Zionism).

Miri repeated words like "slowly" and "baby steps" several times and when the parents did not object to her actions, she felt she was on sure ground and could continue to teach the children appropriate Jewish religious behaviors.

It must be noted that the objective of respectful behavior manifested by the kindergarten teachers in the study was to see religious observance practiced on the kindergarten grounds exclusively, and no efforts were made to persuade the children to take these practices home with them.

The Mesosystem Circle

The realm of the inspectors can be divided into two authorities: the national and the district inspectorate. Each inspectorate works according to its own views. The national inspectorate advocates activism to bring children from secular homes closer to religious observance and see them included in the RSES out of social ideals of national unity. Two mechanisms are used to achieve these ideals. One is to establish a trend which would result, among others, in making the secular Jew an integral part of the RSES tradition. The official RSES anthem, for instance, plays a role in this mechanism, and it is regularly sung at national and district conventions.

> "... all the tribes of Israel/children of any age and diaspora/gather here with grace and charm/and together will build here in the era of redemption/this land, this land of beauty..."[5]

The allusion to "all the tribes of Israel" relates to the togetherness of the secular 'tribes' with those who observe Jewish tradition. This phrase also appears in other RSES documents analyzed for this study. The choice to allude to the secular person in the anthem of the RSES as an integral part of its tradition, suggests the ambition to create national unity by merging the various communities under the auspices of the RSES.

The other mechanism is the use of internal mailings which publish heroic stories of kindergarten teachers who successfully managed to bring the secular pupils closer to religious observance. These stories are based on religious experiences in the kindergarten which served as a bridge between the secular person and the world of Jewish religious observance. These stories are meant as an example to all educators in the RSES branch of Israel's educational system. The head of the RSES administration sends out weekly newsletters to the inspectorate and pedagogical counselors with

---

[5] "grace" and "beauty" are a translation of the Hebrew word HEMED which is also the Hebrew acronym for the religious state education system, translated here as RSES.

educational messages and inspirational voices from the field. Over the two years of this study, reports relating to events from within the kindergartens were subject to analysis, and the findings showed a discourse which gives the kindergarten teacher credit for bringing the secular population under her care closer to the Jewish tradition. The following is an example of a story related by a kindergarten teacher, where she describes how a "Shabbath suitcase"[6] she sent home with a child from a secular background was instrumental in convincing the father and the rest of the family to observe some of the precepts of the Shabbath:

> "one of the children in the kindergarten received this suitcase before the weekend. He came from a secular household, and when the father enrolled his child for the year, he emphatically said, "I know nothing of Judaism, and we both live our separate lives quite well [the parent and Judaism]". I had no idea how the father would react when he received the 'Shabbath suitcase' filled with wine to consecrate the Shabbath as well as other Judaica. The following Sunday the father came to the kindergarten and was very emotional when he said, 'I do not remember ever saying the blessing over the wine. And this past Shabbath I did so. I even bought Hallah bread and we told stories that were relevant. Could we keep that suitcase a few more days?' I breathed a sigh of relief and smiled" (from the RSES administration newsletter).

On the other hand, the district inspectorate has chosen to broaden RSES boundaries, in order to enable the secular child to feel secure within the walls of the RSES kindergarten. Based on this attitude, the inspectorate has labored to protect the secular child from the kindergarten teacher's efforts, or members of the community, to relegate the secular person to religious identity categories on the periphery of Jewish religious law. In one case, the kindergarten inspector related how the kindergarten teacher defended the secular parents against the religious ones, when an argument broke out between them during a PTA meeting in one of the kindergartens in her region.

---

[6] The "Shabbath suitcase" contains symbolic and ritual objects used to usher in and celebrate the Shabbath.

"We still have problems when the parents come to the PTA meetings. It is complicated when secular fathers arrive bareheaded, or mothers wear revealing clothing. They may argue, 'the Torah is not only your premise, and we want to send our children to this kindergarten because we want to live in this neighborhood, and you can't tell us how to dress' […]. On the other hand, one of the observant mothers shouted out, 'excuse me, you know, my husband is a Torah scholar and he brings our son to school. Then he sees these mothers in their sundresses, and it upsets him.' [the lack of modesty] Afterwards this mother complained that the secular parents there started yelling at her and while she had expected the kindergarten teacher to support her and say, 'well, you know, this is an orthodox kindergarten after all! […] and when I in my role as inspector asked the kindergarten teacher about this incident, she said, 'listen, I have a large group of secular parents here, and I would love to open them up to a greater level of observance, but I need to work slowly and carefully and can't make one-sided comments'" (Tzippi, regional inspector of the RSES kindergartens).

The observant parents turned to the inspector and complained that the kindergarten teacher, instead of showing her loyalty to the RSES' religious values and to defend the boundaries of the institution that pays her salary, she allowed the secular parents to violate them. However, the inspector too sided with the secular parents.

The Exosystem Circle

This circle includes the RSES position papers, which views the absorption of secular populations as a clear educational goal "the RSES is also open to pupils from celebrant-but-not-observant households, because one of its goals is to bring them closer to religious observance." (RSES position paper 2008, 38). The RSES, as an essentially religiously observant body, holds that for the greater good, the orthodox educator must see it as his/her sacred mission to bring secular Jews into the fold of religious observance, but emphasizes that this mission must be carried out with great sensitivity and an attitude of respect for those who claim a non-orthodox identity "bringing them closer (to religious observance). must be achieved through kindness and respect for others" (RSES position paper 2008, 19).

The Illusory Multi-Identities Pattern

"multiple interpretations of the Jewish tradition are made possible when the approach is easy-going" (from the Meitarim NPO website).[7]

On the other extreme of the continuum we find the illusory multi-identities pattern in two ecological circles: the microsystem circle and the mesosystem. The microsystem circle is comprised of the kindergarten teacher and the parents. Between them they maintain a relationship of cooperation which, in turn, is supported by the RSES authority as the representative of the mesosystem.

Within this pattern two religious community identities live side by side, while each manifests categories of its own independent religious identity, neither dependent on the other community nor excluding it. As a result, unlike in the case of the two previous patterns described in this article, here, the secular children are exempt from religious observance, also within the kindergarten walls.

This ideological pattern is based on the curriculum of the Meitarim NPO which promotes pluralistic Jewish education. In one of the kindergartens studied, the inspectorate gave the teacher permission to use the Meitarim curriculum, and thus to allow an array of interpretations of the Jewish tradition in the actual practice and pedagogical discourse taking place in the kindergarten.

"Meitarim creates an inclusive educational climate in which learners from diverse Jewish backgrounds co-exist and receive a Jewish education as a central aspect of the educational point of view, without coercion, and enabling multiple interpretations of the Jewish tradition" (From the Meitarim NPO website).

---

[7] https://www.meitarim.org/en/

Making room for secular expression is also spreading to pedagogical practices in the arena of public discourse and is directed at the child's family. Here the identity categories are equally presented over two identities- "some act like this, others like that":

> "I strongly emphasize that some parents say their prayers and others don't and that some people observe the fasts of the Jewish tradition, while other don't. I am inclusive. When I teach a given topic, I do my best to say to the children that it has many different aspects" (Miri, ingroup community, Religious Zionism).

A further example of inclusiveness and giving equal space to the two identities is to hold two different ceremonies concurrently where one is centered around religious practice and the other not. The children are divided into two groups, based on their upbringing, observant or secular:

> "a reading circle and a prayer circle [...] the children enter the library with the teaching aid for storytelling [...] each group is given an activity based on their parents' choices; the secular parents chose storytelling and the observant ones, prayer" (Miri, ingroup kindergarten, Religious Zionism).

Prayer symbolizes the sacred world, while the library symbolizes the profane, however, both are presented with equal status. In order to strengthen the sense of equality, both ceremonies were given the same title, "circle", devoid of religious connotation.

A further pedagogy of equality comes to the fore when the kindergarten does away with dress code; the girls from secular homes may dress as they are accustomed, tank tops and pants. Aside from relaxing rules concerning appearance, there is a more meaningful option of giving space to different identities, namely, the exemption from religious observance: the boys from secular homes are not required to wear skullcaps, one of the essential symbols of the religious hegemony in these kindergartens:

"In this kindergarten, the boy comes without a skullcap or fringed garment" (Hagit, regional inspector of the RSES).

And there is more; the kindergarten teacher will also refrain from making any other demands of the secular child:

"the kindergarten teacher there won't ask the boy to bring a fringed garment" (Zehava, regional inspector of the RSES kindergartens). This restraint extends to blessings before eating: "May refuses to say the blessing [...] I can't force her to do so" (Miri, ingroup kindergarten, Religious Zionism).

In spite of declarations regarding the existence of the multi-identities space which moves in two directions simultaneously, the findings show that they are the result of an illusory prism, meaning that in reality, the religious identity gives up aspects of its identity in order to make space for the existence of the secular one, and this reality comes to the fore in a number of spaces: during the Torah story:

"What I was able to do in other kindergartens, namely to bring in an aspect of Jewish beliefs and rituals, here I was prevented from doing so. [...] I taught the children about the scales of justice that weigh our good and bad deeds, so that HaShem (G-d) can judge us and choose whether to write us into the book of the wicked or the book of life. At this point I understood that I had a problem, that I might do the wrong thing [...] I found that talking about the scales here was complicated because the children might come home and say: 'you don't keep the Shabbath, you will not be written into the book of life'" (Miri, ingroup kindergarten, Religious Zionism).

With great sensitivity, the kindergarten teacher stopped herself from teaching one of the corner stones of Judaism, the principle of reward and punishment. However, this belief may raise conflicts for the children from secular homes and their families. A further example for selective teaching and exclusion is the event of the telling of Torah stories where there are incidences of violence which may go against social, ethical values, and so, the teacher skips these:

> "the topic of the father who sacrifices his son (the sacrifice of Isaac), is very off-putting to secular parents. This is also true of the Cain and Abel story, for instance, where two brothers fight, and one murders the other. They do not like violent stories like that [...] and so I simply skip them" (Miri, ingroup kindergarten, Religious Zionism)

Marginalizing Jewish religious identity categories also occur within the world of pedagogical discourse. In the process of interaction with the children, certain linguistic utterances from the sacred world are adapted to fit the secular one: for example, specific utterances marking them as relating directly to faith are secularized:

> "the word 'tzaddik' when addressing a child is not heard in the kindergarten. I refrain from saying it[8] [...] Instead I address the child as 'good boy', hinting at the idea of keeping the commandments, but not saying it overtly" (Miri, ingroup kindergarten, Religious Zionism).

Even the boundaries of the Halachah are compromised

> "the parents sometimes bring a cake to the kindergarten, and I do not know if it is kosher. In order not to shame the parent, I keep silent [...] it is more important to me that the parents feel comfortable" (Yonit, ingroup kindergarten, Religious Zionism).

Social considerations, then, may lead to actions that transgress the Jewish laws governing consuming only certified kosher food.

---

[8] The Hebrew word "tzaddik" translates as saint, a holy person, but its connotation is a much broader one. It is often used in observant families simply to call the children to the table, to shower, to do homework. This is especially true for young children, and its use is geared to instill the concept of holiness as a way of life. As such, the word 'saint' is not suitable here, and I preferred to use transliteration and a footnote. Moreover, the distance between 'tzaddik' and 'good boy' is enormous and the latter completely misses the mark.

One of the secular mothers tried to explain the advantages of a mixed kindergarten population consisting of children from observant and secular homes, when it is run according to the "illusory multi-identities pattern":

> "It is a fragile, complex reality [...]there is no way a child from a secular family won't be accepted for who he is in an environment that is not overtly religious [...] the educational system makes allowances for such a child [...] if one runs the kindergarten as an overtly religious environment, you won't find children from secular homes there, because it is too single-minded" (a mother from Miri's kindergarten, ingroup community, Religious Zionism).

The consequence of efforts to create a harmonious, educational, cultural fabric where the Modern Orthodox and the secular identity have equal rights to an autonomous existence is that aspects of the observant identity are peripheralized while the secular parents are given the power to determine educational patterns within the RSES: "Clearly, the kindergarten is defined as observant-secular [...] we try so hard not to be overly religious [...] The RSES has two different branches: integrated (observant-secular) and observant (Modern Orthodox) education." (a mother from Miri's kindergarten, ingroup community, Religious Zionism). The two-directional model characterizes the secular education model as equal in value to mainstream Modern Orthodox education.

Summing Up

The illusory multi-identities pattern allegedly advocates pluralism and providing equal space to the Modern Orthodox and secular identities. This would allow the latter their secular identity within the confines of the religious kindergarten and exempt them from participating in the religious rituals also while there. However, this is an optical illusion, as in reality, the secular identity marginalizes the observant one: Sensitive ideas from the Jewish tradition which may contradict modern, social values are selectively removed from the kindergarten. In addition, linguistic utterances of a religious connotation are replaced by those more palatable to the secular world, even to the extent of expressing social preferences which drive out the hegemony of Jewish religious law- Halachah- from within the kindergarten and threatening its religious character, and in this case, the cooperation of the parents is needed. The mandate given to the secular parents to shape the religious identity of the kindergarten gives them the power to "change the cultural, ecological edge" even to the point of taking steps that contradict the RSES' ideological position papers, and may lead to the marginalization of the core beliefs behind the operation of the Modern Orthodox kindergarten.

SUMMARY AND DISCUSSION

The integration of secular populations within the RSES institutions has brought about a cultural encounter between identity communities which are inherently different, perhaps even polar opposites. This meeting point poses a complex social challenge, has given rise to a diversity of coping mechanisms, and in part, has led to changes in categories at the core of the RSES.

The different ecological circles found within the kindergarten and outside, in the community, have different coping patterns. Each pattern represents a different positioning on the part of the identities, observant or secular, along a continuum, with religious glorification on one pole, in parallel with secular exclusion. On the other extreme of the pole- secular glorification in parallel with observant (religious) exclusion, while the pattern of respect lies between the two. Only a few of the ecological circles have the two polar patterns. However, the center of the continuum, where a pattern of respect is located, is supported by all three ecological circles, as is shown in the chart below.

The meeting between the observant and secular identity as a result of the slow entry of communities which do not manifest an observant identity into the cultural, ecological edge of the RSES institutions, has resulted in the establishment of different identity patterns in the RSES kindergarten. These patterns include core characteristics from the central community, Religious Zionism, side by side with secular identity characteristics from the outgroup community (Barak and Gidron 2009; Ben-Rafael and Ben-Haim 2006; Strayer et al. 2003).

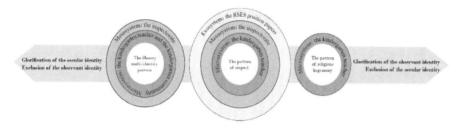

Figure 1. Ecological model of patterns for the establishment of the observant (religious) identity in the RSES kindergarten when the observant (religious) and secular identities meet.

The presence of a number of identity establishment patterns teaches that the ecological circles which surround the kindergarten environment disagree about the desired religious character of the RSES kindergarten, when communities which are not observant enroll in its institutions. The interaction between the ingroup and outgroup communities has changed the RSES kindergarten's community identity (Breakwell 2010; Clemence and Lorenzi-Cioldi 2014; Shavit, Sasson-Levy, and Ben-Porat 2012; Wenger 1998), and added new shades of identity which are reflected in three different identity patterns established in each of the various ecological circles. They are found on a continuum which moves from religious glorification to secular exclusion, and from secular glorification to religious exclusion. The pattern of respect is situated in the center of the continuum and is found in each of the three ecological circles: the teacher, the inspectorate and the RSES position papers. This pattern guards the categories of the RSES' religious identity by using strategies of respect for the secular appropriation of religious spaces, all the while not by excluding categories of secular identity but by turning a blind eye to them. This pattern characterizes an educational system whose departments aspire to allow the existence of a fragile social fabric within its institutions, where it is ready to teach fragments of religious observance to the secular population in a slow and controlled manner, without dismantling the secular identity as long as it does not seek to construct an alternate identity.

However, the findings of the study point out that the cultural edge expanded only in the microsystem circle, which is activated by the kindergarten teachers. The latter created two patterns which represent an edge area which is flexible and open to change and inter-cultural encounters (Cohen 2006; Turner, Davidson-Hunt and O'Flaherty 2003). One, the religious hegemonies pattern, where any behavior not compatible with Jewish Religious Law is excluded and eventually replaced with observant identity categories as binding monolithic patterns. Two, the illusory multi-identities pattern allegedly advocates pluralism and allowing equal space to both the observant and secular identities, however, this is an optical illusion, for in reality the secular identity pushes aside the observant identity's hold over the kindergarten and thus threatens the religious character of the RSES.

The absence of agreement among kindergarten teachers, the inspectorate, and the RSES position papers concerning the character of the edge area have resulted in multi-hued polarized identity patterns which move along the continuum between glorification and exclusion of the secular or observant identity. The variety and the characteristics of such contrasting behavior patterns show that pluralism is an all-present property of the RSES institutions, such as the kindergartens, and it is this dynamic pluralism, where each of the kindergarten teachers is free to establish her own unique pattern of behavior, which reflects the many transformations of the way Judaism is experienced in the RSES kindergarten, all the way up to the exclusion of the other identity.

The range of patterns of behavior established by kindergarten teachers has resulted in ousting certain identities from their classroom. This was possible due to two factors connected to the way the management of the pre-school level of education in Israel diverges from that of the 1-12 education system, where such patterns could not have sprouted: administrative autonomy- most pre-schools are housed in structures that are physically and administratively separate, meaning that they are not an integral part of the grade 1-6 grounds and are separately administered. The advantage is that kindergarten teachers are not required to conform to any set policy, unlike the 1-12 educational system (Frish 2012; Oplatka and Stundi 2011; Schneider 2016; Sverdlov et al. 2010).

Concerning the pedagogical autonomy- in the past decade a number of core curricula for the kindergarten have been published. However, there is still no cohesive social-educational enforcement of such a curriculum in the kindergarten (Amir-Kasif 2013; Frish 2012). In addition, the absence of cohesiveness is especially reflected in the area of the Jewish tradition, where so far, no core curriculum has been written which would serve as a conceptual framework and measuring stick for achievement. The result of this void is the autonomy extended to the kindergarten teacher in making choices based on her own agenda, what values to teach and which methodology to use when she teaches topics connected to the world of Jewish religious observance (Achituv 2012; Odesser 2007; Schneider 2015).

The advantage of having a dynamic system whose principles are fluid and may change based on circumstance and changing needs is two-pronged: a pluralistic educational system whose employees enjoy the autonomous space to design their educational field allows them to offer immediate solutions in a variety of the community fabrics to which they belong (Gross 2011; Lipschitz 2011). At the same time, it makes it possible for new members, i.o.w. the secular population, to be integrated within that community without feeling threatened and without conflict (Cohen 2006; Turner, Davidson-Hunt and O'Flaherty 2003: Zehavi 2011).

Compared to the advantages of the autonomy to include the 'other', the findings in this study demonstrated that the advantages on the community level are a disadvantage on the level of the system. The pluralism, which came to the fore as autonomy given to the field by the organization, put the kindergarten teacher in a position of power which led to the dismantling of the religious boundaries in RSES kindergartens on the cultural ecological edge, even to the point of creating identity patterns contrary to the religious core identity of the RSES kindergarten: on the one hand, the diminishment of the religious entity was reflected in the subsequent diminishment of religious practices as well as the diminishment of the inspectorate's influence over the kindergarten. While this process underscored the strength of the pluralistic educational system which allows the entry of other community identities into the RSES system, and leaves them to find their place in an educational system which allegedly is not compatible with the categories of that community identity, on the other hand, this diminishment points to the weakness of an educational system which fails to control its institutional hegemony when it comes to the outlying areas, far removed from its central core.

This study may shed light on similar tensions, patterns and strategies in other countries and in religious kindergartens of other religions.

REFERENCES

Achituv, Sigal. 2012. "*Early Childhood Educators Tell Their Stories: On the Identity of Religious Pre-School Teachers in Israel.*" PhD diss., Haifa University. Hebrew.

Amir-Kasif, Eileil. 2013. "Instances of Chaotic Order in Education: The Case of a Preschool in South Tel Aviv." In *The Classroom and School, Close-up: Ethnographic Studies of Education*, edited by Braha Alpert and Simha Slusky, 69–107. Tel Aviv: Mahon Mofet. Hebrew.

Arian, Asher., and Ayala, Ceasar-Sugarman. 2009. *Israeli Jews – Portrait: Beliefs, Observing Tradition and Values of Judaism in Israel, 2009.* Jerusalem: The Guttman Center for Public Opinion and Policy Research, The Israel Democracy Institute. Hebrew. Accessed October 25. https://en.idi.org.il/media/5439/guttmanavichaireport2012_engfinal.pdf

Atkinson, Paul., and Martyn, Hammersley. 2000. "Ethnography and Participant Observation." In *Handbook of qualitative research*, edited by Norman K. Denzin and Yvonna S. Lincoln, 248–261. Thousand Oaks, CA: Sage Publications.

Augoustinos, Martha., Iain, Walker., and Ngaire, Donaghue N. 2014. *Social Cognition: An Integrated Introduction.* Thousand Oaks, CA: Sage.

Barak Judith., and Gidron, Ariela. eds. 2009. *Active Collaborative Education – A Story of Teacher-education.* Tel Aviv: Mofet Institute. Hebrew.

Ben-Rafael, Eliezer., and Lior, Ben-Chaim. 2006. *Jewish Identities in an Era of Multiple Modernities*. Ra'anana: The Open University. Hebrew.

Blommaert, Jan. 2005. *Discourse: Key Topics in Sociolinguistics*. Cambridge, UK: Cambridge University Press.

Breakwell, Glynis M. 2010. "Resisting Representations and Identity Processes." *Papers on Social Representations, 19*, 6–1.

Bronfenbrenner, Urie. 1979. *The Ecology of Human Development*. Cambridge, Mass.: Harvard University Press.

Bronfenbrenner, Urie. 1986. "Ecology of Family as a Context For Human Development Research Perspectives." *Developmental Psychology, 22*, 723–742.

Bronfenbrenner, Urie. and Pamela, Morris. 1998. "The Ecology of Developmental Processes." In *Handbook of Child Psychology*, edited by William Damon and Richard Lerner, 993–1028. New York: Wiley.

Buzaglo, Meir. 2005. "The New Traditional Jew and the Halachah Phenomenology." In *Renewal and Tradition: Creating leadership and Cultural Processes among North African Jews*, edited by Moshe Orpali, and Efraim Hazan, 187–204. Jerusalem: The Bialik Institute. Hebrew.

Buzaglo, Meir. 2008. *Language for the Faithful: Thoughts about Tradition*. Jerusalem: Keter. Hebrew.

Carriere, Kevin R. 2013. "Culture Cultivating Culture: The Four Products of the Meaning-Made World." *Integrative Psychological and Behavioral Science, 48*, 270–282. Accessed September 9, 2018. doi: 10.1007/s12124-013-9252-0.

Cicchetti, Dante., and Kristin, Valentino. 2006. An Ecological Transactional Perspective on Child Maltreatment: Failure of the Average Expectable Environment and Its Influence Upon Child Development. In *Developmental Psychopathology*, edited by Dante Cicchetti and Donald J. Cohen, 129–201. Hoboken, N.J.: John Wiley & Sons.

Clemence, Alain., Willem, Doise., and Fabio, Lorenzi-Cioldi. 2014. *The Quantitative Analysis of Social Representations*. New York: Routledge.

Cohen, Asher. 2006. *Non-Jewish Jews in Israel: Israel Jewish Identity and the Challenge to Expand the Jewish People in Israel.* Jerusalem: The Shalom Hartman Institute. Hebrew.

Dagan, Mattityahu. (2006). *Religious Zionist Education in the test of Time and Era.* Tel Aviv: Department of Defense. Hebrew.

Dagan, Mattityahu. 2008. "The RSES Contribution to Society and the State." *Position Paper from the RSES Authority*, 4, 41–48. Hebrew.

Denzin, Norman K. 1978. *The Research Act: A Theoretical Orientation To Sociological Methods.* New York: McGraw-Hill.

Denzin, Norman K. 1994. "Postmodernism and Deconstructionism." In *Postmodernism and Social Inquiry*, edited by David Dickens and Andrea Fontana, 182–202. London: UCL Press.

Diamant, Rosa. 2005. *The kindergarten as part of the child's territorial model – in Isfyia and Kiryat Tivon.* MSc. Thesis, the Technion, Israel Institute of Technology, Haifa. Hebrew.

Dombrowski, Matty. 2010. *From Seclusion to Involvement: The Phenomenon of the Torah Social Action Groups as an Expression of Changes in the Social and Cultural Outlook of Religious Zionism.* PhD dissertation, Bar-Ilan University, Ramat-Gan. Hebrew.

El-Or, Tamar. 2006. *Reserned Seats: Religion, Gender and Ethnicity in Contemporary Israel.* Tel Aviv: Am Oved. Hebrew.

Fairclough, Norman. 1993. "Critical Discourse Analysis and the Marketization of Public Discourse: The Universities." *Discourse & Society*, 4, 133–168.

Fairclough, Norman. 2013. *Critical Discourse Analysis.* Edited by Ruth Wodak. London: Sage.

Frish, Yichiel. 2012. *The Kindergarten Teacher as an Administrator and an Educational Leader: Episodes of Management.* Haifa: Shaanan – The Religious Academic College of Education. Hebrew.

Garred, Michelle G. 2013. "The Power of Mindsets: Bridging, Bonding, and Associational Change in Deeply Divided Mindanao." *Journal of Civil Society*, 9, 21–40.

Gee, James P. 2004. "Discourse Analysis: What Makes It Critical? In *An Introduction to Critical Discourse Analysis in Education*, edited by R. Rogers, 19–50. Mahwah, N.J.: Lawrence Erlbaum Associates.

Gilchrist, Alison, Melanie, Bowles, and Margaret, Wetherell. 2010. *Identities and Social Action: Connecting Communities for a Change*. London: Community Development Foundation.

Glaser, Barney G. and Anselm, L. Strauss. 2017. *Discovery of Grounded Theory: Strategies for Qualitative Research*. New York: Routledge.

Goodman, Yehuda, and Yossi, Yonah. 2004. "Introduction". In *Maelstrom of Identities: A Critical Look at Religion and Secularity in Israel*, edited by Yossi Yonah and Yehuda Goodman, 9–45. Tel Aviv: Hakibbutz Hameuchad Publishing House. Hebrew

Grbich, C. 2007. *Qualitative Data Analysis: An Introduction*. London: Sage Publications.

Gross, Zehavit. 2011. "The RSES between Integration and Isolationism." In *This is Hemed: One Hundred Years of Religious-Zionist Education*, edited by Lilach Rosenberg-Fridman, and Yitzhak S. Recanati, 33-47. Jerusalem: Yad Yitzhak Ben-Tzvi. Hebrew

Guba, Egon G., and Yvonna, S. Lincoln. 2005. "Paradigmatic Controversies, Contradictions, and Emerging Confluences." In *The Sage Handbook of Qualitative Research*, edited by Norman K. Denzin, and Yvonna S. Lincoln, 191–216. Thousand Oaks, CA: Sage Publications.

Hammersley, Martyn, and Paul, Atkinson. 2007. *Ethnography: Principles in Practice*. New York: Routledge.

Handelman, Don., and Lea, Shamgar-Hendelman. 2004. "Celebration of the National: Holiday Occasion in Kindergartens." In *Nationalism and the Israeli State: Bureaucratic Login in Public Event*, edited by Don Handelman, 61–66. Oxford: Berg.

Hart, Christopher, and Christopher, Cap. eds. 2014. *Contemporary Critical Discourse Studies*. London and New York: Bloomsbury Publishing.

Keel, Yehuda. 1987. *The RSES: Its Roots, History and Problems*. Jerusalem: Ministry of Education and Culture. Hebrew.

Kasen, Lea., and Michal, Kromer-Nevo. 2010. Introduction to qualitative data analysis. In *Qualitative Data Analysis*, edited by Leah Kessin and Michal Kromer-Nevo, 18-1. Beer-Sheva: Ben-Gurion. University Publishing House. Hebrew.

Kupferberg, Irit. 2010. "A model for the four words of interactive discourse analysis." In *Qualitative Data Analysis*, edited by Leah Kessin and Michal Kromer-Nevo, 155–180. Beer-Sheva: Ben-Gurion University Publishing House. Hebrew.

LeBaron, Michelle, and Mohammed, Abu-Nimer. 2003. *Bridging Cultural Conflicts: A New Approach for a Changing World*. San Francisco: Jossey-Bass.

Leon, Nisim. 2009. *Soft Ultra-Orthodoxy: The Religious Renewal among Oriental Jews*. Jerusalem: Yad Ben-Zvi Institute. Hebrew.

Lewis, Sarah. 2015. "Qualitative Inquiry and Research Design: Choosing Among Five Approaches." *Health promotion practice*, *16*, 473–475.

Lipschitz, Abraham. 2011. "The RSES: Looking Toward the Future." In *This is Hemed: One Hundred Years of Religious-Zionist Education*, edited by Lilach Rosenberg-Fridman and Yitzhak S. Recanati, 385–396. Jerusalem: Yad Yitzhak Ben-Tzvi. Hebrew.

Morrison, Kimberly R., and Oscar, Ybarra. 2008. "The Effects of Realistic Threat and Group Identification on Social Dominance Orientation." *Journal of Experimental Social Psychology*, *44*, 156–163.

Moses, Hanan. 2009. *From Religious Zionism to Post-Modern Religion: Trends and Processes among Religious Zionism since Rabin's Assassination*. PhD Dissertation, Bar-Ilan University, Ramat Gan. Hebrew.

Nir-Yaniv, Nehama. 1984. *To Educate and be Educated: Educational Approaches and the Educator's Personal Development*. Tel Aviv: Sifriath Hapoalim. Hebrew.

Odesser, Luzit. 2007. *The Biblical Story in the RSES Kindergarten as a Reflection of the Kindergarten Teacher's Role in light of the Pentateuch*. MA. Thesis, Hebrew University, Jerusalem. Hebrew.

Oplatka, Izhar, and Masada, Stundi. 2011. "The Components and Determinants of Preschool Teacher Organisational Citizenship

Behaviour." *International Journal of Educational Management*, 25, 223–236. Hebrew

Pianta, Robert C., Bridget, Hamre, and Masada, Stuhalman. 2003. "Relationships Between Teachers and Children." In *Handbook of psychology*, edited by William Reynolds and Gloria Miller, 199–234. New York: Wiley.

Sagi, Avi. 2006. *The Jewish-Israeli Voyage: Questions of culture and identity*. Jerusalem: Shalom Hartman Institue. Hebrew.

Sagi, Avi. 2017. *This Era: Jewish Thought in the Test of the Present*. Jerusalem: Grafit. Hebrew.

Schiffrin, Deborah, Deborah, Tannen, and Heidi, E. Hamilton. 2001. "Introduction." In *The Handbook of Discourse Analysis*, edited by Deborah Schiffrin, Deborah Tannen, and Heidi E. Hamilton, 1–10. Malden, MA: Blackwell.

Schneider, Orna. 2015. "The RSES Kindergarten in the Maelstrom of Identities." *Shaanan, 21*, 151–178. Hebrew.

Schneider, Orna, and Deborah, Court. 2016. "The Pedagogy of a well-run community." *Mayim MeDlaleyav, 27*, 6–36. Hebrew.

Schwartz, Dov. 2003. *Religious Zionism: History and Ideology*. Tel Aviv: Ministry of Defence. Hebrew.

Shavit, Zeev, Orna, Sasson-Levy, and Guy, Ben-Porat. 2013. *Point of Reference: Changing Identities and Social Positioning in Israel*. Jerusalem: Van Leer Institute. Hebrew.

Shkedi, Asher. 2011. *The Meaning Behind the Words: Methodologies for Qualitative Research – Theory and Practice*. Tel Aviv: Ramot. Hebrew.

Sluski, Simha, and Braha, Alpert. 2007. *Guidelines for writing qualitative research papers*. Tel Aviv: MOFET Institute. Hebrew.

Spradley, James P. 2016. *Participant Observation*. Long Grove, IL: Waveland Press.

Stake, Robert E. 2006. *Multiple Case Study Analysis*. New York: The Guildford Press.

Stake, Robert E. 2013. *Multiple Case Study Analysis*. New York: The Guilford Press.

Strauss, Anselm, and Juliet, M. Corbin. 1997. *Grounded Theory in Practice.* Thousand Oaks: Sage.

Sverdlov, Aviva, and Ora, Goldhirsch. 2010. *The Educational Work in the Kindergarten: Guidelines for the educational staff.* Jerusalem: Dept. of Publications, the Ministry of Education. Retrieved 9 September, 2018. http://cms.education.gov.il/nr/rdonlyres/5cb32d8a-03b1-4bfb-bc65-76d9f8e70573/105673/kavimmanhim1209.pdf.

Turner, Nancy J., Iain, J. Davidson-Hunt., and Michael, O'Flaherty. 2003. "Living on the Edge: Ecological and Cultural Edges as Sources of Diversity for Social Ecological Resilience." *Human Ecology, 31*, 439–461.

Van, Dijk., and Teun, A. 2001. "Discourse Analysis and Narrative." In *The Handbook of Discourse Analysis*, edited by Deborah Schiffrin, Deborah Tannen, and Heidi E. Hamilton, 71–352. Malden, MA: Blackwell.

Van, Dijk. 2015. "Critical Discourse Studies: A Sociocognitive Approach." In *Methods of critical discourse studies analysis*, edited by Ruth Wodak and Michael Meyer, 62–86. London: Sage.

Wenger, Etienne. 1998. *Communities of Practice: Learning, Meaning, and Identity.* Cambridge: Cambridge University Press.

Yadgar, Yaacov. 2010. *Modernity without Secularization.* Jerusalem: The Shalom Hartman Institute. Hebrew.

Yadgar, Yaacov. 2012. *Boyond Secularization: Traditionism and the Critique of Israeli Secularism.* Jerusalem: The Shalom Hartman Institute. Hebrew.

Yin, Robert. 2009. *Case Study Research: Design and Methods.* Los Angeles, CA: Sage.

Zehavi, Ram. 2011. "Between Halachah and Traditionalism in the RSES in Israel." In *This is Hemed: One Hundred Years of Religious-Zionist Education*, edited by Lilach Rosenberg-Fridman and Yitzhak S. Recanati, 363–377. Jerusalem: Yad Yitzhak Ben-Tzvi. Hebrew.

BIOGRAPHICAL SKETCH

Orna Schneider

Affiliation: Shaanan College, Haifa, Israel

Education: PhD

Research and Professional Experience: The focus of my work is qualitative, ethnographic research and studies of the rich cultural population disparity in Israel's state education, and its pedagogical consequences. Another aspect of my research concerns teacher training with a focus on ecological systems at work within the educational system.

Professional Appointments: Head of the Faculty of Early Childhood Education at Shaanan College.

Publications from the Last 3 Years:

Schneider, Orna. 2015. "The RSES Kindergarten in the Maelstrom of Identities". *Shaanan, 21*, 151–178.

Schneider, Orna., and Deborah, Court. 2016. "The Pedagogy of a well-run community." *Mayim MeDlaleyav, 27*, 6–36.

Schneider, Orna., and Deborah, Court. 2016. "The Kindergarten Ceremony in the service of Religious Zionism". *Kaet, 2*, 184-201.

Schneider, Orna., and Deborah, Court. 2019. In press ."A Pedagogical - Religious Model for Formation of Religious Identity: Between Theological and Sociological". *Iyunim Behinuch,* 17-18.

In: Religious Education
Editor: Richard Coudert

ISBN: 978-1-53615-832-8
© 2019 Nova Science Publishers, Inc.

Chapter 3

SHARING CHRISTIAN SPIRITUALITY AT SECULAR UNIVERSITIES

Nuria Toledano[*]
Business Management and Marketing Department,
University of Huelva, Huelva, Spain

ABSTRACT

This chapter discusses the possibilities opened up for learning from Christian spirituality in the framework of a post-modern European university. On the one hand, the study is framed within the current debates around the purpose and meaning of the public – secular – University. On the other hand, it deals with the challenges that modern universities are facing for attending students' religious needs. The insights come from an initiative undertaken by a Spanish university with the aim of enlivening the commitments of the youth with the nature and demands of ultimate questions. The study suggests that introducing religious insights in the context of a secular education is an area that is by no means easy to approach, but where there are opportunities to draw bridges between reason and religious spirituality.

---

[*] Corresponding Author's E-mail: toledano@dem.uhu.es.

Keywords: Christian spirituality, religion, university, higher education

INTRODUCTION

In 1641 René Descartes (1596-1650) wrote in his Meditation on First Philosophy about his experience of religious and spiritual search for certainty and security in the midst of what he saw as a chaotic world. Paradoxically, Descartes' solution to his own dilemma (the known formula "*Cogito ergo sum*" –I think therefore I am) ended up placing the human reason as the cornerstone for human knowledge. There was then a need for cultivating the secular reasoning thorough and optimistic humanism and, in this context, universities became the great temples for doing it. In this sense, it is generally admitted that modern universities are a product of the enlightenment (Baratta and Smith 2018; Fourie and Fourie 2009). Throughout centuries there has been a strong faith on the positive role of universities for the intellectual and moral progress of humanity, as they promote the values of reason, rationality and scepticism (Porter 2001; Guest et al. 2013). But such prestige of universities as standard bearers of knowledge came to marginalize the reasonable knowledge derived from religious traditions (Weller, Hooley and Moore 2011; Yancey 2012). Therefore, any insight associated with a religious faith was excluded from the daily life of higher educational institutions and public universities were increasingly to be associated with secular universities (Ecklund, Park and Veliz 2008; Hyers and Hyers 2008).

Over the last years, however, the increasing diversity of religions all over the world is opening new scenarios for religions in universities and other spheres of public life –as workplaces (Hicks 2003; Toledano 2018; Toledano and Karanda 2017a). Even within secular universities, there are members who are expressing the need of welcoming openly religious influences in the university campus. Some of them are also keen to creating spaces where learning from religion becomes one of the "normal" options that universities can offer to both local and international students (Biddington 2013; Johnson and Laurence 2012).

This chapter builds on the experience undertaken in a public European University – the University of Huelva, in Spain – for sharing Christian spirituality among the university members. Being Christianity the major spiritual tradition in Europe (Kim, Fisher and McCalman 2009), it is justified to bring about initiatives related to this religious tradition in the European university context. Moreover, Christian influence has been powerful in every sphere of European thought and life; philosophy, art, and many fundamental principles to social life have found inspirations in Christianity, even though the religious language has been taken away (Toledano and Karanda 2017a). Nonetheless, from this must not follow that other experiences that represent different faith religious – whether western or eastern faith traditions – cannot have room in the campus. Rather, most campuses will find it today desirable to provide facilities for the different religious needs of students and faculty (Johnson and Laurence 2012). Yet, in this chapter our focus will be placed on initiatives developed to share Christian spirituality. The rest of the chapter will be structured as follows. First, we will contextualize this study in the framework of the current discussions around the purposes of the public – secular – university. We will then summarize the main aspects of Christian spirituality and provide some methodological notes. Afterwards, we will present the novel experience undertaken at the University of Huelva. Finally, the chapter will end with a brief discussion about the initiatives developed for providing university members with opportunities to sharing Christian spirituality and the main conclusions of the work.

RETHINKING THE MISSION OF PUBLIC UNIVERSITIES AT THE 21ST CENTURY

The University has been recognized as the second-oldest institution in the Western world with an unbroken history after the Roman Catholic Church (Iyanga 2000). Its unbroken evolution began in the late sixth century with the cathedral-based schools, which gave rise to the world's first university in 1088: the University of Bologna. (Lozano Aguilar et al. 2008). Afterwards, the universities of Oxford (in 1167), Paris (in 1170) and Salamanca (in 1230) were created. As a result of their natural evolution of cathedral and monastery schools, the universities, at that time, were seats of religious instruction, debate, and research; they were concerned with the need to establish the truth (Kennedy, 2017). However, the modern public university, as we know today, appears to have lost the thrill for seeking of true knowledge. Instead, it seems that nowadays higher education is understood in predominantly instrumentalist terms (Panton, 2017), that is, as instruments serving the public interest (Christensen and Gornitzka 2017; Christensen and Lægreid 2007, 2014). Some recent works refer to this idea by saying that universities are "socially embedded" (Ramirez 2010; Stensaker 2018).

Without denying the importance of having universities related to their environments, the point we want to stress here is that this fact may also bring us some problems. Indeed, the fact of having "socially embedded universities" – a reality that is increasingly gaining ground – might probably be at the root of the fragmentation and confusion about the mission of universities. And, of course, this also means that universities are being transformed from being institutions into becoming organizations (Ramirez 2010) highly influenced by their environments. Accordingly, they are open to the influence of the discourses generated by professionals on how best the university should function as organization (Ramirez 2006, 2010).

With the advent of this instrumental culture in the life of the university, many questions have raised for those of us involved in higher education. This new scenario suggests that the pursuit of the truth that was at the heart of the universities in their origins has been replaced by the transmission of knowledge that generates the capacities to allow fulfilling the needs of the labour market and the marketplace in a better way. In fact, a socially embedded university emphasizes its social usefulness whether in terms of being a medium to increase the opportunities to get a job or in terms more directly linked to the progress, as in Clark's (1998) vision of the entrepreneurial university. In fact, the notion of a "core curriculum" is centred on the STEM disciplines (science, technology, engineering, and mathematics) almost exclusively. Although we give full credit to these subjects, the "problem" is that all of them are mainly ordered toward utility, such that the focus is, as we have noted, on forming professionals who will succeed when it comes to employability and ultimately achieve financial goals (Hornsby and Morello 2017). But what is more worrying is that the employment in a good company or the creation of new successful businesses become not only the primary determinant of the content of education, but also the standard under which the quality and success of an university is measured (Panton 2017). At times the purpose of education is in part subordinated towards the end of getting as many students as possible into university (Ramirez 2010; Stensaker 2018). But paradoxically, we also find teachers that are encouraged, in one way or other, to pay more attention to the number of publications they get each year than to the teaching achievement of their students. Besides, teaching achievements are on occasions the result of what students display in a final exam (Toledano and Karanda 2017a).

While we believe that the university has an important role to play in the development of society by providing young people well trained, the point is that it should not be limited to this. If the language that we use to talk about universities represents them as a service organization – or an enterprise – embedded in a competitive market (Christensen and Lægreid 2007, 2014), then we might end up with universities that are far beyond the universities which were created with the purpose to seek the truth and nurture critical thinking. Recognising the contingent economic and social demands that characterize contemporary societies and the secular and market values that govern public universities today, we might be running the risk of forgetting what is indispensable in any level of education: the formation of human persons.

Placing the formation of the human person at the centre of the university's goals will lead us to reflect on the ideal of humanity that we wish; and, of course, to reflect also on the mission of universities at the 21st century. Universities may be spaces where people learn how to live their lives, achieve cultural growth, receive vocational training and engage in the pursuit of the common good (Hollenbach 1998). They could become again those spaces that provided opportunities to extend and deepen human understanding about the person, the world, but also about all that transcend the material world. Envisioning the future of the university in terms of research, Collini (2012) has emphasized the need for the kind of intellectual inquiry that goes beyond the research and development laboratories of large corporations, which despite that pursue inquiry in a variety of topics, they probably do it for some practical purpose (Collini 2012). As several authors have suggested (Collini, 2012; Golding 2016), including John Newman's well known works and highly cited lecturers, higher education is a public good and not simply a good for those who happen to get the private benefit from it at any given moment.

The challenge we, the academics, face today is to find out how the transformations of our societies and their demands can be reconciled with the values that characterized the origins of the university. Undoubtedly, higher education must guide students to face the reality of the worlds they are living in, but it should do it by transmitting a sense of responsibility and giving enough opportunities to think about the transcendental attributes that give human life meaning: Truth and Goodness. In order to walk through this road, we believe that creating spaces to share the Christian spirituality that has been at the roots of the universities in the western world may be a good starting point. To comment on the main aspects of this spirituality we turn now.

CHRISTIAN SPIRITUALITY AT THE AGE OF SECULAR UNIVERSITIES

The term "Spirituality" comes from the Hebrew word ruach (spirit, breath, wind), which can be interpreted as that which gives life and animation to something (Melé and Fontrodona 2017). Although this word is today used in different religions and by people with no religious beliefs, its origins were Christian and referred to living life under the influence of God's Spirit (Sheldrake 2012). Indeed, the discourses around spirituality in the past used to be associated with religious life, while nowadays spirituality is generally defined independently of religion (Melé and Fontrodona 2017), such as that many people today claim to be spiritual but not religious. We clarify both concepts spirituality and Christian spirituality in the next subsections.

Spirituality

Spirituality, when detached from its religious roots it is considered a human phenomenon, a "secular" spirituality, rather than an explicit belief in God. Different behaviours or events are in the heart of this spirituality (Eisler and Montouori 2003; Perrin 2007; Stringfellow 2006). William Stringfellow, for example, in his book *The Politics of Spirituality* provides a broad spectrum of such behaviours/events (Stringfellow, 2006). According to this author, behaviours related to a "secular" spirituality can range from stoic attitudes, yoga discipline, hospitality or generosity till occult phenomena – just citing some (Stringfellow, 2006). In occasions, this kind of spirituality is associated with a "soft spirituality" because it emphasizes external actions instead of internal motivations (Perrin 2007; Simchai 2017). However, beyond these external actions, in some people there may be underlying deeper motivations related to the seeking of meaning in life; in such cases, scholars speak about "authentic spiritualities" (Perrin, 2007).

According to Perrin (2007, p.18), "authentic spiritualities refer to a commitment to look critically at oneself and one's relationships as well as an openness to question objectively and regularly all aspects of living." Perrin (2007) points out four characteristics to identify authentic spirituality. First, it is in general related with the search for meaning, values, and purpose in life; moreover, the question of meaning relates to an understanding of personality development in which interpersonal relationships, volunteering time or taking part in certain rituals regularly are all seen as ways of nurturing the humanistic development. Second, authentic spirituality is intimately related with having a conscience of reality that goes beyond the material world; it may refer to brooders understandings of the numinous, the undefined depths of human existence or the mysteries of the cosmos, so it considers, somehow, the human capacity for self-transcendence. Third, there are practices, rituals and behaviours that shape the way of life. And fourth, it often implies some forms of studying spirituality. In sum, authentic spirituality would imply a type of spirituality that involves the integration of all aspects of life in a unified whole. Yet, it is not necessarily associated with belief in God, although it does not exclude it either.

In their healthiest forms, the goal of authentic spiritualities is to construct hope and meaning in the midst of daily life (Perrin 2007). The assumption is that spirituality is an innate human characteristic and may be understood as an inner push that requires us to find a coherent sense to the life we are living; it pushes us to prove that the story of our life matters, that it makes sense, even though at times it may appear incomprehensible to us or with events that seem disparate or unconnected to each other. Therefore, spirituality, in a secular – humanist – perspective, stresses the human spirit in the sense of human consciousness as a constitutive (fundamental) dimension of human beings (Fry 2003; Perrin 2007). It involves the human capacity to be self-conscious, which means that human beings can be intentional about who they are and what the reasons are because they exist. In this context, spirituality is a phenomenon that is in some manner mirrored within our universities (Baratta and Smith 2018; Sabri et al. 2008). Yet, at the same time this process of self-conscious reflection requires the work of human spirit; because it is in this spiritual centre where the place of surrender to authenticity and love unfolds (Perrin 2007). Yet there has also been recognition that such secular spiritually may also be destructive (Perrin, 2007), a risk that tends to disappear when spirituality is unfolded and well framed in its religious roots – with the exception of religious fundamentalisms. In the Christian tradition, the spirituality involves a quest for the sacred, which in turn is related to beliefs about the Triune God.

Christian Spirituality

As already noted, Christian spirituality, in contrast to secular or humanistic spiritualities, has the Christian God as the ultimate concern of the person's life (Melé and Fontrodona 2017; Sheldrake 2012). The belief in transcendence is distinctive to this spirituality. Moreover, Christian spirituality is dependent on the dynamic relationship between the Spirit of God and the human spirit. And this relationship is, precisely, what more characterizes spirituality for the Christian.

At the centre of Christian spirituality is God's animating, graceful presence. A spiritual person in this context means a person who lives in the Spirit, guided by the Spirit of God – the third person of the Trinity (Emery 2011). Because it is God's Spirit alive in people's lives, that moves them beyond the boundaries of their fragile selves to give their lives in many different ways to others (Perrin 2007). This ethical side of Christian spirituality is aimed at trying to be a fully human person in joyful communion with others in God. Around this notion of becoming fully human, Perrin (2007, p. 32) provides a definition of Christian spirituality as "the experience of transformation in the Divine – human relationship as modelled by Jesus Christ and inspired by the Holy Spirit." Indeed, if we reduce Christian spirituality to its essence we may associate it with following the teachings of Jesus Christ or imitating his values (Sheldrake 2012). But this occurs only as a result of entering a loving relationship with Him, in communion with God. Christian spirituality implies, first of all, a personal relationship to the event/person who inaugurated it: Jesus Christ (Goergen 2002).

The word "discipleship," or "following Christ," summarizes in a great part this relationship that leads to a particular way of life. It involves a friendship relationship between Jesus and his disciples, as ideally may exist today in the university context between teacher and student. Yet, it also implies that the Christian disciple absorbs a whole way of existence by being alongside the teacher (Sheldrake 2012). It has two elements. The first one is a call to personal transformation; in other words, a conversion to turn away from previously flawed ways of behaving in response to a call from God. The second element is actively to follow the way of Jesus; and this involves both a new way of life and joining in building the Kingdom of God – that is, continuing Jesus' mission to transform the world in a place of love (Goergen 2002; Sheldrake 2012). Thus, disciples are also profoundly united to Jesus as a person and through that union share in Jesus' own intimate relationship with God.

Another important feature of Christian spirituality is that it is a theological based spirituality (Aumann 1985). Christian spirituality has a great richness of concepts and approaches (Scorgie et al. 2011). However, as we have seen, Christian spirituality is more than just following certain devotional practices or to accept some abstract theory; it involves the personal relationship with a person – Jesus Christ. Thus, while embracing Christian traditions and beliefs, Christian spirituality is always open to new and unexpected expressions of that relation as well as the different times and places in which it has been experienced by people throughout centuries.

As Christian spirituality is deeply associated to a personal relationship with Jesus Christ – it grew out of spiritual practice rather than out of abstract theory –, it is not surprising that within Christian spirituality can be identified many sub-spiritualities (Melé and Fontrodona 2017; Sheldrake 2012). Sheldrake (2012), for instance, distinguishes five types of Christian spiritualities: the ascetical, mystical, active, aesthetic and the prophetic type. The ascetical type is often associated with monasticism and highlights discipline and detachment from material pleasures as the pathway to spiritual growth. The mystical type focuses on the desire for an immediacy of presence to, and intuitive knowledge of, God, frequently via contemplative practice. The active type promotes everyday life and service to other people as the context for spiritual growth. The aesthetic type covers a range of ways in which the spiritual journey is expressed in and shaped by the arts, music, and literature. And the prophetic type of spirituality, embraces an explicit commitment to social justice and the transformation of society.

All the above makes obvious that Christian spirituality speak with robust but diverse voices. Delbecq (1999, p. 345) reminds us the diverse witness within the Catholic tradition: from the mountains, the desert Fathers, John of the Cross, and the Contemporary Carmelite Thomas Merton; from the valleys, St. Francis and the contemporary Teilhard de Chardin; from the city, Augusitine, Aquinas, Ignatius, Newman, and the contemporary (Sta.) Mother Theresa. Among the great reformer voices of Christianity, Delbecq

(1999) cites to Luther, Calvin, Wesley; within black Christian spirituality to Martin Luther King, and among the feminist voices to Dorothy Day. Despite the great diversity, Christian spiritual traditions share their biblical roots – Jewish and Christian scriptures – so that the love of God and neighbour rests at the heart of all of them. Besides, the traditions of Christian spirituality increasingly engage with important issues of social and cultural transformation – e.g., peace, ecological questions, the world of business, the meaning of healthcare – which can be an invitation to share in university contexts.

A METHODOLOGICAL NOTE

The insights presented here reports the initiatives undertaken by a multidisciplinary group of six teachers (including the author) and a Catholic priest to provide a space for Christian spirituality in a secular public European university –the University of Huelva. Founded in 1993, the University of Huelva is a public university situated in the urban setting of the town of Huelva (Andalusia), in the south-west corner of Spain. The university is recognized as an International Campus of Excellence, especially in the agri-food and sea fields. The staff is comprised of approximately one thousand lecturers and more than four hundred administrative and support staff. Moreover, over 12,000 students attend the University of Huelva each course, including 400 carrying out post graduate studies. Even though the University of Huelva is a secular university, it has an institutional service – SARUH – that could offer religious assistance in the framework of the Catholic faith to those of the university community who demand it. It is worth noting that such religious assistance is voluntary for university members and is supposed to be applied under the principle of respect to all religious traditions. In the practice, however, SARUH has only worked sporadically.

To a large extent, the initiative that we report here arose from the desire of its promoters to fuelling the SARUH's activities and renovating the existing facilities that were not being used. Ultimately, however, it responded to the general commitment of universities to the students' development, but adding to their professional development the possibility of contributing to their development as spiritual beings. More specifically, the main goal of the initiative was enlivening the commitments of the youth with the nature and demands of ultimate questions such as the meaning of life and death, and their association with the purpose of work and the goals of university education. Inspired by the Synod of the Youth convened by the Holy Father, Pope Francis, for October 2018, during the course 2017-2018 it was decided to undertake several activities to creating existential spaces that made possible interchange "signals of transcendence" based on students' own experiences, and where it could be possible to discuss how to seek a response to them. At the level of the student, it was sought that each person's religious or secular beliefs or outlook could be positioned in relation to such questions.

Informal conversations, group discussions, and participant observation were all part of the methodological tools used to bring clarification to the ideas here shown. In this respect, it is important to note that the information presented in this chapter is focused exclusively on the first phase of the initiative. Therefore, the following section provides a descriptive account, which is substantive, processual and contextualized, as it is typical of similar researches when they provide partial results in their initial steps.

THREE ILLUSTRATIVE INITIATIVES FOR SHARING CHRISTIAN SPIRITUALITY

In light of the above, three actions were undertaken during the first semester of the course 2018/2019. Two of them lied on the traditional approach of public universities' purpose; they were an educational and a researching initiative. The last one mirrored more clearly the religious approach: a prayer initiative. We comment on their main characteristics in the following paragraphs.

An educational-learning experience.- The educational-learning experience involved a 45 minutes of biweekly coffee-meeting in which teachers and students discussed topics of current interest for students. The topics could belong to different disciplines but the purpose was to find a Christian reading that provided a fresh perspective on the theme. Even though a broader religious reading may also be given to the topics – depending of the people who attended the coffee-meetings –, the foundations of the religious interpretations were normally supposed to be found on the Christian spiritual tradition, since, as was mentioned earlier, it is the tradition that is behind the Western culture and, therefore, the faith that most students and teachers were familiar with –independently they belonged to it or not. The format of the activity was the dialogue and the focus was on discussing those aspects of the topics that may be a clue for seeing a possibility of human experience in which the Transcendence may be somehow noticeable. The essence of the activity was to find from what students claim to know through their daily experiences, what they learn as university students, what they apply, the footprints of the Transcendence. In other words, the key issue was the notion of finding God in the everydayness of students' classes, challenges or, putting differently, to look for where God was at work at a public university. An important assumption is that students not only learn in the classrooms but also from informal dialogues with people who they may have not met before. Meetings guided by free dialogues were seen as a way of pushing people to think "out of the box" and trigger them to challenge previous partial views. In this context, some of the main topics for the discussion had to do with the occidental understanding of mindfulness, the notion of servant leadership in the current entrepreneurial world, the recent Spanish use of feminism language and the development of empathy.

The development of a research line.- The research side of the experience was premised on the need to give more consideration to the investigation of the religious aspect within higher education. As the workforce is becoming more religiously diverse, professional, and especially future managers and leaders, need to be able to creating healthy and pluralistic workplaces; so, it was considered important to investigate the weakness and strengths that currently have higher educational institutions in

this aspect (Groen 2008). In this context, it was seen appropriated to formalize the creation of a research group whose research line was focused on how universities are providing education for facing the role that the increased religious and spiritual diversity is playing in the market and work places. A part of that research has begun to be developed as theoretical proposals that defend the use of religious sources to approach ethical issues within different disciplines (e.g., businesses, entrepreneurship, social work, finances) (Toledano 2018 ; Toledano and Karanda 2015, 2017a, 2017b). Another line of research is planned to adopt action research so that it can be developed and tested as learning experiments such as the one that we are reporting here (Toledano and Anderson 2017). More investigation in which different disciplines are involved is clearly necessary, considering the holistic approach that religion implies to give a perspective of the human person, the world, and God. The future of this initiative, however, will be in part dependent that such interdisciplinary collaboration and resulting research become more acceptable by both journals' editors and the institutions that evaluate research's results.

A prayer experience.- Providing a prayer experience was developed under the practice of Eucharistic Adoration. This ancient practice of worshiping within the Catholic devotion invites one to pray, whether in private prayer or shared with others, in the presence of Jesus Christ under the appearance of a consecrated host. It is a practice performed under the belief that Christ – his body, blood, soul, and divinity, is really present in the Eucharist. Throughout centuries it has been practice in Catholic churches and believers have found that this worship experience helps to experience a deeper connection with God and enter more deeply in the mystery of the Trinity. At the University of Huelva never before had it been put into place a prayer initiative of this nature. It was implemented as a weekly practice available in a little chapel. The goal was to offer a space for silence so that attendants can have a break in the academic tasks and have a space for nurturing the spiritual part of themselves. Nonetheless, although all are welcome to pray in contemplative silence during the prayer time, some worship music could occasionally be listened to, and some spiritual readings could serve to guide the prayer. So, the idea was that each week there could

be some new worship activities accompanying the experience of adoration such as could be the prayer of the rosary[1].

DISCUSSION AND CONCLUSION

Whether the ethos of an individual higher education institution is self-consciously secular or based on a religious heritage, all universities have had to address shifts in the role and nature of religion or belief in wider society (Groen 2008; Weller, Hooley and Moore 2011). In many contemporaneous discussions regarding their role in the learning of our students, it has been noted the importance of returning to the roots that justified the creation of universities. From this follows the interest in recovering the idea of the university as a place for reflection, for sharing opinions and contributing to the development of the youth not just as professionals but also as persons (Hyers and Hyers 2008; Sabri et al. 2008). The experiences recently undertaken at the University of Huelva and showed here fit well with this idea. By focusing on the spiritual development of the youth it has developed several initiatives aimed at encouraging both students and teachers to seek the impact of the Transcendence in their daily activities. Although it is still soon to evaluate the impact that these experiences are having, especially in the students, this chapter has attempted to put over the table the ideas that are serving to go back to the roots of the University, even though it has focused on doing it from a Christian perspective. The above activities have showed some possibilities to meet the need that exists in the University to make room for experimental approaches that focus on the spiritual development of the youth beyond their professional development (Johnson and Laurence 2012)

---

[1] The rosary consists in the recitation of fifteen decades of Hail Marys, each introduced by the Lord's Prayer and concluded with the Doxology. To assist the memory during the recitation of the decades is common to count the prayers with a string of beads. While the rosary, being a prayer known by its excessive simplicity, may be seen as inappropriate in a complex and intellectual context as it may be the university, it is worth mentioning that it has been recognized a prayer of "true simplicity" (Radcliffe 1998), that is, a simplicity of the heart, of the clear eye, and in essence, a simplicity that can only be attained with God's grace. In other words, simplicity is not considered as opposing but rather as synonymous of true wisdom.

The experiences undertaken at the University of Huelva have a common element. In some way, all of them treated to provide an answer to the question of how to cultivate a learning space that expanded the limited meaning that the university curriculum gives to spiritual questions. The educational-learning activity, for example, echoes the six paradoxical tensions within the teaching and learning space proposed two decades ago by Parker Planer (1998), but still useful for creating spaces within the field of spirituality in education (Groen 2008). These tensions can be summarized as follows: the space to the learning experience should be open and hospitable; it should invite the voice of the individual as well as the voice of the group, by honouring both the "little" personal stories of the individual and "big" narratives of groups who come from similar disciplines; and finally, it should welcome both silence and speech (spoken and written) (Planer 1998).

Furthermore, the different experiences developed found common ground through the process of engaging teachers and students in relationships nurtured by friendship and dialogue. With respect to friendship, the "fathers" of the initiative strongly believed that sharing Christian spirituality required an appropriate context. Specifically, the space, the time, the climate that should be created in order that the initiatives could be developed appropriately were thought to be characterized by an intimacy in the interpersonal relations, so that barriers between teachers and students fell down and true friendship could emerge. This was the reason for entitling the educational-learning experience "coffee-meetings." Friendship is a disinterested and unqualified type of relationship. And spiritual and disinterested friendships can be more or less intimate, but at their greatest they encompass all the activities of the souls engaging in them.

As far as dialogue is concerned, it is worthy mentioning that dialogue is aimed at fostering shared meaning through critical reflection (Kawalilak 2004). In fact, from the time of Socrates, education was based on dialogue guided by a teacher. And from then, active discussion is considered as one of the best ways to drawing students in to participate (Hornsby and Morello 2017). In this sense, the coffee-dialogue biweekly was considered a proper option. The same friendship spirit was in the foundations of the research and prayer experience as the friendship with colleagues and God was supposed to be at the heart of the activities.

In conclusion, the idea of sharing Christian spirituality at the University of Huelva allows not only embracing the original idea of university (Kennedy 2017) but also the current need of students for developing a spiritual conscience that helps them to face their future challenges as professionals in diverse religious work environments. Centred on the development of the whole person, and affirming the principle that education at universities should not close the door to religious spiritualities, this chapter has shown the importance of offering alternatives that could fulfil some of the unmet need of our students. The idea may be seen as a new concept in a secular and postmodern higher education institution but at the same time it might mark the revival of what we have seen that dates back many centuries ago (Lozano Aguilar et al. 2008). So, it may be considered both a new beginning but also, in some way, a return to the University tradition.

Finally, even though we have focused here in sharing Christian spirituality in a public and secular university, the whole idea is not necessarily reserved for this religious tradition. In fact, this does not mean that the experiences outlined cannot serve of inspiration or have a translation to the integration of other faith religions to university campus. As universities are facing the challenge of accommodating students' wide variety of religious needs, multi-faith centres seems to be one of the trends that will grow in the coming years (Johnson and Laurence 2012). Whether such centres can begin with initiatives focused on Christian spirituality or on spiritualities that belong to other religious traditions will probably depend on the community context – students, teachers, and societies around. As cardinal Grocholewski (2014) said in the congregation for Catholic education in 2014, science and transcendence are not mutually exclusive, but come together for a greater and better understanding of man and the world.

REFERENCES

Aumann, J. (1985). *Christian spirituality in the Catholic tradition*. London: Bloomsbury.

Baratta, A. and Smith, P. V. (2018). "The Confrontation of Identities: How University Students Manage Academic and Religious Selves in Higher Education." *Educational Studies*, https://doi.org/10.1080/03055698.2018.1534084.

Biddington, T. (2013). "Towards a Theological Reading of Multifaith Spaces." *International Journal of Public Theology*, 7: 315-328.

Christensen, T. and Gornitzka, Å. (2017). "Reputation Management in Complex Environments. A Comparative Study of University Organizations." *Higher Education Policy*, 30:123-140.

Christensen, T. and Lægreid P. (2014). "Reputation Management in Times of Crisis." In *Organizational Reputation in the Public Sector*, edited by A. Wæraas, and M. Maor, 117-140. New York: Taylor and Francis.

Christensen, T. and Lægreid, P. (2007). *Transcending new public management : the transformation of public sector reforms*. Aldershot: Ashgate.

Clark, B. R. (1998). *Creating Entrepreneurial Universities: Organisational Pathways of Transformation*. London: Emerald Group Publishing Limited.

Collini, S. (2012). *What are Universities For?* London: Penguin books.

Delbecq, A. L. (1999). "Christian Spirituality and Contemporary Business Leadership." *Journal of Organizational Change Management*, 12(4): 345-354.

Ecklund, E. H., Park, J. Z. and Veliz, P. T. (2008). "Secularization and Religious Change among Elite Scientists, *Social Forces*, 86(4): 1805-1839.

Emery, G. O.P. (2011). *An Introduction of the Catholic Doctrine on the Triune God* (Translated by Matthew Levering). Washington, D.C.: The Catholic University of America Press.

Fourie, J., and Fourie, W. (2009). *Let's Talk About Varsity*. South Africa: Gabbema Books.

Fry, L. W. (2003). "Toward a theory of spiritual leadership." *Leadership Quarterly*, 14(6), 693-727.
Goergen, D. (2002). *The Jesus of Christian History. A theology of Jesus. Volume 3.* Eugene: Wipf and Stock Publishers.
Golding, P. (2016). "The UK Experience in Higher Education: A Negative Model for the Twenty-First Century?" In *What are universities for? On the current state and the future of universities,* edited by H. Nieminen and K. Rahkonen, 9-20. Helsinki: University of Helsinki.
Grocholewski, Z. (2014). *Educating today and tomorrow: A renewing passion. Instrumentum laboris.* Retrieved from: http://www.vatican.va/roman_curia/congregations/ccatheduc/documents/rc_con_ccatheduc_doc_20140407_educare-oggi-e-domani_en.html.
Groen, J. (2008). "Paradoxical tensions in creating a teaching and learning space within a graduate education course on spirituality." *Teaching in Higher Educaiton*, 13(2): 193-204.
Guest, M., Aune, K., Sharma, S., and Warner, R. (2013). *Christianity and the university experience: Understanding student faith.* A&C Black.
Hicks, D. A. (2003). *Religion and the workplace: Pluralism, spirituality, leadership.* New York, NY: Cambridge University Press.
Hollenbach, D. (1998). "The Catholic University and the Common Good." *Conversations on Jesuit Higher Education*, 13(1), 5–15.
Hornsby, C. and Morello, S. (2017). "Beyond the secular university." In *Beyond McDonaldization: Visions of Higher Education,* edited by D. Hayes, 57-67. Abingdon, Oxon; New York, NY: Routledge.
Hyers, L. L. and Hyers, C. (2009). "Everyday Discrimination Experienced by Conservative Christians at the Secular University." *Analyses of Social Issues and Public Policy*, 8(1): 113-137.
Iyanga, A. (2000). *Hystory of the University in Europe* (Historia de la Universidad en Europa), Universistat de Valencia, Valencia.
Johnson, K. and Laurence, P. (2012). "Multi-Faith Religious Spaces on College and University Campuses." *Religion & Education*, 39(1): 48-63.
Kawalilak, C. (2004). *Illumination – An adult educator's journey: Dialogues with adult educators and adult learners in Indigenous*

Western Australia. Unpublished doctoral dissertation. University of Calgary, Alberta, Canada.

Kennedy, A. (2017). "Beyond McUniversity. The university as it should be." In *Beyond McDonaldization: Visions of Higher Education*, edited by D. Hayes, 47-56. Abingdon, Oxon; New York, NY: Routledge.

Kim, D., Fisher, D. and McCalman, D. (2009). "Modernism, Christianity, and business ethics: A worldview perspective." *Journal of Business Ethics*, 90(1): 115-121.

Lozano Aguilar, J. F., Pérez Zafrilla, P. J. & González Esteban, E. (2008). "The limits of tolerance in public universities." *Politics in Central Europe* 4(2): 9-25.

Melé, D. and Fontrodona, J. (2017). "Christian Ethics and Spirituality in Leading Business Organizations: Editorial Introduction." *Journal of Busines Ethics*, 145(4): 671-679.

Panton, J. (2017). "Beyond McThinking." In *Beyond McDonaldization: Visions of Higher Education*, edited by D. Hayes, 84-92. Abingdon, Oxon; New York, NY: Routledge.

Perrin, D. B. (2007). *Studying Christian Spirituality*. New York and London: Routledge.

Porter, R. (2001). *The Enlightenment*. Basingstoke: Palgrave.

Radcliffe, T. Fr. OP (1998). *The Rosary. The identity of religious today.* Retrieved: http://www.dominicans.ca/Documents/masters/Radcliffe/rosary.html.

Ramirez, F. O. (2006). "The Rationalization of the University." In *Transnational governance: Institutional dynamics of regulation,* edited by M. L. Dejelic and K. Sahlin-Anderson, 225-244. Cambridge: Cambridge University Press.

Ramirez, F. O. (2010). "Accounting for Excellence: Transforming Universities into Organizational Actors." In *Higher Education, Policy, and the Global Competition Phenomenon*, edited by L. M. Portnoy, V. D. Rust, and S. S. Bagley, 43-58. New York: Palgrave Macmillan.

Sabri, D., Rowland, C., Wyatt, J., Stavrakopoulou, F., Cargas, S. and Hartley, H. (2008). "Faith in Academia: Integrating Students' Faith

Stance into Conceptions of Their Intellectual Development." *Teaching in Higher Education* 13(1): 43-54.

Scorgie, G. G., Chan, S., Smith, G. T., & Smith, J. D. I. (Eds.). (2011). *Dictionary of Christian spirituality*. Grand Rapids, MI: Zondervan.

Sheldrake, P. (2012). *Spirituality. A very short Introduction*. Oxford: Oxford University Press.

Simchai, D. (2017). "Paradox in cultural change: New Age Rituals as Case Study." In *Contemporary alternative Spiritualities in Israel*, edited by S.Feraro and J. R. Lewis, 95-114. New York: Palgrave MacMillan.

Stensaker B. (2019). "Socially Embedded Universities and the Search for Meaning." In *Universities as Agencies. Public Sector Organizations*, edited by T. Christensen, A. Gornitzka and F. Ramirez, 251-269. Palgrave Macmillan, Cham.

Stringfello, W. (2006). *The Politics of Spirituality*. Wipf & Stock Publishers. Eugene, Oregon.

Toledano, N. (2018). "Promoting Ethical Reflection in the Teaching of Social Entrepreneurship: A Proposal Using Religious Parables." *Journal of Business Ethics*, DOI: 10.1007/s10551-018-4077-x.

Toledano, N., & Karanda, C. (2015). "Virtuous Entrepreneurs: A Rethinking of the Way to Create Relational Trust in a Global Economy." *International Journal of Business and Globalisation*, 14(1): 9-20.

Toledano, N. and Anderson, A. R. (2017). "Theoretical Reflections on Narrative in Action Research." *Action research*. DOI: 10.1177/ 1476750317748439.

Toledano, N. and Karanda, C. (2017a). "Morality, Religious Writings and Entrepreneurship Education." *Journal of Moral Education*, 46(2): 195-211.

Toledano, N. and Karanda, C. (2017b). "Virtues and Temptations in Entrepreneurial Relationships: Learning from Christian Narratives." *Journal of Biblical Integration in Business*, 20(1): 68-77.

Weller, P., Hooley, T. and Moore, N: (2011). *Religion and Belief in Higher Education: The Experiences of Staff and Students.* London: Equality Challenge Unit.

Yancey, G. (2012). "Recalibrating Academic Bias." *Academic Questions*, 25(2): 267–278.

BIBLIOGRAPHY

"I still see the talibés begging": government program to protect talibé children in Senegal falls short.

LCCN	2017433627
Type of material	Book
Personal name	Seibert, Lauren, author.
Main title	"I still see the talibés begging": government program to protect talibé children in Senegal falls short.
Published/Produced	[New York, New York]: Human Rights Watch, [2017] ©2017
Description	i, 40 pages: illustrations (some color), color map; 27 cm
Links	View full text of publication. https://www.hrw.org/report/2017/07/11/i-still-see-talibes-begging/government-program-protect-talibe-children-senegal
ISBN	9781623134952 1623134951
LC classification	HV4627.7.A4 S45 2017

Bibliography

Related names — Human Rights Watch (Organization), issuing body, publisher.

Summary — "Across Senegal, more than 50,000 talibé children living in traditional Quranic boarding schools, or daaras, are forced to beg for daily quotas of money, rice or sugar by their Quranic teachers. The children are often beaten, chained, bound, and subjected to other forms of abuse. In June 2016, the Senegalese government demonstrated meaningful political will by introducing a new program to "remove children from the streets" and crack down on forced child begging. One year later, the program - implemented exclusively in Dakar - has hardly made a dent in the alarming numbers of children subject to exploitation, abuse and neglect daily. ... [This report], based on interviews with more than 90 people conducted in Dakar, in Saint-Louis and by phone, examines the successes and failings of the first year of the program"--Page 4 of cover.

Contents — Map of Senegal and Guinea-Bissau -- Summary -- Methodology -- I. Background -- II. "Retrait" program fails to ensure children's rights, justice -- III. Resurgence in child begging -- IV. Violence and abuses against talibés -- Recommendations and next steps -- Acknowledgments.

Subjects — Boarding school students--Abuse of--Senegal.
Muslim students--Abuse of--Senegal.
Child abuse--Senegal.
Begging--Senegal.
Forced labor--Senegal.
Child labor--Senegal.
Islamic religious education--Senegal.

Bibliography

Notes   "This report was researched and written by Lauren Seibert, West Africa Associate for the Africa Division at Human Rights Watch"--Page 40.
Includes bibliographical references.

"I won't be a doctor, and one day you'll be sick": girls' access to education in Afghanistan

LCCN	2018300418
Type of material	Book
Personal name	Barr, Heather, author.
Main title	"I won't be a doctor, and one day you'll be sick": girls' access to education in Afghanistan / [written by Heather Barr].
Published/Produced	[New York, N.Y.]: Human Rights Watch, [2017]. ©2017
Description	ii, 132 pages: color map, color photographs, color portraits; 27 cm
Links	https://www.hrw.org/report/2017/10/17/i-wont-be-doctor-and-one-day-youll-be-sick/girls-access-education-afghanistan
ISBN	9781623135348 (paperback)
	1623135346 (paperback)
Portion of title	Girls' access to education in Afghanistan
Spine title	Afghanistan, "I won't be a doctor, and one day you'll be sick"
Related names	Human Rights Watch (Organization), publisher, issuing body.
Summary	"This report describes how, as security in the country worsens and international donors disengage from Afghanistan, progress made toward getting girls into school has stalled. It is based on 249 interviews in Kabul, Kandahar, Balkh, and Nangarhar provinces, mostly with

Contents

girls ages 11 to 18 who were not able to complete their education"--Publisher's description. Summary and Key Recommendations: Numbers -- Schooling in Afghanistan -- Barriers to girls education outside of the school system -- Barriers to girls' education within the school system -- Donor support to educaiton in Afghanistan -- Legal obligations -- To the Afghan govemnment: Methodology -- I. Background: Number of Girls in School -- Compulsory Education in Afghanistan -- Choice of Schools: Government Schools -- Community-Based Education Programs -- Religious Education -- Private Schools -- Demand for Girls' Education -- II. Barriers to Girls' Education Outside the School System: Social Barriers, including Harmful Gender Norms: Child and Forced Marriage -- Poverty -- Child Labor -- Impact of the War on Girls' Access to Education -- Attacks on Education -- Military and Insurgent Use of Schools and Recruitment of Child Soldiers -- Dangers and Threats on the Way to School: Abduction and Kidnapping -- Sexual Harassment -- III. Barriers to Girls' Education within the School System: Lack of Schools and Distance to School: School Shortages -- Distance to School -- Education Costs -- Challenges Providing Good Quality Education: Poor Infrastructure, Lack of Supplies -- Access to Water and Toilets -- Poor Quality of Instruction -- Insufficient Numbers of Teachers -- Administrative Barriers -- Barriers to Education for Internally Displaced People and Returnees -- Identification and School Records -- Exclusion from Study as Internally Displaced

People and Returnees, and Discrimination -- Challenges with Community-Based Education Programs in Afghanistan: Difficult Transition from Community-Based Education Programs to Government Schools -- Lack of Assistance for Children with Disabilities and Trauma -- Corruption and Lack of Transparency -- IV. International Funding--Generous, but at Risk: V. Afghanistan's Obligations Under Afghan and International Law: Right to Education -- Non-Discrimination in Education -- Quality of Education -- Protection from Child Marriage and Child Labor -- Right to Inclusive and Accessible Education -- Protection from Violence, including Corporal Punishment and Cruel and Degrading Forms of Punishment -- Recommendations: To the President and Chief Executive -- To the Ministry of Education: Increase Access to Education for Girls -- Formalize Community-Based Education and Make it Sustainable -- Improve Retention of Girls in School -- Enforce Compulsory Education -- Improve the Quality of Education -- Meet the Needs of Children with Disabilities and Mental Health Needs -- Improve Transparency and Accountability -- To Ministry of Labor, Social Affairs, Martyrs and Disabled -- To Ministry of Interior -- To Ministry of Defense and Ministry of Interior -- To Ministry of Finance -- To Ministry of Women's Affairs -- To the Taliban and Other Non-State Armed Groups -- To International Donors and Agencies Supporting Education in Afghanistan -- Acknowledgments.

Subjects 2000-2099
Girls--Education--Afghanistan--21st century.

	Right to education. Education--Afghanistan--21st century. Children's rights--Afghanistan. Children--Afghanistan--Social conditions. Education and state--Afghanistan. Children--Social conditions. Children's rights. Education. Education and state. Girls--Education. Politics and government. Right to education. Afghanistan--Politics and government--21st century. Afghanistan.
Notes	"October 2017"--Table of contents page. "This report was written by Heather Barr, senior researcher on women's rights"--Page 131, Acknowledgments. Includes bibliographical references.

...And yet they learned: education of Jewish children in Nazi occupied areas between 1933-1945

LCCN	2016916036
Type of material	Book
Personal name	Silver, Jacqueline, author.
Main title	...And yet they learned: education of Jewish children in Nazi occupied areas between 1933-1945 / Jacqueline Silver.
Published/Produced	North Charleston, South Carolina: CreateSpace Independent Publishing Platform, [2015]
Description	163 pages: illustrations; 23 cm
ISBN	9781537796352 1537796356

LC classification	LC3585.G3 S55 2015
Subjects	Jewish children--Education--Germany--History--20th century.
	Jewish religious education of children--Germany--History--20th century.
	Jewish children--Education--Europe--History--20th century.
	Jewish religious education of children--Europe--History--20th century.
	Holocaust, Jewish (1939-1945)
Notes	Includes bibliographical references (pages 147-162).

101 inclusive and SEN citizenship, PSHE and religious education lessons: fun activities and lesson plans for children aged 3-11

LCCN	2018041184
Type of material	Book
Personal name	Brewer, Claire, author.
Main title	101 inclusive and SEN citizenship, PSHE and religious education lessons: fun activities and lesson plans for children aged 3-11 / Claire Brewer and Kate Bradley.
Published/Produced	London; Philadelphia: Jessica Kingsley Publishers, 2019.
ISBN	9781785923685
LC classification	LB1584 .B667 2019
Variant title	One hundred and one inclusive and SEN citizenship, PSHE and religious education lessons
Related names	Bradley, Kate (Kathryn D.), author.
Subjects	Civics--Study and teaching (Elementary)--Activity programs.
	Social sciences--Study and teaching (Elementary)--Activity programs.

Health education (Elementary)--Activity programs.
Religion--Study and teaching (Elementary)--Activity programs.
Special education--Activity programs.
Inclusive education--Activity programs.

13 very surprising sayings and why Jesus said them
LCCN 2017952579
Type of material Book
Personal name Keefer, Mikal.
Main title 13 very surprising sayings and why Jesus said them / Mikal Keefer.
Published/Produced Colorado Springs, CO: David C Cook, 2018.
ISBN 9781434712554 (pbk.: alk. paper)
9780830772971 (ebk.: alk. paper)

2014 papers: the church, theological education and violence in the earth community: the Nigeria experience
LCCN 2017453447
Type of material Book
Corporate name West African Association of Theological Institutions. (Nigeria Zone). Biennial Conference (2014: Ibadan, Nigeria)
Main title 2014 papers: the church, theological education and violence in the earth community: the Nigeria experience / edited by Emmanuel O. Oyemomi, PhD, Stephen O.Y. Baba, PhD, Helen I. A. Oyekanmi, PhD.
Published/Produced Ilorin (Nigeria): Published for WAATI by Amazing Grace Press, [2016]
Description xi, 349 pages; 21 cm
ISBN 9781878673
9789781878671

LC classification	BT736.4 .W47 2014
Portion of title	Church, theological education and violence in the earth community
Related names	Oyemomi, Emmanuel O., editor.
	Baba, Stephen O. Y. (Stephen Oluwarotimi Y.), 1967- editor.
	Oyekanmi, Helen I. A., editor.
Contents	List of contributors -- Preface / Rev. Dr. Stephen O.Y. Baba, Secretary WAATI (Nigeria zone) -- Chapter One: Domestic violence and disruption in Nigerian homes: a search for peace / Helen I.A. Oyekanmi, PhD -- Chapter Two: The role of the church in curbing violence within the Nigerian society / Ven. J.O. Adeloye -- Chapter Three: The church and marital violence: the Nigerian experience / Z.A. Adeniji -- Chapter Four: A call to the liturgical assembly to address marital violence against women in Nigeria / E.C. Anagwo, PhD -- Chapter Five: Promoting peace in the earth community through the agencies of education / E.O. Ayandokun, PhD -- Chapter Six: Philosophical perspective of theological education and violence in the earth: the Nigerian historic experience / W.A.O. Egbetakin, PhD -- Chapter Seven: Theological education and violence: the dilemma of the ecclesiastical society / George O. Folarin, PhD / -- Chapter Eight: Impact of violence on Christianity in northern Nigeria: a case study of Boko Haram insurgency / O.P. Jegede, PhD -- Chapter Nine: The prevalence of gender-based violence in Nigeria: implications for the church / Joseph Oladeinde -- Chapter Ten: Nehemiah's pragmatic approach as a sustainable peaceful coexistence among the Jews: a panacea

for Nigeria situation / J.O. Ojo, PhD -- Chapter Eleven: The role of theological education in building security consciousness in Nigeria society / Dr. Moses Goddey -- Chapter Twelve: Christian apologetics as a response of the church in religious antagonism in Nigeria / M.A. Ogunewu -- Chapter Thirteen: Terrorism and theological challenges in Africa: the Boko Haram example / M.O. Oladeji and S.F. Kehinde -- Chapter Fourteen: Old Testament strategies for countering terrorism and enhancing peace-time national development in Nigeria / G.O. Olaniyan, PhD -- Chapter Fifteen: Biblical perspectives and Christian response to domestic violence in Nigeria / S.K. Oyeku -- Chapter Sixteen: Violence in human and earth community: the Nigerian situation / E.O. Oyemomi, PhD -- Chapter Seventeen: Confronting conflicts in a Christian community: how relevant is Matthew 18:15-35 to Christ Apostolic Church (CAC)? / O.D. Oyeniyi -- Chapter Eighteen: Preparing youths for a peaceful society: the challenge of the church in Nigeria / S.S. Salami -- Chapter Nineteen: Violence against humanity in the case of Boko Haram in northern Nigeria / Simon Kolawole, PhD -- Chapter Twenty: A Christian education response to religious violence in Nigeria / Helen Ishola-Esan, PhD.

Subjects Peace--Religious aspects--Christianity--Study and teaching--Nigeria--Congresses.
Peace building--Nigeria--Congresses.
Violence--Religious aspects--Christianity--Congresses.
Violence--Nigeria--Prevention--Congresses.

Notes	Religious education--Nigeria--Congresses. Includes bibliographical references.

A fresh look at Islam in a multi-faith world: a philosophy for success through education

LCCN	2014018723
Type of material	Book
Personal name	Wilkinson, M. L. N. (Matthew L. N.)
Main title	A fresh look at Islam in a multi-faith world: a philosophy for success through education / Matthew L.N. Wilkinson.
Published/Produced	London; New York: Routledge, 2015.
Description	xxvi, 278 pages; 25 cm
ISBN	9780415813198 (hardback)
LC classification	BP161.3 .W547 2015
Summary	"A Fresh Look at Islam in a Multi-Faith World provides a comprehensively theorised and practical approach to thinking systematically and deeply about Islam and Muslims in a multi-faith world. It makes the case for a contemporary educational philosophy to help young Muslims surmount the challenges of post-modernity and to transcend the hiatuses and obstacles that they face in their interaction and relationships with non-Muslims and visa-versa.It argues that the philosophy of critical realism in its original, dialectical and metaReal moments so fittingly 'underlabours' (Bhaskar, 1975) for the contemporary interpretation, clarification and conceptual deepening of Islamic doctrine, practice and education as to suggest a distinctive branch of critical realist philosophy, specifically suited for this purpose. This approach is called Islamic Critical Realism.The book proceeds to

explain how this Islamic Critical Realist approach can serve the interpretation of the consensual elements of Islamic doctrine, such as the six elements of Islamic belief and the five 'pillars' of Islamic practice, so that these essential features of the Muslim way of life can help Muslim young people to contribute positively to life in multi-faith liberal democracies in a globalising world.Finally, the book shows how this Islamic Critical Realist approach can be brought to bear in humanities classrooms by history, religious education and citizenship teachers to help Muslim young people engage informatively and transformatively with themselves and others in multi-faith contexts."-- Provided by publisher.

"A Fresh Look at Islam in a Multi-Faith World: A Philosophy for Success through Education provides a comprehensively theorised and practical approach to thinking systematically and deeply about Islam and Muslims in a multi-faith world. It makes the case for a contemporary educational philosophy to help young Muslims surmount the challenges of post-modernity and to transcend the hiatuses and obstacles that they face in their interaction and relationships with non-Muslims and visa-versa. It argues that the philosophy of critical realism in its original, dialectical and metaReal moments so fittingly 'underlabours' (Bhaskar, 1975) for the contemporary interpretation, clarification and conceptual deepening of Islamic doctrine, practice and education as to suggest a distinctive branch of critical realist philosophy, specifically suited for this purpose. This approach is called

	Islamic Critical Realism. The book proceeds to explain how this Islamic Critical Realist approach can serve the interpretation of the consensual elements of Islamic doctrine, such as the six elements of Islamic belief and the five 'pillars' of Islamic practice, so that these essential features of the Muslim way of life can help Muslim young people to contribute positively to life in multi-faith liberal democracies in a globalising world"-- Provided by publisher.
Subjects	Islam.
	Critical realism.
	Education--Philosophy.
	Islam--Relations.
Notes	Includes bibliographical references (pages 256-269) and index.
Series	New studies in critical realism and education (Routledge critical realism)

A hermeneutics of religious education

LCCN	2015015347
Type of material	Book
Personal name	Aldridge, David, author.
Main title	A hermeneutics of religious education / by David Aldridge.
Published/Produced	London; New York: Bloomsbury, Bloomsbury Academic, an imprint of Bloomsbury Publishing, Plc, [2015]
Description	vi, 217 pages; 24 cm
ISBN	9781441114426 (HB)
LC classification	BV1464 .A47 2015
Subjects	Religious education--Philosophy.
	Religious education--England.
	Religious education--Wales.

Notes	Includes bibliographical references (pages 200-212) and index.

Addressing special educational needs and disability in the curriculum: religious education

LCCN	2016059004
Type of material	Book
Personal name	Hunt, Dilwyn, author.
Main title	Addressing special educational needs and disability in the curriculum: religious education / Dilwyn Hunt.
Edition	Second Edition.
Published/Produced	London; New York: Routledge, 2018.
Description	xviii, 168 pages: illustrations; 30 cm.
ISBN	9781138683761 (Hardback)
	9781138683778 (Paperback)
LC classification	LC4036.G7 H865 2018
Contents	Introduction -- Chapter 1. Meeting Special Educational Needs: Your responsibility -- Chapter 2. The inclusive religious education classroom -- Chapter 3. Teaching and learning -- Chapter 4. Monitoring and assessment -- Chapter 5. Managing support -- Chapter 6. Real pupils in real classrooms.
Subjects	Children with disabilities--Education--Great Britain.
	Special education--Great Britain.
	Religious education--Great Britain.
Notes	"First edition published by Routledge 2004"--T.p. verso.
	Includes webography.
	Includes bibliographical references (pages 160-161) and index.

Series Addressing Special Educational Needs and Disability in the Curriculum

Advancing the learning agenda in Jewish education
LCCN 2018024454
Type of material Book
Main title Advancing the learning agenda in Jewish education / Jon A. Levisohn and Jeffrey S. Kress, editors.
Published/Produced Boston: Academic Studies Press, 2018.
Description 1 online resource.
ISBN 9781618117540 ()
LC classification LC715
Related names Levisohn, Jon A., editor.
Kress, Jeffrey S., editor.
Contents Introduction: what the "learning agenda" is and why it matters / Jon A. Levisohn and Jeffrey S. Kress -- Activating Jewish learners: positioning youth for persistent success in Jewish learning and living / Rena Dorph and Christian D. Schunn -- Fostering identity and disposition development in jewish education: a view from the learning sciences / Janet L. Kolodner -- Learning about learning in Jewish education / Ari Y. Kelman -- Old traditions, new practices: a proposal for a return to text study as a centerpiece of Jewish community and family life / Daniel P. Resnick and Lauren B. Resnick -- Observing havruta learning from the perspective of the learning sciences / Baruch Schwarz -- Learning the whole game of Shabbat / Joseph Reimer -- What we can learn about learning from Holocaust education / Simone Schweber -- Is this a real story?: learning

	critical history and learning its limits / Sam Wineburg.
Subjects	Jews--Education.
	Jewish religious education.
	Judaism--Study and teaching.
Notes	Includes bibliographical references.
Additional formats	Print version: Advancing the learning agenda in Jewish education Boston: Academic Studies Press, 2018 9781618117533 (DLC) 2018023237

Advancing the learning agenda in Jewish education

LCCN	2018023237
Type of material	Book
Main title	Advancing the learning agenda in Jewish education / edited by Jon A. Levisohn and Jeffrey S. Kress.
Published/Produced	Boston: Academic Studies Press, 2018.
Description	vi, 219 pages: illustrations; 23 cm
ISBN	9781618117533 (hardcover)
	9781618118790 (pbk.)
	9781618117540 (ebook)
LC classification	LC715 .A33 2018
Related names	Levisohn, Jon A., editor.
	Kress, Jeffrey S., editor.
Contents	Introduction: what the "learning agenda" is and why it matters / Jon A. Levisohn and Jeffrey S. Kress -- Activating Jewish learners: positioning youth for persistent success in Jewish learning and living / Rena Dorph and Christian D. Schunn -- Fostering identity and disposition development in jewish education: a view from the learning sciences / Janet L. Kolodner -- Learning about learning in Jewish education / Ari Y. Kelman -- Old traditions, new practices: a proposal for a

	return to text study as a centerpiece of Jewish community and family life / Daniel P. Resnick and Lauren B. Resnick -- Observing havruta learning from the perspective of the learning sciences / Baruch Schwarz -- Learning the whole game of Shabbat / Joseph Reimer -- What we can learn about learning from Holocaust education / Simone Schweber -- Is this a real story?: learning critical history and learning its limits / Sam Wineburg.
Subjects	Jews--Education.
	Jewish religious education.
	Judaism--Study and teaching.
Notes	Includes bibliographical references.
Additional formats	Online version: Advancing the learning agenda in Jewish education Boston: Academic Studies Press, 2018 9781618117540 (DLC) 2018024454

After study hours: exploring the Madrassah mindset.

LCCN	2018306386
Type of material	Book
Main title	After study hours: exploring the Madrassah mindset.
Edition	Edition first.
Published/Produced	Islamabad: Pak Institute for Peace Studies, 2018.
Description	1 online resource (132 pages): color illustrations, digital, PDF file
Links	https://www.pakpips.com/web/wp-content/uploads/2018/01/Exploring_the_Madrassah_Mindset.pdf
ISBN	9789699370298
LC classification	LC910.P3
Portion of title	Exploring the Madrassah mindset
Related names	Pak Institute for Peace Studies.

Subjects	Islamic education--Pakistan.
	Islamic religious education--Pakistan.
	Madrasahs--Pakistan.
Notes	Includes bibliographical references.

An argument open to all: reading The Federalist in the twenty-first century

LCCN	2015940161
Type of material	Book
Personal name	Levinson, Sanford, 1941- author.
Main title	An argument open to all: reading The Federalist in the twenty-first century / Sanford Levinson.
Published/Produced	New Haven: Yale University Press, [2015]
Description	xiii, 350 pages; 25 cm
ISBN	9780300199598 (cloth: alk. paper)
	0300199597 (cloth: alk. paper)
LC classification	KF4515 .L48 2015
Summary	"In An Argument Open to All, renowned legal scholar Sanford Levinson takes a novel approach to what is perhaps America's most famous political tract. Rather than concern himself with the authors as historical figures, or how The Federalist helps us understand the original intent of the framers of the Constitution, Levinson examines each essay for the political wisdom it can offer us today. In eighty-five short essays, each keyed to a different essay in The Federalist, he considers such questions as whether present generations can rethink their constitutional arrangements; how much effort we should exert to preserve America's traditional culture; and whether The Federalist's arguments even suggest the desirability of world government."--Dust jacket.

Contents

Publius, our contemporary: an introduction -- Part 1. Something must be done to save the Union. On the frequency of "reflection and choice" by "we the people" -- How much pluribus within a single unum? -- Federalism and foreign policy -- "Concerning dangers from foreign force" -- In union there is strength -- Humankind as "ambitious, vindictive, and rapacious" -- Endless sources of conflict (and war), even within the United States -- On the rise of a militarized state -- Part 2. Bigger is, in fact, better. The new (and improved) science of politics -- Can moral or religious education overcome natural tendencies toward faction? -- It's a harsh and competitive world out there -- Commerce and state finance -- Economies of scale -- Publius and permanent revolution (or, at least, improvement) -- Part 3. Why "confederation" is both "odious" and an "imbecility." "The imbecility of our government" -- Why confederation is "odious" and a national government is necessary -- The political sociology of federalism (part I) -- Ancient history as caution -- The defects of multiple sovereigns -- The Dutch provide the final cautionary example -- On the importance of sanctions -- Publius as majoritarian -- Part 4. The state and the machinery of death (or, at least, defense): standing armies. "Common defence" and (un)limited government -- The inconvenience of militia service -- More on the merits of standing armies -- In whom do we place our "confidence"? -- Further reflections on confidence in the national government -- The necessity of force -- "Concerning the militia" -- Part 5. How does one pay for the services supplied by the Union? On taxes and the taxing power. First death, now taxes -- On the inutility of specified limits -- Taxation and constitutional interpretation -- The irrelevance of text -- Drafting a constitution with the long view in mind -- Who will allocate the tax burdens, and why should we trust them? -- State and national officials as partners or adversaries -- Part 6. To err is human (and perfect clarity is chimerical). Human (and even divine) fallibility and written constitutions -- The best as the enemy of the good--and the necessary -- Federalism, "compact," and the specter of secession -- Part 7. On the limits of the "rule of law." Exigency and fidelity to law -- Existential dangers and legal fidelity -- Part 8. National and state prerogatives (and maintenance of a federal political order). Who should control naturalization (and immigration)? -- Controlling internal insurrections -- Confidence, money, and debt -- Evaluating the constitutional order -- The political sociology of federalism (part II) -- Is "separation of powers" a helpful maxim? -- "Parchment barriers" -- Part 9. Veneration versus reflection. "Veneration" versus "reflection and choice" -- Maintaining constitutional fidelity -- Part 10. Institutional design: the legislature. Designing institutions for devils (who organize themselves into political parties) -- Suffrage and representation -- For how long should representatives serve? -- Who counts as worthy of representation, and for how much? -- Does size matter, and if not, what does? -- "Local knowledge" and representation -- Does "representation" mean "mirroring"? -- Does the "iron law of oligarchy" apply to the House of Representatives? -- Part 11. Who should be in charge of elections? The death of state autonomy? -- Manipulating elections -- What is a propitious time to choose representatives? -- Part 12. On the senate. On the "lesser evil" -- Let sleeping sovereigns lie? -- The Senate's superior wisdom on foreign affairs -- The Senate's confirmation and impeachment powers -- The past is a different country -- Part 13. On the executive. A monarchical president? -- Selecting the president -- Comparing the president with the/a king -- Unity in the executive -- How long should a president be able to serve? -- You can't get too much of a good president -- Why the presidential veto? -- The presidential prerogative to pardon -- The complicated process of making or refusing to make treaties -- The appointment power -- The constitutional bona fides of a unilateral authority to remove executive branch officials -- Part 14. The roles of the national judiciary. Is the judiciary "above politics"? -- Fixed salaries--but what about inflation? -- The importance of federal courts -- Discipling judges by threatening impeachment? -- A judiciary for the whole -- Trial by jury -- Part 15. Reprise: the importance of institutions and the necessity of a strong national government. The limited importance--if not outright dangers--of bills of rights -- "A nation [with] a national government."

Subjects   Federalist--Influence.
Federal government--United States.
Constitutional history--United States.

Notes	United States--Politics and government--21st century. Includes bibliographical references (pages 335-343) and index.

Assessment in ethics education: a case of national tests in religious education

LCCN	2017930930
Type of material	Book
Personal name	Franck, Olof.
Main title	Assessment in ethics education: a case of national tests in religious education / Olof Franck.
Published/Produced	New York, NY: Springer Berlin Heidelberg, 2017.
ISBN	9783319507682

Catechetical leadership: what it should look like, how it should work, and whom it should serve

LCCN	2017953327
Type of material	Book
Personal name	Herrera, Adrián Alberto, author.
Main title	Catechetical leadership: what it should look like, how it should work, and whom it should serve / Adrián Alberto Herrera.
Published/Produced	Chicago: Loyola Press, [2017] ©2017
Description	vi, 134 pages; 23 cm
ISBN	9780829445268 0829445269
LC classification	BX1968 .H46 2017
Contents	Put away the pedestal: what leadership in ministry looks like -- Where are you taking us?: leadership and articulating a vision -- Avoiding the superhero approach: leadership, collaboration, and

	delegation -- Got what it takes?: leadership and core competencies -- If it takes a village, better build one: leadership and fostering communio -- Let no one disregard you: leadership and legitimate authority -- Getting to know the terrain: leadership in a changing landscape -- Make up your mind: leadership and decision making -- Smoothing out the rough spots: leadership and conflict -- Unabashedly Catholic: leadership and robust Catholic identity.
Subjects	Catechetics--Catholic Church.
	Christian leadership--Catholic Church.
	Christian education directors.
	Directors of religious education.
Notes	Includes bibliographical references.
Series	The effective catechetical leader

Catholic Primary Religious Education in a Pluralist Environment

LCCN	2016302817
Type of material	Book
Personal name	Hession, Anne
Main title	Catholic Primary Religious Education in a Pluralist Environment / Anne Hession
Published/Produced	Dublin: Veritas, 2015.
Description	236 pages; 22 cm
ISBN	9781847305923

Children's voices: theological, philosophical and spiritual perspectives

LCCN	2015417428
Type of material	Book
Main title	Children's voices: theological, philosophical and spiritual perspectives / Petra Freudenberger-Lötz, Gerhard Büttner (Hrsg.).

Published/Produced	Kassel: Kassel University Press, [2015]
Description	167 pages: some illustrations (some color); 21 cm.
ISBN	9783862199228 (pbk.)
LC classification	BV1475.3 .C455 2015
Related names	Freudenberger-Lötz, Petra, editor.
	Büttner, Gerhard, editor.
Subjects	Religious education of children.
	Christian education.
Notes	Includes bibliographical references.
Additional formats	9783862199235 (online)
	(GyWOH)har155011442
Series	Beiträge zur Kinder- und Jugendtheologie; Band 32

Chinuch with heart: a veteran mechanech answers pressing questions

LCCN	2017278982
Type of material	Book
Personal name	Bender, Yaakov, author.
Main title	Chinuch with heart: a veteran mechanech answers pressing questions / Rabbi Yaakov Bender.
Edition	First edition.
Published/Produced	Brooklyn, N.Y.: Mesorah Publications; [Far Rockaway]: in conjunction with Yeshiva Darchei Torah, January 2018.
Description	451 pages; 24 cm
ISBN	1422619672
	9781422619674
LC classification	BM103 .B4554 2018
Related names	Yeshivah Darkhe Torah (Far Rockaway, New York, N.Y.)
Subjects	Jewish religious education of children--United States--Miscellanea.
Notes	"The Lowinger edition."
Series	ArtScroll series

Circuits of faith: migration, education, and the Wahhabi mission

LCCN	2016029388
Type of material	Book
Personal name	Farquhar, Michael (Michael J.), author.
Main title	Circuits of faith: migration, education, and the Wahhabi mission / Michael Farquhar.
Published/Produced	Stanford, California: Stanford University Press, [2017]
Description	xiii, 269 pages; 24 cm
ISBN	9780804798358 (cloth: alk. paper) (electronic)
LC classification	LG359.M47 F37 2017
Contents	Transformations in the late Ottoman Hijaz -- Wahhabi expansion in Saudi-occupied Mecca -- National politics and global mission -- Migration and the forging of a scholarly community -- Rethinking religious instruction -- A Wahhabi corpus in motion -- Leaving Medina.
Subjects	Jāmi'ah al-Islāmīyah bi-al-Madīnah al-Munawwarah--Influence.
	Jāmi'ah al-Islāmīyah bi-al-Madīnah al-Munawwarah--Foreign students.
	Islamic religious education--Saudi Arabia.
	Wahhābīyah--Saudi Arabia--Influence.
	Islam and state--Saudi Arabia.
	Islamic fundamentalism.
	Transnationalism.
Notes	Includes bibliographical references (pages [237]-259) and index.
Series	Stanford studies in Middle Eastern and Islamic societies and cultures

Created in their image: evangelical Protestantism in Antigua and Barbados, 1834-1914

LCCN	2015904134
Type of material	Book
Personal name	Kirton-Roberts, Winelle J. author
Main title	Created in their image: evangelical Protestantism in Antigua and Barbados, 1834-1914 / Winelle J. Kirton-Roberts.
Published/Produced	Bloomington, Indiana: Authorhouse, [2015] ©2015
Description	xiv, 338 pages; 24 cm
ISBN	9781504901000 1504901002
LC classification	BR645.B37 K57 2015
Contents	Evangelical Protestantism -- The meaning of Freedom -- Gender and female roles -- Christian religious education -- Equipping black leaders -- Evangelical Faith -- Evangelical privileges -- Black sexuality and sin -- Image: The evangelical black.
Subjects	Protestantism--Antigua and Barbuda--Antigua. Protestantism--Barbados. Protestantism. Religion. Antigua--Religion. Barbados--Religion. Antigua and Barbuda--Antigua. Barbados.
Notes	Includes bibliographical references.

Critical religious education in practice: a teacher's guide for the secondary classroom

LCCN	2017053099
Type of material	Book

Personal name	Easton, Christina, author.
Main title	Critical religious education in practice: a teacher's guide for the secondary classroom / Christina Easton, Angela Goodman, Andrew Wright and Angela Wright.
Published/Produced	Abingdon, Oxon; New York, NY: Routledge, 2018.
ISBN	9781138123212 (hbk)
	9781138123229 (pbk)
LC classification	LC410.G7 E36 2018
Contents	Critical religious education: an Introduction -- Critical religious education: handling controversy in the classroom -- Critical religious education: an introductory scheme of work (year 7) -- Critical religious education and world religions: an exemplar scheme of work for teaching Islam (year 8) -- Critical religious education and philosophy: an exemplar scheme of work for teaching science and religion (year 9) -- Critical religious education and ethics: an exemplar scheme of work for introducing moral decision making (year 9) -- Critical religious education and GCSE religious studies -- Critical religious education and assessment -- Critical religious education and differentiation.
Subjects	Religious education--Great Britain.
	Religion--Study and teaching (Secondary)--Great Britain.
	Critical pedagogy--Great Britain.
Notes	Includes bibliographical references.

Crossings and crosses: borders, educations, and religions in Northern Europe

LCCN	2015001479

Type of material	Book
Main title	Crossings and crosses: borders, educations, and religions in Northern Europe / edited by Jenny Berglund, Thomas Lundén, and Peter Strandbrink.
Published/Produced	Boston: De Gruyter, [2015]
Description	viii, 241 pages: illustrations, map; 24 cm.
ISBN	9781614517542 (hardcover 23 x 15,5: alk. paper)
LC classification	BL980.E853 C76 2015
Related names	Berglund, Jenny, editor.
Subjects	Religion and politics--Europe, Northern. Religious education--Europe, Northern. Europe, Northern--Religion.
Notes	Includes bibliographical references and index.
Series	Religion and society, 1437-5370; Volume 63

Culture and human rights: the Wroclaw commentaries

LCCN	2016478863
Type of material	Book
Main title	Culture and human rights: the Wroclaw commentaries / edited by Andreas Joh. Wiesand, Kalliopi Chainoglou, Anna Śledzińska-Simon; in collaboration with Yvonne Donders.
Published/Produced	Berlin; Boston: De Gruyter, [2016] ©2016
Description	xxxi, 326 pages; 25 cm
ISBN	9783110440508 (hbk.: alk. paper) 3110440504 (hbk.: alk. paper)
LC classification	K3240 .C845 2016
Related names	Wiesand, Andreas Johannes, editor. Chainoglou, Kalliopē, editor. Śledzińska-Simon, Anna, editor.
Summary	The City of Wroclaw, in cooperation with the National Cultural Centre (Warsaw), has asked

Andreas Joh. Wiesand to prepare, together with experts from many different countries, a basic handbook which cover all relevant legal questions as well as main political consequences related to human rights and culture. The publication is to be presented in the context of the programme for Wroclaw, European Capital of Culture 2016 -- Source other than Library of Congress.

Contents

Culture and human rights: concepts, instruments and institutions -- Freedom of expression in the arts and media -- Cultural diversity and cultural identity in human rights -- Access to culture, media, information in the digital age -- Rights and protection of social/socio-cultural groups -- Freedom of religion or belief -- Cultural heritage in the human rights system -- Access control technologies -- Administration -- Affirmative action -- African human rights system -- Alliance of civilizations -- Archaeological heritage -- Architectural heritage -- Armed conflict -- Artists' freedom of expression -- Arts education -- Asian values -- Assembly and association -- Authors' rights/copyright -- Belief -- Blasphemy -- Caricatures/cartoons -- Censorship -- Charter of Fundamental Rights of the European Union (CFR) -- Children -- Churches -- Circumcision -- Citizenship -- Clash of civilisations -- Common values -- Community identification -- Constitutional courts -- Conversion -- Council of Europe (CoE) -- Court of Justice of the European Union (CJEU) -- Cultural autonomy -- Cultural dimensions of human rights -- Cultural expressions -- Cultural genocide -- Cultural identity -- Cultural institutions/infastructure --

Cultural policy -- Defamation -- Development -- Digital media -- Disabilities -- Disability and copyright -- Discrimination -- Dissidents -- ECHR cultural protocal debates/CAHMIN -- Equality -- European Committee of Social Rights -- European Convention on Human Rights (ECHR) -- European Court of Human Rights (ECtHR) -- European Union -- European Union Agency for Fundamental Rights (FRA) -- Female genital mutilation -- Food -- Free trade -- Fundamentalism -- Gender stereotypes -- Golden rule -- Governments -- Hate crimes -- Hijab -- Historical truth -- Housing -- Human diginity -- Human Rights Council -- Human security -- Hybridity -- Illicit trafficking of cultural objects -- Impact assessment -- Indigenous peoples -- Information -- Intangible cultural heritage -- Intellectual property and human rights -- Inter-American human rights system -- Intercultural competence -- International Covenant on Economic, Social and Cultural Rights (ICESCR) -- Internet access -- Internet content suppression -- Investigative journalism -- Journalists -- Landscapes -- Language rights in Europe -- Language of migrants -- LGBT -- Libraries -- Literary expressions -- Margin of appreciation -- Media content -- Migrants -- Movement of cultural objects -- Names -- National minorities -- Older persons -- Organisation for Security and Cooperation in Europe (OSCE) -- Parody -- Participation in cultural life -- Peoples' rights -- Pornography/obscenity -- Poverty -- Press freedom -- Privacy -- Procedures -- Public broadcasting -- Public space -- Refugees --

	Regional and minority languages -- Religious education -- Religious minorities -- Religious symbols -- Restitution and return of cultural objects -- Right to science and culture -- Roma culture -- Secularism and Islamic law -- Social media -- Status of artists -- Trolling and shitstorms -- UN treaty bodies -- Underwater cultural heritage -- UNESCO -- Universal Declaration of Human Rights (UDHR) -- Universalism and cultural relativism -- Urban planning -- Values -- Whistleblowing -- Youth.
Subjects	Human rights.
	Civil rights.
	International law and human rights.
Notes	Includes bibliographical references and index.

Didaktikos: journal of theological education.
LCCN	2017203110
Type of material	Periodical or Newspaper
Uniform title	Didaktikos (Bellingham, Wash.)
Main title	Didaktikos: journal of theological education.
Published/Produced	Bellingham, WA: Lexham Press, part of Faithlife Corporation, [2017-]
Publication history	Began with: Volume 1, Issue 1 (November 2017).
Current frequency	Five issues yearly
ISSN	2575-0127
LC classification	BV4019 .D53
Serial key title	Didaktikos
Subjects	Theology--Study and teaching--Periodicals.
	Religious education--Periodicals.
	Religious education.
	Theology--Study and teaching.
Form/Genre	Periodicals.

Discourses of religion and secularism in religious education classrooms
LCCN 2017944626
Type of material Book
Personal name Flensner, Karin Kittelmann.
Main title Discourses of religion and secularism in religious education classrooms / Karin Kittelmann Flensner.
Published/Produced New York, NY: Springer Berlin Heidelberg, 2017.
ISBN 9783319609485

Does religious education matter?
LCCN 2016016604
Type of material Book
Main title Does religious education matter? / edited by Mary Shanahan.
Published/Produced London; New York: Routledge, Taylor & Francis Group, 2017.
Description ix, 278 pages; 24 cm
ISBN 9781472484321 (hardback: alk. paper)
LC classification BL42 .D64 2017
Related names Shanahan, Mary (College teacher), editor.
Contents Part I. The distinctness of religious education -- Part II. Religious education in the school context -- Part III. Exploring the potential of religious education.
Subjects Religious education.
Notes Includes bibliographical references and index.

Echoes of enlightenment: the life and legacy of the Tibetan Saint Sönam Peldren
LCCN 2015044398
Type of material Book

Personal name	Bessenger, Suzanne M., author.
Main title	Echoes of enlightenment: the life and legacy of the Tibetan Saint Sönam Peldren / Suzanne M. Bessenger.
Published/Produced	New York, NY: Oxford University Press, [2016]
Description	viii, 296 pages; 25 cm
ISBN	9780190225285 (paperback: alk. paper)
	9780190225278 (cloth: alk. paper)
LC classification	BQ942.S5965 B48 2016
Summary	"Echoes of Enlightenment explores the issues of gender and sainthood raised by the recently discovered 'liberation story' of the fourteenth-century Tibetan female Buddhist practitioner Sönam Peldren. Born in 1328, Sönam Peldren spent most of her adult life as a nomad in eastern Tibet until her death in 1372. She is believed to have been illiterate, lacking religious education, and unconnected to established religious institutions. For that reason, and because as a woman her claims of religious authority would have been constantly questioned, Sönam Peldren's success in legitimizing her claims of divine identity appear all the more remarkable. Today the site of her death is recognized as sacred by local residents. Suzanne Bessenger draws on the new-found biography of the saint to understand how the written record of the saint's life is shaped both by the hagiographical agendas of its multiple authors and by the dictates of the genres of Tibetan religious literature, including biography and poetry. She considers Sönam Peldren's enduring historical legacy as a fascinating piece of Tibetan history that reveals much about the social and textual machinations of saint

Contents production. Finally, she identifies Sönam Peldren as one of the earliest recorded instances of a historical Tibetan woman successfully using the uniquely Tibetan hermeneutic of deity emanation to achieve religious authority."-- Provided by publisher.

Contents Acknowledgments -- Introduction -- Chapter One: The Life of Sönam Peldren -- Chapter Two: Composing the Life of Sönam Peldren -- Chapter Three: The Religion of Sönam Peldren -- Chapter Four: "Low Birth but High Thought": Depictions of Gender and Female Bodies in the Life of Sönam Peldren -- Chapter Five: The Posthumous Careers of Sönam Peldren -- Conclusion -- Appendix A: Outlines of Two Manuscripts of the Life of Sönam Peldren -- Appendix B: Life Prayer of the Wisdom Dakini Sönam Peldren -- Appendix C: Ya Nga Jamda Ganden Khachö Ling Nunnery and Its Surroundings -- Appendix D: Mapping the Life and Death of Sönam Peldren -- Bibliography -- Index.

Subjects Bsod-nam-dpal-'dren, 1328-1372.
Buddhist saints--Biography.
Buddhism--Tibet Region--History.
Religion / Buddhism / History.

Notes Includes bibliographical references (pages 279-287) and index.

Additional formats Online version: Bessenger, Suzanne M., author. Echoes of enlightenment New York: Oxford University Press, 2016 9780190225292 (DLC) 2016028667

Education and religion
LCCN 2016008667

Type of material	Book
Main title	Education and religion / edited by James Arthur and Philip Barnes.
Published/Produced	Abingdon, Oxon; New York, NY: Routledge, 2017.
ISBN	9781138827769 (set: alk. paper)
	9781138827776 (volume 1: alk. paper)
	9781138827783 (volume 2: alk. paper)
	9781138827790 (volume 3: alk. paper)
	9781138827806 (volume 4: alk. paper)
LC classification	LB1027.2 .E35 2017
Related names	Arthur, James, 1957- editor.
	Barnes, Philip (L. Philip), editor.
Contents	v. 1. Aims and purposes of religious education -- v. 2. Religion in education -- v. 3. Religion, diversity and education -- v. 4. Debates in religion and education.
Subjects	Education--Religious aspects.
	Religion in the public schools.
	Religious education.
Notes	Includes bibliographical references and index.
Series	Major themes in education

Education law, policy, and practice: cases and materials

LCCN	2017018224
Type of material	Book
Personal name	Kaufman, Michael J., 1958- author.
Main title	Education law, policy, and practice: cases and materials / Michael J. Kaufman, J.D., Dean, Founding Director of Education Law and Policy Institute, and Professor of Law, Loyola University Chicago School of Law and Sherelyn R. Kaufman, J.D, M.A., in teaching C.A.S. in Early Childhood Administration, Professor of Early

	Childhood Administration, Erikson Institute, Graduate School in Child Development.
Edition	Fourth edition.
Published/Produced	New York: Wolters Kluwer, [2018]
Description	xxxiii, 1087 pages; 26 cm.
ISBN	9781454883326 (hbk)
LC classification	KF4119 .K38 2018
Related names	Kaufman, Sherelyn R., 1957- author.
Contents	An overview of the book: the integration of education law, policy, and practice -- The structure of American education law, finance practice, and policy -- The limits of public education -- The right to a public education and the equitable, distribution of public educational resources -- The law and policy of early childhood education -- The establishment clause and the lemon test: publice resources for religious education -- The modification of lemon and the rise of private choice and vouchers -- Religious observance in the public school -- The use of school facilities -- The legal structure of school governance -- The legal and practical mechanics of school board governance -- Equal educational opportunities -- The rights of students -- Students with educational disabilities -- Traditional common law torts in the educational environment -- Evolving duties in the educational environment -- The constitutional and statutory rights of teachers -- The professional and contractual responsibilities and rights of teachers.
Subjects	Educational law and legislation--United States.
Form/Genre	Casebooks (Law).
Notes	Includes bibliographical references (pages 1039-1048) and index.

Series   Aspen casebook series

Ethical English: teaching and learning in English as spiritual, moral and religious education

LCCN	2014016240
Type of material	Book
Personal name	Pike, Mark A., author.
Main title	Ethical English: teaching and learning in English as spiritual, moral and religious education / Mark A. Pike.
Published/Created	London; New York: Bloomsbury Academic, An imprint of Bloomsbury Publishing Plc, 2015.
Description	xv, 233 pages; 24 cm
Links	Cover image http://www.netread.com/jcusers2/bk1388/835/9781472576835/image/lgcover.9781472576835.jpg
ISBN	9781472576835 (HB)
	9781472576828 (PB)
LC classification	PR51.G7 P55 2015
Summary	"Ethical English addresses the 'ethos' of English teaching and draws attention to its 'spirit' and fundamental character, identifying the features that English teaching must exhibit if it is to continue to sustain us morally as a liberal art and to provide the learners of increasingly plural societies with a broad ethical education. Mark A. Pike provides practical examples from the classroom, including assessment and teaching, knitting these with an ethical critique of practice, stimulating readers to engage in critical reflection concerning the teaching of English. This book not only shows readers how to teach English but also helps them to critically evaluate the ethics of the

	practice of English teaching"-- Provided by publisher.
Contents	Foreword, David Stevens Foreword, Thomas Lickona Acknowledgements Introduction: Why 'Ethical' English Teaching? Part 1: Ethical English as Spiritual Education 1. Ethical English 2. Well-Being in English 3. The Art of Assessing and Planning English 4. The Spirit of Professional Learning in English Part 2: Ethical English as Moral Education 5. Educational Foundations for English 6. English as Moral and Character Education 7. Learning Citizenship and Character in English 8. The Character of Professional Learning Part 3: Ethical English as Religious Education 9. English as Pseudo-Religion 10. Multicultural English 11. English as Secularist Subject 12. Believing in Professional Learning Appendix Bibliography Index.
Subjects	English literature--Study and teaching--Great Britain.
	English teachers--Training of--Great Britain.
	Moral education--Great Britain.
	Education / Philosophy & Social Aspects.
	Education / General.
	Education / Teaching Methods & Materials / Arts & Humanities.
Notes	Includes bibliographical references (pages 209-224) and index.

European perspectives on Islamic education and public schooling
LCCN	2018012272
Type of material	Book
Main title	European perspectives on Islamic education and public schooling / edited by Jenny Berglund.

Published/Produced	Sheffield, UK; Bristol, CT: Equinox Publishing, 2018.
ISBN	9781781794845 (hb)
LC classification	BP43.E85 E87 2018
Related names	Berglund, Jenny, editor.
Subjects	Islamic education--Europe.
	Islam--Study and teaching--Europe.
	Islamic religious education--Europe.
Notes	Includes bibliographical references and index.
Additional formats	Online version: European perspectives on Islamic education and public schooling Sheffield, UK; Bristol, CT: Equinox Publishing, 2018 9781781797754 (DLC) 2018013558

European perspectives on Islamic education and public schooling

LCCN	2018013558
Type of material	Book
Main title	European perspectives on Islamic education and public schooling / edited by Jenny Berglund.
Published/Produced	Sheffield, UK; Bristol, CT: Equinox Publishing, 2018.
Description	1 online resource.
ISBN	9781781797754 (ePDF)
LC classification	BP43.E85
Related names	Berglund, Jenny, editor.
Subjects	Islamic education--Europe.
	Islam--Study and teaching--Europe.
	Islamic religious education--Europe.
Notes	Includes bibliographical references and index.
Additional formats	Print version: European perspectives on Islamic education and public schooling Sheffield, UK; Bristol, CT: Equinox Publishing, 2018 9781781794845 (DLC) 2018012272

Excellence in ministry: best practices for successful catechetical leadership

LCCN	2017948967
Type of material	Book
Personal name	Quinlan, Tom, author.
Main title	Excellence in ministry: best practices for successful catechetical leadership / Tom Quinlan.
Published/Produced	Chicago: Loyola Press, [2017] ©2017
Description	vii, 157 pages: illustrations; 23 cm
ISBN	9780829445329 0829445323
LC classification	BX1968 .Q56 2017
Portion of title	Best practices for successful catechetical leadership
Contents	Forming and sharing the vision -- Planning and evaluating catechetical ministries -- Fitting within church structures -- Catechetical resources and models -- Operational aspects: out front and behind the scenes -- Marketing and catechetical ministry -- Pastoral approaches to gathering and engaging God's people -- Catechesis and liturgy belong together -- Parents and evangelization -- Mentoring the next generation of leaders.
Subjects	Catechetics--Catholic Church. Christian education directors. Christian leadership--Catholic Church. Directors of religious education. Lay ministry. Parish life coordinators. Religious education. Catechetics--Catholic Church. Christian education directors. Christian leadership--Catholic Church.

Notes	Directors of religious education. Lay ministry. Parish life coordinators. Religious education. Includes bibliographical references.
Series	The effective catechetical leader Effective catechetical leader.

Formation of a religious landscape: Shi'i higher learning in Safavid Iran

LCCN	2017056411
Type of material	Book
Personal name	Moazzen, Maryam, author.
Main title	Formation of a religious landscape: Shi'i higher learning in Safavid Iran / by Maryam Moazzen.
Published/Produced	Leiden; Boston: Brill, 2018.
Description	1 online resource.
ISBN	9789004356559 (E-book)
LC classification	BP194.9.E3
Summary	In Formation of a Religious Landscape: Shi'i Higher Learning in Safavid Iran, Maryam Moazzen offers the first systematic examination of Shi'i educational institution and practices by exploring the ways in which religious knowledge was produced, authenticated, and transmitted in the second half of Safavid rule (1588-1722). By analyzing the deeds of endowment of the Madrasa-yi Sulṭānī and other mosque-madrasas built by the Safavid elite, this study sheds light on the organizing mechanisms and structures utilized by such educational foundations. Based on the large number of ijazās and other primary sources including waqfiyyas, biographical dictionaries and autobiographies, this study also reconstructs

Contents	the Safavid madrasas' curriculum and describes the pedagogical methods used to transmit religious knowledge as well as issues that faced Shi'i higher learning in early modern times. The Mosque-Madrasas of Safavid Isfahan -- The Madrasa-yi Sulṭānī: Waqfs, Administrative Structure, and Academic Life -- Reshaping Shi'a Cultural Memory: Commemorative Rituals and Constructing Identity -- The Safavid Curriculum: Conflicting Visions, Contested Triumphs -- Engagement with Religious Knowledge: Dialogical and Hermeneutical Modes of Transmission -- Safavid Pedagogical Approaches: Theories, Application, and Practices.
Subjects	Madrasahs--Iran--History.
	Islamic religious education--Iran--History.
	Shiites--Education--Iran--History.
	Islamic education--Iran--History.
Notes	Includes bibliographical references and index.
Additional formats	Print version: Moazzen, Maryam, author. Formation of a religious landscape Leiden; Boston: Brill, 2018 9789004355293 (DLC) 2017050564

Formation of a religious landscape: Shi'i higher learning in Safavid Iran

LCCN	2017050564
Type of material	Book
Personal name	Moazzen, Maryam, author.
Main title	Formation of a religious landscape: Shi'i higher learning in Safavid Iran / by Maryam Moazzen.
Published/Produced	Leiden; Boston: Brill, [2018]
Description	xiii, 290 pages; 25 cm
ISBN	9789004355293 (hardback: alk. paper)

	(ebook)
LC classification	BP194.9.E3 M63 2018
Summary	In Formation of a Religious Landscape: Shi'i Higher Learning in Safavid Iran, Maryam Moazzen offers the first systematic examination of Shi'i educational institution and practices by exploring the ways in which religious knowledge was produced, authenticated, and transmitted in the second half of Safavid rule (1588-1722). By analyzing the deeds of endowment of the Madrasa-yi Sulṭānī and other mosque-madrasas built by the Safavid elite, this study sheds light on the organizing mechanisms and structures utilized by such educational foundations. Based on the large number of ijazās and other primary sources including waqfiyyas, biographical dictionaries and autobiographies, this study also reconstructs the Safavid madrasas' curriculum and describes the pedagogical methods used to transmit religious knowledge as well as issues that faced Shi'i higher learning in early modern times.
Subjects	Madrasahs--Iran--History.
	Islamic religious education--Iran--History.
	Shiites--Education--Iran--History.
	Islamic education--Iran--History.
Notes	Includes bibliographical references (pages and indexes254-283) and indexes.
Additional formats	Online version: Moazzen, Maryam, author. Formation of a religious landscape Leiden; Boston: Brill, 2018 9789004356559 (DLC) 2017056411

Fundamentalist U: keeping the faith in American higher education
LCCN 2017277919

Type of material	Book
Personal name	Laats, Adam, author.
Main title	Fundamentalist U: keeping the faith in American higher education / Adam Laats.
Published/Produced	New York, NY, United States of America: Oxford University Press, [2018]
Description	x, 348 pages: illustrations; 25 cm
ISBN	0190665629 hardcover
	9780190665623 hardcover
LC classification	LC586.F85 L33 2018
Summary	Adam Laats offers a provocative and definitive new history of conservative evangelical colleges and universities, institutions that have played a decisive role in American politics, culture, and religion. This book looks unflinchingly at the issues that have defined these schools, including their complicated legacy of conservative theology and social activism.
	Colleges, universities, and seminaries do more than just transfer knowledge to students. They sell themselves as "experiences" that transform young people in unique ways. The conservative evangelical Protestant network of higher education has been no different. In the twentieth century, when higher education sometimes seemed to focus on sports, science, and social excess, conservative evangelical schools offered a compelling alternative. On their campuses, evangelicals debated what it meant to be a creationist, a Christian, a proper American, all within the bounds of Biblical revelation. Instead of encouraging greater personal freedom and deeper pluralist values, conservative evangelical schools thrived by imposing stricter rules on their

students and faculty. In Fundamentalist U, Adam Laats shows that these colleges have always been more than just schools; they have been vital intellectual citadels in America's culture wars. These unique institutions have defined what it has meant to be an evangelical and have reshaped the landscape of American higher education. Students at these schools have been expected to learn what it means to be an educated evangelical in a secularizing society. This book asks new questions about that formative process. How have conservative evangelicals hoped to use higher education to instill a uniquely evangelical identity? How has this identity supported the continuing influence of a dissenting body of knowledge? In what ways has it been tied to cultural notions of proper race relations and proper relations between the sexes? And perhaps most important, how have students responded to schools' attempts to cultivate these vital notions about their selves? In order to understand either American higher education or American evangelicalism, we need to appreciate the role of this influential network of dissenting institutions. Only by making sense of these schools can we make sense of America's continuing culture wars.

Contents Introduction: Higher (power) education -- College and Christ -- In the beginning -- A mote in the eye -- "I came to be went with" -- Billy Graham was a transfer student -- What is college for? -- Nightmare on College Avenue -- Is the Bible racist? -- Learn one for the Gipper -- Epilogue: Sandals of the evangelical mind.

Subjects Evangelicalism--United States.

	Christian universities and colleges--United States. Religious education--Political aspects--United States. Fundamentalism--United States. Education / Higher. Religion / Christian Education / Children & Youth. Religion / Education. Christian universities and colleges. Evangelicalism. Fundamentalism. United States.
Notes	Includes bibliographical references and index.

Generational IQ: Christianity isn't dying, millennials aren't the problem, and the future is bright

LCCN	2015019768
Type of material	Book
Personal name	Shaw, Haydn.
Main title	Generational IQ: Christianity isn't dying, millennials aren't the problem, and the future is bright / Haydn Shaw, with Ginger Kolbaba.
Published/Produced	Carol Stream, IL: Tyndale House Publishers, Inc., 2015.
Description	275 pages; 22 cm
ISBN	9781414364728 (hc)
LC classification	BR121.3 .S53 2015
Subjects	Christianity. Intergenerational religious education. Intergenerational relations--Religious aspects--Christianity. Intergenerational communication--Religious aspects--Christianity. Generations.

Age groups.

Global perspectives on Catholic religious education in schools.
LCCN	2018968091
Type of material	Book
Main title	Global perspectives on Catholic religious education in schools.
Published/Produced	New York, NY: Springer Berlin Heidelberg, 2019.
ISBN	9789811361265

Have a little faith: religion, democracy, and the American public school
LCCN	2016005055
Type of material	Book
Personal name	Justice, Benjamin, 1971- author.
Main title	Have a little faith: religion, democracy, and the American public school / Benjamin Justice, Colin Macleod.
Published/Produced	Chicago: The University of Chicago Press, [2016]
Description	vii, 180 pages; 24 cm.
ISBN	9780226400310 (cloth: alk. paper)
	9780226400457 (paper.: alk. paper)
LC classification	LC111 .J89 2016
Related names	Macleod, Colin M. (Colin Murray), 1962- author.
Contents	Religion and education: a democratic perspective -- The founding fathers, religion, and education -- Religion and the origins of public education -- Religion and public education in the era of progress -- Religion and public education since 1960 -- Finding faith in democracy: three cases.
Subjects	Religion in the public schools--United States--History.
	Religious education--United States--History.

	Democracy--United States--Religious aspects.
	Church and state--United States--History.
Notes	Includes bibliographical references and index.
Series	History and philosophy of education series

History, remembrance and religious education

LCCN	2014028211
Type of material	Book
Main title	History, remembrance and religious education / Stephen G. Parker, Rob Freathy and Leslie J. Francis (eds).
Published/Produced	Oxford: Peter Lang, [2015]
Description	x, 413 pages: illustrations; 23 cm.
ISBN	9783034317207 (alk. paper)
	3034317204 (alk. paper)
LC classification	BV1471.3 .H57 2015
Related names	Parker, Stephen G., 1965-
	Freathy, Rob.
	Francis, Leslie J.
Subjects	Religious education--Cross-cultural studies.
	Collective memory--Cross-cultural studies.
	Group identity--Cross-cultural studies.
	Moral education--Cross-cultural studies.
Notes	Includes bibliographical references and indexes.
Series	Religion, education, and values, 2235-4638; volume 7
	Religion, education and values; v. 7. 2235-4638

Holy Rus': the rebirth of Orthodoxy in the New Russia

LCCN	2016948024
Type of material	Book
Personal name	Burgess, John P., 1954- author.
Main title	Holy Rus': the rebirth of Orthodoxy in the New Russia / John P. Burgess.

Published/Produced	New Haven: Yale University Press, [2017] ©2017
Description	xii, 264 pages: illustrations; 25 cm
ISBN	9780300222241 (alk. paper)
	0300222246 (alk. paper)
LC classification	BX493 .B87 2017
Portion of title	Rebirth of Orthodoxy in the New Russia
Summary	A fascinating, vivid, and on-the-ground account of Russian Orthodoxy's resurgence. A bold experiment is taking place in Russia. After a century of being scarred by militant, atheistic communism, the Orthodox Church has become Russia's largest and most significant nongovernmental organization. As it has returned to life, it has pursued a vision of reclaiming Holy Rus': that historical yet mythical homeland of the eastern Slavic peoples; a foretaste of the perfect justice, peace, harmony, and beauty for which religious believers long; and the glimpse of heaven on earth that persuaded Prince Vladimir to accept Orthodox baptism in Crimea in A.D. 988. Through groundbreaking initiatives in religious education, social ministry, historical commemoration, and parish life, the Orthodox Church is seeking to shape a new, post-communist national identity for Russia. In this eye-opening and evocative book, John Burgess examines Russian Orthodoxy's resurgence from a grassroots level, providing Western readers with an enlightening, inside look at the new Russia.
Contents	Envisioning Holy Rus' -- The rebirth of Orthodoxy -- Religious education -- Social ministry -- The New martyrs -- Parish life -- The future.

Subjects	Russkaia pravoslavnaia tserkov'--Influence.
	Nationalism--Religious aspects--Russkaia pravoslavnaia tserkov'.
	Church renewal--Russkaia pravoslavnaia tserkov'--History--21st century.
	National characteristics, Russian--History--21st century.
	Christianity and culture--Russia (Federation)--History--21st century.
	11.53 Eastern Churches.
	Russia (Federation)--Church history--21st century.
Notes	Includes bibliographical references and index.

Identity, history and trans-nationality in Central Asia: the mountain communities of Pamir

LCCN	2018020995
Type of material	Book
Main title	Identity, history and trans-nationality in Central Asia: the mountain communities of Pamir / edited by Dagikhudo Dagiev and Carole Faucher.
Published/Produced	London; New York: Routledge, Taylor & Francis Group, 2019.
Description	xvi, 299 pages: illustrations; 25 cm.
ISBN	9780815357551 (hardback)
LC classification	DK929.5.P36 I34 2019
Related names	Faucher, Carole, 1956- editor.
	Dagiev, Dagikhudo editor.
Contents	Locating Pamiri communities in Central Asia / Carole Faucher and Dagikhudo Dagiev -- Identity formation, borders and political transformations -- Geography, ethnicity and cultural heritage in interplay in the context of the Tajik Pamiri identity / Sunatullo Jonboboev -- Pamiri ethnic

identity and its re-emergence in post-Soviet Tajikistan / Dagikhudo Dagiev -- Transformations and lost in the Wakhi language / Sherali Gulomaliev -- The Tajiks of China: identity in the age of transition / Amier Saidula -- Archaeology, myths, intellectual and cultural heritage -- A Badakhshani origin for Zoroaster / Yusufsho Yaqubov and Dagikhudo Dagiev -- The Silk Road castles and temples: ancient Wakhan in legends and history / Abdulmamad Iloliev -- Nasir-i Khusraw's intellectual contribution: the meaning of pleasure and pain in his philosophy / Ghulam Abbas Hunzai -- Religious identity in the Pamirs: the institutionalisation of the Ismaili dawa in Shughnan / Daniel Beben -- Forgotten figures of Badakhshan: Sayyid Munir al-Din Badakhshani and Sayyid Haydar Shah Mubarakshahzada / Muzaffar Zoolshoev -- Social cohesion, interactions and globalization -- Blessed people in a barren land: the Bartangi and their success catalyser Barakat / Stefanie Kicherer -- Promoting peace and pluralism in the rural, mountainous region of Chitral, Pakistan, Mir Afzal Tajik / Ali Nawab, Abdul Wali Khan -- A "shift" in values: mother's educational role in the Gorno-Badakhshan Region / Nazira Sodatsayrova -- Project identity: the discursive formation of Pamiri identity in the age of the internet / Aslisho Qurboniev -- Religious education and self-identification among Tajik Pamiri youth / Carole Faucher.

Subjects   Pamir--History.
Pamir--Civilization.

Notes	Includes bibliographical references (pages 265-291) and index.
Series	Central Asian studies series; 33

In good faith: secular parenting in a religious world

LCCN	2017001465
Type of material	Book
Personal name	Polonchek, Maria, 1979- author.
Main title	In good faith: secular parenting in a religious world / Maria Polonchek.
Published/Produced	Lanham: Rowman & Littlefield, [2017]
Description	xii, 193 pages; 24 cm
ISBN	9781442270664 (cloth: alk. paper)
LC classification	HQ755.8 .P65 2017
Contents	Acknowledgments -- Introduction: on making it personal -- Baggage claim -- Religious education -- Morality -- Awe and wonder -- Death -- Meaning and purpose -- Family -- Holidays, traditions, and rituals -- Conclusion: on needing community -- Bibliography -- Index.
Subjects	Parenting.
	Secularism.
	Religious education.
Notes	Includes bibliographical references (pages 185-188) and index.
Additional formats	Online version: Polonchek, Maria, 1979- author. In good faith Lanham, MD: Rowman & Littlefield, [2017] 9781442270671 (DLC) 2017030523

Inspiring wonder, awe, and empathy: spiritual development in young children

LCCN	2017022211
Type of material	Book

Personal name	Schein, Deborah L., author.
Main title	Inspiring wonder, awe, and empathy: spiritual development in young children / Deborah Schein, PhD.
Edition	First edition.
Published/Produced	St. Paul, MN: Redleaf Press, [2018]
Description	ix, 156 pages: illustrations; 23 cm
ISBN	9781605544847 (pbk.:acid-free paper)
LC classification	BL625.5 .S34 2018
Contents	The developing self -- Spiritual development in relationship to other developmental domains -- Curriculum, play, and spiritual development -- Nature and spiritual development: being in nature and with nature -- Cultivating spiritual moments with young children -- Preventing bullying by nurturing spiritual development.
Subjects	Children--Religious life. Spirituality. Religious education of children.
Notes	Includes bibliographical references and index.
Additional formats	Online version: Schein, Deborah L., author. Inspiring wonder, awe, and empathy First edition. St. Paul, MN: Redleaf Press, [2018] 9781605544854 (DLC) 2017036409

International journal of Christianity & education.

LCCN	2016204626
Type of material	Periodical or Newspaper
Main title	International journal of Christianity & education.
Published/Produced	London, England: Sage, 2015-
Publication history	Vol. 19, issue 1 (March 2015)-
Description	volumes; 23 cm. Continues the numbering of Journal of education and Christian belief.

Current frequency	Three times a year
ISSN	2056-9971
LC classification	BV1460 .I6257
	LC368
Continues in part	Journal of Christian education 0021-9657 (OCoLC)03306795
	Journal of education and Christian belief 1366-5456 (OCoLC)37135980
Variant title	International journal of Christianity and education
Subjects	Church and education--Periodicals.
	Christian education--Periodicals.
	Religious education--Periodicals.
	Education (Christian theology)--Periodicals.
	Christian education.
	Church and education.
	Education (Christian theology)
	Religious education.
Form/Genre	Periodicals.
Notes	Formed by the merging of 'Journal of Christian education' and 'Journal of education and Christian belief'.
Additional formats	Also available online.
	International Journal of Christianity & Education 2056-9971

Islam and citizenship education

LCCN	2014958971
Type of material	Book
Main title	Islam and citizenship education / Ednan Aslan, Marcia Hermansen (eds.); in cooperation with Minela Salkic Joldo.
Published/Produced	Wiesbaden: Springer VS, [2015] ©2015.
Description	342 pages; 21 cm.

Links	Contributor biographical information http://www.loc.gov/catdir/enhancements/fy1601/2014958971-b.html
	Publisher description http://www.loc.gov/catdir/enhancements/fy1601/2014958971-d.html
	Table of contents only http://www.loc.gov/catdir/enhancements/fy1601/2014958971-t.html
ISBN	9783658086022 (pbk.)
	3658086025 (pbk.)
	(ebook)
LC classification	BP173.63 .I735 2015
Related names	Aslan, Ednan, 1959- editor.
	Hermansen, Marcia K., 1951- editor.
	Joldo, Minela Salkic, editor.
Summary	The scholarly contributors to this volume investigate various means to stimulate and facilitate reflection on new social relations while clarifying the contradictions between religious and social affiliation from different perspectives and experiences. They explore hindrances whose removal could enable Muslim children and youth to pursue equal participation in political and social life, and the ways that education could facilitate this process. Contents Muslims in Europe Citizenship Education Religion and Citizenship Education Values and Citizenship Education Target Groups Researchers and students interested in Public, Academics-Education, Religious and Migration Studies The Editors Dr. Ednan Aslan is Chair of the Institute for Islamic Studies and Islamic Religious Education at the Center for Teacher Education at the University of Vienna. Dr. Marcia Hermansen is Director of the Islamic World Studies program at Loyola

	University Chicago where she teaches courses in Islamic Studies and Religious Studies as a Professor in the Theology Department.
Contents	Section one Western European cases -- Section two The Balkans and the Middle East -- Section Three Eastern Europe and Russia -- Section Four North America -- Appendix Messages of Felicitation
Subjects	Islam and civil society--Congresses. Muslims--Education--Congresses. Citizenship--Study and teaching--Religious aspects--Islam--Congresses.
Notes	These diverse studies are based on communications initially presented at a conference on citizenship, education and Islam convened in Tirana, Albania in November, 2013 by the Faculty of Philosophy and Education, Department of Education, University of Vienna, the University of Tirana, and Bedër University -- Page 13. Includes bibliographical references (pages 323-342).
Additional formats	Also available online: Islam and citizenship education. Wiesbaden [Germany]: Springer VS, [2015] 9783658086039 (OCoLC)900276835 (GyWOH)har150067335
Series	Wiener Beiträge zur Islamforschung

Islamic education in Africa: writing boards and blackboards

LCCN	2016030077
Type of material	Book
Main title	Islamic education in Africa: writing boards and blackboards / edited by Robert Launay.

Published/Produced	Bloomington; Indianapolis: Indiana University Press, [2016]
Description	ix, 323 pages; 24 cm
ISBN	9780253022707 (cloth: alk. paper)
	9780253023025 (pbk.: alk. paper)
LC classification	BP43.A357 I85 2016
Related names	Launay, Robert, 1949- editor.
Subjects	Islamic religious education--Africa, Sub-Saharan--History.
	Islamic education--Africa, Sub-Saharan--History.
	Muslims--Education--Africa, Sub-Saharan--History.
	Education--Africa, Sub-Saharan.
	Africa, Sub-Saharan--Colonial influence.
Notes	Includes bibliographical references and index.
Additional formats	Online version: Islamic education in Africa Bloomington; Indianapolis: Indiana University Press, 2016 9780253023186 (DLC) 2016030765

Islamic education in Britain: new pluralist paradigms

LCCN	2015007960
Type of material	Book
Personal name	Scott-Baumann, Alison, author.
Main title	Islamic education in Britain: new pluralist paradigms / Alison Scott-Baumann and Sariya Cheruvallil-Contractor.
Published/Produced	London; New York: Bloomsbury Academic, an imprint of Bloomsbury Publishing Plc, Bloomsbury, 2015.
Description	xv, 218 pages; 25 cm
ISBN	9781472569387 (hardback)
LC classification	BP43.G7 S36 2015
Related names	Scott-Baumann, Alison.

Summary

"The Western world often fears many aspects of Islam, without the knowledge to move forward. On the other hand, there are sustained and complex debates within Islam about how to live in the modern world with faith. Alison Scott-Baumann and Sariya Contractor-Cheruvallil here propose solutions to both dilemmas, with a particular emphasis on the role of women. Challenging existing beliefs about Islam in Britain, this book offers a paradigm shift based on research conducted over 15 years. The educational needs within several groups of British Muslims were explored, resulting in the need to offer critical analysis of the provision for the study of classical Islamic Theology in Britain. Islamic Education in Britain responds to the dissatisfaction among many young Muslim men and women with the theological/secular split, and their desire for courses that provide combinations of these two strands of their lived experience as Muslim British citizens. Grounded in empirical research, the authors reach beyond the meta-narratives of secularization and orientalism to demonstrate the importance of the teaching and learning of classical Islamic studies for the promotion of reasoned dialogue, interfaith and intercultural understanding in pluralist British society"-- Provided by publisher.

Contents

1. Introduction: British Islam and Education for British Muslims 2. Understanding and Defining Classical Islamic Studies in Britain 3. Mapping the Provision for Classical Islamic Studies in Britain 4. Imams on the Street: What do they do? 5. Arabic: The Centrality of a Living World

	Language 6. Muslim Women's Voices, Feminisms, and Theologies 7. Collaborative Partnerships in Higher Education 8. Conclusion: Classical Islamic Studies, Pluralism and British Life Bibliography Index.
Subjects	Islamic religious education--Great Britain. Islamic education--Great Britain. Islam--Study and teaching--Great Britain. Religion / Education. Religion / Islam / Sufi. Social Science / Islamic Studies.
Notes	Includes bibliographical references (pages 206-215) and index.

Jesus Christ: his mission and ministry

LCCN	2018303724
Type of material	Book
Personal name	Pennock, Michael, author.
Main title	Jesus Christ: his mission and ministry / catechetical writing team: Michael Pennock, Michael Amodei, Sarah Kisling, Gloria Shahin, Justin McClain.
Edition	Second edition.
Published/Produced	Notre Dame, Indiana: Ave Maria Press, [2017] ©2017
Description	346 pages: color illustrations; 28 cm
ISBN	9781594716249 (paperback)
LC classification	BX930 .P44 2017
Related names	Amodei, Michael, author. Kisling, Sarah, author. Shahin, Gloria, author. McClain, Justin, author.
Subjects	Religious education--Textbooks. Christian education--Textbooks.

Form/Genre	Christian education. Religious education. Textbooks.
Notes	"Framework course II / Scripture"--Back cover. "Engaging minds, hearts and hands for faith is a trademark of the Ave Maria Press, Inc."--Title page verso. Includes indexes.
Series	The encountering Jesus series

Jewish values in Exodus: if i could ask Miriam: lesson plan manual

LCCN	2015042255
Type of material	Book
Personal name	Schultz, Rachael Gelfman, author.
Main title	Jewish values in Exodus: if i could ask Miriam: lesson plan manual / by Rachael Gelfman Schultz.
Published/Produced	Springfield, NJ: Behrman House, [2016] ©2016
ISBN	9780874419283
LC classification	BS1245.55 .S382 2016
Subjects	Bible. Exodus--Study and teaching (Elementary) Jewish ethics--Study and teaching (Elementary) Jewish religious education--Teaching methods.

Jewish values in Exodus: if I could ask Miriam

LCCN	2015037689
Type of material	Book
Personal name	Schultz, Rachael Gelfman, author.
Main title	Jewish values in Exodus: if I could ask Miriam / by Rachael Gelfman Schultz.
Published/Produced	Springfield, NJ: Behrman House, Inc., [2016] ©2016
ISBN	9780874419276
LC classification	BS1245.55 .S38 2016

Contents	Introduction -- How do I find courage? The midwives in Egypt; Gevurah: courage -- What makes a good leader? Moses at the Burning Bush; Manhigut: leadership -- How can I fight for justice? Moses confronts Pharaoh; Tzedek: justice -- What am I thankful for? Song of the Sea; Hodaya: thankfulness -- To what am I committed? Receiving the Torah; Brit: covenant and commitment -- How Can I learn to forgive? The Golden Calf; Selichah: forgiveness -- What can I give? Building the Tabernacle; Netinah: giving -- Bringing Torah into my life: my community project.
Subjects	Bible. Exodus--Textbooks for children. Jewish ethics--Biblical teaching--Textbooks for children. Jewish religious education--Activity programs.
Notes	This book is complemented by a "Lesson plan manual" for the educator--Title page verso.

Jewish values in Genesis: if I could ask Abraham: lesson plan manual

LCCN	2014046364
Type of material	Book
Personal name	Schultz, Rachael Gelfman, author.
Main title	Jewish values in Genesis: if I could ask Abraham: lesson plan manual / by Rachael Gelfman Schultz.
Published/Produced	Springfield, NJ: Behrman House, [2015] ©2015
ISBN	9780874419269
LC classification	BS1239 .S382 2015
Contents	Structure of the Course -- Using this teacher resource book -- Teaching strategies and tips -- Chapter 1: Who am I? Creation: Lesson 1-Lesson 2 -- Chapter 2: What do I stand for? Noah and the

	flood: Lesson 1-Lesson 2 -- Chapter 3: Where do I find faith and hope? Abraham and Sarah: Lesson 1- Lesson 2 -- Chapter 4: How can I pay It forward? Rebekah at the well: Lesson 1- Lesson 2 -- Chapter 5: Should I always tell the truth? Jacob and Esau: Lesson 1- Lesson 2 -- Chapter 6: What can I do about feeling jealous? Joseph and his brothers: Lesson 1-Lesson 2 -- Chapter 7: How can I take responsibility? Judah and Benjamin: Lesson 1-Lesson 2 -- Living Values Project.
Subjects	Bible. Genesis--Study and teaching (Elementary). Jewish ethics--Study and teaching (Elementary) Jewish religious education--Teaching methods.
Notes	"This work consists of two complementary books. The Student Response Journal includes creative, interactive activities, integrating Jewish texts with journal writing, drama, art, music, movement, and more. The Teacher Resource presents 14 ready-to-use lesson plans of approximately 50 minutes each for Jewish values in Genesis: If I Could Ask Abraham. It includes suggestions for teaching every element of the Student Response Journal"--Introduction.

Jewish values in Genesis: if I could ask Abraham

LCCN	2014046367
Type of material	Book
Personal name	Schultz, Rachael Gelfman, author.
Main title	Jewish values in Genesis: if I could ask Abraham / by Rachael Gelfman Schultz.
Published/Produced	Springfield, New Jersey: Behrman House, [2015] ©2015
Description	72 pages: color illustrations; 26 cm
ISBN	9780874419252

LC classification	BS1239 .S38 2015
Summary	"Jewish Values in Genesis helps students in Jewish congregational schools explore core values by studying stories from the Book of Genesis--Abraham and Sarah's faith and trust in journeying to a new land, Rebecca's kindness at the well, the jealousy and betrayal of Joseph by his brothers, and more. Through the ups and downs of our biblical ancestors, students will discover values that can guide them in their lives today. This book includes stories, skits, journaling prompts, projects, and more"-- Provided by publisher.
Contents	1. Who am I? Creation: B'tzelem Elohim=In the image of God -- 2. What do I stand for? Noah and the flood: Ometz leiv=Strength of heart -- 3. Where do I find faith and hope? Abraham and Sarah: Bitachon=Trust -- 4. How can I pay it forward? Rebekah at the well: Chesed=Kindness -- 5. Should I always tell the truth? Jacob and Esau: Emet=Truth -- 6. What can I do about feeling jealous? Joseph and his brothers: Kinah=Jealousy -- 7. How can I take responsibility? Judah and Benjamin: Acharayut=Responsibility -- Bringing Torah into my life: my project.
Subjects	Bible. Genesis--Textbooks for children. Jewish ethics--Biblical teaching--Textbooks for children. Jewish religious education--Activity programs.
Notes	"This work consists of two complementary books. The Student Response Journal includes creative, interactive activities, integrating Jewish texts with journal writing, drama, art, music, movement, and

more. The Teacher Resource presents 14 ready-to-use lesson plans of approximately 50 minutes each for Jewish values in Genesis: If I Could Meet Abraham. It includes suggestions for teaching every element of the Student Response Journal"-- Introduction.
Grades 4-6.

Jumpstart! RE: games and activities for ages 7-12
LCCN	2017059034
Type of material	Book
Personal name	Mogra, Imran, author.
Main title	Jumpstart! RE: games and activities for ages 7-12 / Imran Mogra.
Published/Produced	Milton Park, Abingdon, Oxon; New York, NY: Peter Lang, 2018.
Description	1 online resource.
ISBN	9781315437491 ()
LC classification	BV1475.3
Portion of title	Jumpstart! religious education
Summary	"Jumpstart! Religious Education presents a collection of simple to use games and activites that will jumpstart student's understanding of religions. This indispensable and practical guide provides activities to explore all major belief systems including Judaism, Christianity, Islam, Humanism, Hinduism, Buddhism, Sikhism, Jainism and Far East traditions. Activities are based around six main themes - sacred beliefs, sacred texts, sacred spaces, leaders, festivals and rites. If you are one of the thousands of teachers looking for a range of practical and fun ideas to teach about religion engagingly, then this is the perfect book for you"-- Provided by publisher.

Contents	Christian beliefs -- Hindu beliefs -- Humanist beliefs -- Jain beliefs -- Jewish beliefs -- Muslim beliefs -- Sikh beliefs -- Taoist beliefs -- Leadership in Buddhism -- Leadership in Christianity -- Leadership in Confucianism -- Leadership in Islam -- Leadership in Judaism -- Leadership in Sikhism -- The Bible -- Guru Granth Sahib -- Quran -- Tipitaka -- Torah -- Vedas -- The church -- The gurdwara -- The kuan -- The mandir -- The mosque -- The pagoda -- The synagogue -- Pilgrimage in Buddhism -- Pilgrimage in Christianity -- Pilgrimage in Hinduism -- Pilgrimage in Islam -- Pilgrimage in Judaism -- Pilgrimage in Sikhism -- Pilgrimage in ancient traditions -- Chinese new year -- Gurpurbs -- The day of Arafat -- Deepavali -- Easter -- The sabbath.
Subjects	Religious education of children. Games in religious education. Religious education--Activity programs.
Additional formats	Print version: Mogra, Imran, author. Jumpstart! RE Milton Park, Abingdon, Oxon; New York, NY: Peter Lang, 2018 9781138218529 (DLC) 2017029205

Jumpstart! religious education: games and activities for ages 7-12

LCCN	2017029205
Type of material	Book
Personal name	Mogra, Imran, author.
Main title	Jumpstart! religious education: games and activities for ages 7-12 / Imran Mogra.
Published/Produced	London; New York: Routledge, Taylor & Francis Group, 2018
Description	xi, 173 pages; 22 cm

ISBN	9781138218529 (hardback)
	9781138218536 (pbk.)
LC classification	BV1475.3 .M64 2018
Summary	"Jumpstart! Religious Education presents a collection of simple to use games and activites that will jumpstart student's understanding of religions. This indispensable and practical guide provides activities to explore all major belief systems including Judaism, Christianity, Islam, Humanism, Hinduism, Buddhism, Sikhism, Jainism and Far East traditions. Activities are based around six main themes - sacred beliefs, sacred texts, sacred spaces, leaders, festivals and rites. If you are one of the thousands of teachers looking for a range of practical and fun ideas to teach about religion engagingly, then this is the perfect book for you"-- Provided by publisher.
Contents	Christian beliefs -- Hindu beliefs -- Humanist beliefs -- Jain beliefs -- Jewish beliefs -- Muslim beliefs -- Sikh beliefs -- Taoist beliefs -- Leadership in Buddhism -- Leadership in Christianity -- Leadership in Confucianism -- Leadership in Islam -- Leadership in Judaism -- Leadership in Sikhism -- The Bible -- Guru Granth Sahib -- Quran -- Tipitaka -- Torah -- Vedas -- The church -- The gurdwara -- The kuan -- The mandir -- The mosque -- The pagoda -- The synagogue -- Pilgrimage in Buddhism -- Pilgrimage in Christianity -- Pilgrimage in Hinduism -- Pilgrimage in Islam -- Pilgrimage in Judaism -- Pilgrimage in Sikhism -- Pilgrimage in ancient traditions -- Chinese new year -- Gurpurbs -- The day of Arafat -- Deepavali -- Easter -- The sabbath.

Subjects	Religious education of children.
	Games in religious education.
	Religious education--Activity programs.
Additional formats	Online version: Mogra, Imran, author. Jumpstart! RE Milton Park, Abingdon, Oxon; New York, NY: Peter Lang, 2018 9781315437491 (DLC) 2017059034

Late Ottoman educational system in the Balkans in the light of the ijāzahs

LCCN	2017345708
Type of material	Book
Personal name	Idriz, Mesut, author.
Main title	Late Ottoman educational system in the Balkans in the light of the ijāzahs / Mesut İdriz.
Edition	1st edition.
Published/Produced	İstanbul: Libra Kitapçılık, 2017.
Description	119 pages: facsimiles, 21 cm.
ISBN	9786059022934
	6059022936
LC classification	LA941 .I37 2017
Summary	"The study of ijāzah tradition, its history and its impact is somehow neglected by both Muslim and non-Muslim researchers and scholars alike. This significantly unique tradition of the Muslim educational system has a long history as it emerged and developed parallel to Islamic education itself, and was in practice for more than a millennium. However, after adapting the new educational system during the late 19th century and throughout 20th century until the present, the tradition of granting ijāzah drastically began to decline and to extent became a part of history as it was practised among countable scholars, who

express their will to keep this distinctive Muslim tradition alive. During the 3rd century of Hijrah/9th century of C.E., this tradition had a strong impact to the higher learning institutions of Europe, where it is believed that granting diploma/license was the product of the Muslim tradition of ijāzah, but in terms of the form and content the former differed completely from the latter. Besides the central regions of the Muslim world, the ijāzah system appeared and practised extensively in the periphery, where this can be clearly seen in the regions of Southeast Asia and Southeast Europe. Though modern-day diploma replaced ijāzah, this practice is still alive in certain parts of these regions; however, it is not recognised "officially" by the government higher learning institutions. Up to this moment, this research managed to interview and discuss with number of 'ulamā who have been granted ijāzah from their preceding scholars from various countries of the Balkans. Thank to this 'ulamā, this work have managed to obtain copies of their original ijāzahs. In this study, based on these invaluable sources available to the researcher, it studies the detailed information contained in these documents from various aspects, such curriculum, books, studied, and transmission of knowledge. After doing so, it tries to compare and contrast with the practice and the content of this tradition in other parts of the Muslim world."--Page [4] of cover.

Subjects   Turkey--Education--History.
Balkan Peninsula--Education--History.

Subject keywords	Islamic religious education, Turkey, Ottoman period, Balkan territories
Notes	"190"--Title page verso.
	Includes bibliographical references (pages 109-115) and index.
	Text in English with facsimiles in Ottoman Turkish.
Series	History; 171
	Tarih dizisi (Libra Kitapçılık ve Yayıncılık); 171.

Leading financial sustainability in theological institutions: the African perspective

LCCN	2017394542
Type of material	Book
Personal name	Bellon, Emmanuel O., author.
Main title	Leading financial sustainability in theological institutions: the African perspective / Emmanuel O. Bellon; foreword by Tite Tiénou.
Published/Produced	Eugene, Oregon: Pickwick Publications, 2017.
Description	xv, 245 pages; 23 cm
ISBN	9781498291880 (paperback)
	1498291880
	9781498291903 (hardcover)
	1498291902
LC classification	BV4167 .B45 2017
Summary	The role of theological institutions in Christian mission is likened to the crucible that shapes the hearts and minds of those leading the charge to reconcile the world to God. Nevertheless, it is also the weakest link in the chain of Christian ministry, and efforts to sustain the unique contribution of institutions have been enigmatic. So why should we be concerned about theological institutions? What if there were no theologians, missiologists,

trained pastors, or missionaries in Christian ministry? What if there were no theological institutions? What if the existing theological institutions collapsed, shut down for lack of resources? How effective would the witness of the Christian church be without theological institutions in a world in need of God? Over the centuries, various models for supporting theological training have been tried in institutions, but very few of these have been successful. Time, cost, and quality of education (among others) have been the driving forces behind the changing models, and yet financial sustainability has been elusive. Only informed leadership that draws insights from historical, biblical, and practical wisdom is necessary in achieving this goal. This book is your faithful companion in the quest to achieve financial sustainability in theological institutions. -- Provided by publisher.

Subjects   Theological seminaries--Finance.
Religious education--Economic aspects.
Missions--Finance.
Finance--Religious aspects--Christianity.

Notes   Includes bibliographical references (pages 233-236) and index.

Learning to teach religious education in the secondary school: a companion to School experience

LCCN	2017008419
Type of material	Book
Main title	Learning to teach religious education in the secondary school: a companion to School experience / edited by L. Philip Barnes.
Edition	Third Edition.

Published/Produced	London; New York: Routledge, 2018.
Description	xxii, 239 pages; 25 cm
ISBN	9781138783713 (hardback)
	9781138783720 (paperback)
LC classification	LC410.G7 W75 2018
Related names	Barnes, Philip (L. Philip), editor.
Subjects	Religious education--Great Britain.
	Religion--Study and teaching (Secondary)--Great Britain.
Notes	"Second edition published 2009 by Routledge"--T.p. verso.
	The books in this series complement Learning to teach in the secondary school and its companion, Starting to teach in the secondary school.
	Includes bibliographical references and index.
Series	Learning to Teach Subjects in the Secondary School series

Living the future in dialogue: towards a new integral and transformative model of religious education for Nigeria in the 21st century

LCCN	2015031667
Type of material	Book
Personal name	Ugbor, Chizurum Ann, 1974- author.
Main title	Living the future in dialogue: towards a new integral and transformative model of religious education for Nigeria in the 21st century / Chizurum Ann Ugbor.
Published/Produced	Frankfurt am Main; New York: Peter Lang Edition, [2015]
Description	529 pages; 22 cm
ISBN	9783631663806
LC classification	BV1470 .N5 U33 2015
Subjects	Christian education--Nigeria.

	Religious education--Nigeria.
	Christianity and other religions--Islam.
	Islam--Relations--Christianity.
Notes	Includes bibliographical references (pages 481-529).
Series	African theological studies; VOLUME 8

Losing our religion: how unaffiliated parents are raising their children

LCCN	2015019843
Type of material	Book
Personal name	Manning, Christel.
Main title	Losing our religion: how unaffiliated parents are raising their children / Christel Manning.
Published/Produced	New York: NYU Press, [2015]
Description	ix, 245 pages; 23 cm.
ISBN	9781479874255 (cl: alk. paper)
	9781479883202 (pb: alk. paper)
LC classification	BL2525 .M3565 2015
Contents	Who are the Nones? -- What do Nones believe and practice? -- The importance of time -- The importance of place -- What are we, mom? -- The meaning of choice in religion -- The risks and benefits of raising children without religion.
Subjects	Non church-affiliated people--United States.
	Religious education of children--United States.
	United States--Religion.
Notes	Includes bibliographical references and index.
Series	Secular studies

Madrassa reforms in Pakistan between islamization and enlightened moderation

LCCN	2017332695
Type of material	Book

Personal name	Lodhi, Maryam Siddiqa, author.
Main title	Madrassa reforms in Pakistan between islamization and enlightened moderation / Maryam Siddiqa Lodhi.
Edition	Ist edition.
Published/Produced	Islamabad: Iqbal International Institute for Research and Dialogue, International Islamic University, 2016.
Description	x, 167 pages; 26 cm
ISBN	9789697576036
LC classification	BP43.P18 L63 2016
Cover title	Politics of Madrassa reforms in Pakistan: Islamization and enlightened moderation
Related names	International Islamic University (Islāmābād, Pakistan). Iqbal International Institute for Research & Dialogue.
Subjects	Madrasahs--Pakistan.
	Islamic religious education--Pakistan.
	Education and state--Pakistan.
	Islamic religious education--History.
Notes	Includes bibliographical references and index.

Making European Muslims: religious socialization among young Muslims in Scandinavia and Western Europe

LCCN	2014013977
Type of material	Book
Main title	Making European Muslims: religious socialization among young Muslims in Scandinavia and Western Europe / edited by Mark Sedgwick.
Published/Produced	New York: Routledge, [2015]
Description	xi, 296 pages; 24 cm
ISBN	9781138789500 (hardback)
LC classification	BP188.3.C5 M35 2015

Related names	Sedgwick, Mark J.
Scope and content	"Making European Muslims provides an in-depth examination of what it means to be a young Muslim in Europe today, where the assumptions, values and behavior of the family and those of the majority society do not always coincide. Focusing on the religious socialization of Muslim children at home, in semi-private Islamic spaces such as mosques and Quran schools, and in public schools, the original contributions to this volume focus largely on countries in northern Europe, with a special emphasis on the Nordic region, primarily Denmark. Case studies demonstrate the ways that family life, public education, and government policy intersect in the lives of young Muslims and inform their developing religious beliefs and practices. Mark Sedgwick's introduction provides a framework for theorizing Muslimness in the European context, arguing that Muslim children must navigate different and sometimes contradictory expectations and demands on their way to negotiating a European Muslim identity"--Provided by publisher.
Contents	1. Introduction: Families, Governments, Schools, Alternative Spaces and the Making of European Muslims / Mark Sedgwick -- Part 1. Islamic Religious Socialization: 2. Islam in the Family: The Religious Socialization of Children in a Danish Provincial Town / Marianne Holm Pedersen -- 3. "Freedom has Destroyed the Somali Family": Somali Parents' Experiences of Epistemic Injustice and its Influence on their Raising of Swedish Muslims / Rannveig Haga -- 4. Dilemmas of Educating Muslim Children in the

Dutch Migration Context / Trees Pels -- Part 2. Government Policies: 5. Religion and Citizenship in France and Germany: Models of Integration and the Presence of Islam in Public Schools / Margrete Søvik -- 6. Negotiating Identity, Difference and Citizenship in Finnish Islamic Education: Building a Foundation for the Emergence of "Finnish Islam?" / Inkeri Rissanen -- 7. Religious Diversity and Muslim Claims-making: Conflicts over the Danish Folkeskole / Lene Kühle -- 8. Islam in Christianity: Religious Education in the Danish Folkeskole / Mark Sedgwick -- Part 3. Public Schools: 9. Being a Good, Relaxed or Exaggerated Muslim: Religiosity and Masculinity in the Social Worlds of Danish Schools / Laura Gilliam -- 10. Muslimness and Prayer: The Performance of Religiosity in Everyday Life in and Outside School in Denmark / Iram Khawaja -- 11. Likable Children, Uneasy Children: Growing up Muslim in Small-town Danish Schools / Sally Anderson -- Part 4. Alternative Spaces: 12. Islamic Private Schooling in Austria: a Case-Study of Parents' Expectations / Elif Medeni and Barbara Breen-Wenninger -- 13. Brainwashed at School?: Deprogramming the Secular Among Young Neo-orthodox Muslims in Denmark / Christian Suhr.

Subjects Muslim children--Religious life--Scandinavia.
Muslim children--Religious life--Europe, Western.
Muslim children--Education--Scandinavia.
Muslim children--Education--Europe, Western.
Muslim families--Scandinavia.
Muslim families--Europe, Western.

	Socialization--Scandinavia.
	Socialization--Europe, Western.
	Islam--Social aspects--Scandinavia.
	Islam--Social aspects--Europe, Western.
Notes	Includes bibliographical references (pages 273-290) and index.
Series	Routledge studies in religion; 40

Mandatory separation: religion, education, and mass politics in Palestine

LCCN	2017022011
Type of material	Book
Personal name	Schneider, Suzanne, 1983- author.
Main title	Mandatory separation: religion, education, and mass politics in Palestine / Suzanne Schneider.
Published/Produced	Stanford, California: Stanford University Press, 2018.
Description	xi, 262 pages; 23 cm
ISBN	9781503604148 (cloth: alk. paper)
	9781503604155 (pbk.: alk. paper)
LC classification	BL42.5.P19 S35 2018
Contents	Religious education in the modern age -- Educational modernity in Palestine -- Education and community under sectarian rule -- New schooling for an "old" order -- The boundaries of "religious" knowledge -- Border clashes -- Conclusion: the invisible cross.
Subjects	Religious education--Palestine--History--20th century.
	Jewish religious education--Palestine--History--20th century.
	Islamic religious education--Palestine--History--20th century.

	Education and state--Palestine--History--20th century.
	Education--Political aspects--Palestine--History--20th century.
	Palestine--Politics and government--1917-1948.
Notes	Includes bibliographical references (pages [205]-250) and index.
Additional formats	Online version: Schneider, Suzanne, 1983- author. Mandatory separation Stanford, California: Stanford University Press, 2018 9781503604520 (DLC) 2017047749

Methods of teaching in religious education: learning by heart or by experience?: proceedings of the conference held in Sofia, Bulgaria, June 17-21 2014

LCCN	2016399041
Type of material	Book
Meeting name	Orthodox Christian Religious Education Association Conference (2014: Sofia, Bulgaria) author.
Main title	Methods of teaching in religious education: learning by heart or by experience?: proceedings of the conference held in Sofia, Bulgaria, June 17-21 2014 / [edited by Risto Aikonen and Andrian Aleksandrov].
Published/Created	Sofia: [Regional Development Foundation [for] the Orthodox Christian Religious Education Association (OCREA)], 2015.
Description	265 pages: illustrations (chiefly color); 24 cm
ISBN	9789549294095
	9549294099
LC classification	BV1475.3 .O77 2014
Related names	Aikonen, Risto, editor.
	Aleksandrov, Andrian, editor.

Contents

Section I. Methodological discussions, religious education practices and new solutions: Teaching Orthodox Christianity today: challenges to methodologies / Anton C. Vrame -- Aims and teaching methods in Orthodox Christian education / Alexandros Koptsis and Petros Panagiotopoulos -- Earlier methods and means of religious education for modern times / Miron Erdei -- Case studies in religious education as a method of experiential learning / Magdalena Legkostup -- Religious education in a modern pluralistic society: the case of Orthodoxy / Niki Papageorgiou -- Historical moments in Greek Orthodox missions / Petros Panagiotopouios and Georgios A. Krapis -- Learning by sharing experience: cooperation between the teacher of religion and the priest for the successful education of children in the Romanian Orthodox Church / Vasile Gordon -- The right of individual freedom and the reliigious consciousness in teaching religion reflected in Professor Dumitru Staniloae's theology / Adrian Ivan -- Religious education in Bulgaria: past and present / Andrian Aleksandrov -- One possible approach to religious education in Bulgaria: concept, implementation and results / Polina Spirova -- History of religions: the young person's guide to a correct worldview / Klara Toneva -- Integration of learning objects in educational scenarios for teaching religious education / Vasiliki Mitropoulos -- Exploratory learning and reflective pedagogy: an interdisciplinary approach to the status of women in the Orthodox Church for first lyceum class pupils / Ioanna Komninou -- Encountering technological devices and WEB 2.0 applications to religious education in Finnish comprehensive schools: some perspectives from fifth and ninth grade / Risto Aikonen -- Section II. Classroom amd biblical contents: a kindergarten and school perspective: Religious education in European Union countries / Polyxena Matsouka -- Teaching about the Virgin Mary and the Orthodox Christian religion in kindergarten / Kyriakos Stavrianos and Vasileios Oikonomidis -- National and religious tradition in the textbooks of fifth and sixth classes of Greek primary school / Eleftheria G. Zampoulaki --The pedagogy of the Neptic Fathers / Evangelia Makridaki -- Teaching the Cana marriage miracle in kindergarten / Krystallo Pelaka -- The Parable of the sower: a patristic approach / Kyriakos Stavrianos -- Teaching the Parable of the sower in kindergarten / Athina Koutantou -- Saints, St. Nicholas and young children / Cristina Tsaka -- Pedagogical ideas in the book of Proverbs /

Subjects Christian education of children--Congresses.
Christian education of children--Teaching methods--Congresses.
Religious education--Orthodox Eastern Church--Congresses.

Notes Includes bibliographical references.

Modern Jewish scholarship in Hungary: the "Science of Judaism" between East and West
LCCN 2016056633
Type of material Book

Main title	Modern Jewish scholarship in Hungary: the "Science of Judaism" between East and West / edited by Tamás Turán and Carsten Wilke.
Published/Produced	Berlin; Boston: Walter de Gruyter, [2017]
Description	vii, 414 pages; 24 cm.
ISBN	9783110330212 (hardcover)
LC classification	LC746.H8 M53 2017
Related names	Turán, Tamás, editor. Wilke, Carsten, 1962- editor.
Summary	"Hungarian Jewish scholarship had a lasting impact on the Wissenschaft des Judentums ("Science of Judaism"). Its unique profile was shaped by Ashkenazi Yeshiva traditions, Jewish modernization movements, and Magyar politics that boosted academic Orientalism in the context of patriotic historiography. This volume presents an overview of a century of Hungarian Jewish scholarly achievements, examining their historical context and assessing their ongoing relevance"-- Provided by publisher.
Subjects	Jews--Education--Hungary--History. Jewish religious education--Hungary--History. Jewish learning and scholarship--Hungary--History.
Notes	Includes bibliographical references and index.
Series	Europäisch-jüdische Studien Beiträge, 2192-9602; Band 14

Modernizing Jewish education in nineteenth century Eastern Europe: the school as the shrine of the Jewish enlightenment

LCCN	2015041129
Type of material	Book
Personal name	Zalḳin, Mordekhai, author.
Uniform title	El hekhal ha-haśkalah. English

Main title	Modernizing Jewish education in nineteenth century Eastern Europe: the school as the shrine of the Jewish enlightenment / by Mordechai Zalkin.
Published/Produced	Leiden; Boston: Brill, [2016] ©2016
ISBN	9789004308206 (hardback: alk. paper)
LC classification	LC3585.E852 Z3513 2016
Summary	"In Modernizing Jewish Education in Nineteenth Century Eastern Europe, Mordechai Zalkin offers a new path through which the Eastern European traditional Jewish society underwent a rapid and significant process of modernization - the Maskilic system of education. Since the beginning of the nineteenth century a few local Jews, affected by the values and the principles of the European Enlightenment, established new private modern schools all around The Pale of Settlement, in which thousands of Jewish boys and girls were exposed to different disciplines such as sciences and humanities - a process which changed the entire cultural structure of contemporary Jewish society"-- Provided by publisher.
Subjects	Jews--Education--Europe, Eastern--History--19th century. Jewish religious education--Europe, Eastern--History--19th century.
Notes	Includes bibliographical references and index.
Additional formats	Online version: Zalḵin, Mordekhai, author. Modernizing Jewish education in nineteenth century Eastern Europe Leiden; Boston: Brill, [2016] 9789004307513 (DLC) 2015042787

Muslim schools, communities and critical race theory: faith schooling in an Islamophobic Britain?

LCCN	2017949540
Type of material	Book
Personal name	Breen, Damian, author.
Main title	Muslim schools, communities and critical race theory: faith schooling in an Islamophobic Britain? / Damian Breen.
Published/Produced	London, United Kingdom: Palgrave Macmillan, [2018]
Description	xiv, 201 pages; 22 cm
ISBN	9781137443960
	1137443960
LC classification	LC912.G7 B64 2018
Subjects	Islamic religious education--Great Britain.
	Muslims--Education--Great Britain.
	Education and state--Great Britain.
Notes	Includes bibliographical references (pages 187-195) and index.

My Last Year in Mitzrayim: a Jewish boy's ancient diary

LCCN	2017279360
Type of material	Book
Personal name	Grinboim, Ḥayim.
Main title	My Last Year in Mitzrayim: a Jewish boy's ancient diary / Chaim Greenbaum.
Published/Produced	Brooklyn, N.Y: Mesorah Publications, Ltd. 2018. ©2018
Description	215 pages; 24 cm
ISBN	9781422619988
	1422619982
Related names	Lazewnik, Libby, adaptor, translator.
Subjects	Bible. Exodus--Juvenile fiction.

	Bible--History of Biblical events--Juvenile fiction.
	Bible. Exodus.
	Jews--Egypt--History--To 1200 B.C.
	Exodus, The--Juvenile fiction.
	Jewish religious education of children--Juvenile fiction.
	Exodus, The.
	Jews.
	Jewish religious education of children.
	Egypt.
Form/Genre	Fiction.
	Juvenile works.
Series	ArtScroll youth series.

Net: an eJournal of faith-based distance learning.

LCCN	2016203115
Type of material	Periodical or Newspaper
Uniform title	Net (St. Louis, Mo.)
Main title	Net: an eJournal of faith-based distance learning.
Published/Produced	[St. Louis, MO]: The Faith-Based Online Learning Directors (FOLD), 2015-
Publication history	Began with: Volume 1, Number 1 (Winter 2015)
Current frequency	Semiannual
ISSN	2473-7860
LC classification	BV1610
Variant title	Distance learning in theological education
	eJournal of faith-based distance learning
Serial key title	Net (St. Louis, Mo.)
Related names	Faith-Based Online Learning Directors.
	Council of Distance Learning Directors in Theological Education.
Subjects	Christian education--Computer-assisted instruction--Study and teaching--Periodicals.

	Religious education--Computer-assisted instruction--Study and teaching--Periodicals.
	Distance education--Periodicals.
	Distance education.
Form/Genre	Periodicals.
Reproduction no./Source	Faith-Based Online Learning Directors (FOLD), 5705 Rhodes Ave., St. Louis, MO 63109

New ways of living the gospel: spiritual traditions in Catholic education

LCCN	2014481247
Type of material	Book
Main title	New ways of living the gospel: spiritual traditions in Catholic education / edited by Jim and Therese D'Orsa.
Published/Produced	Mulgrave, VIC: Vaughn Publishing, [2015]
Description	v, 246 pages; 23 cm.
ISBN	0987306057
	9780987306050 (paperback)
LC classification	LC509 .N49 2015
Related names	D'Orsa, Jim, editor.
	D'Orsa, Therese, editor.
Subjects	Catholic Church--Education--Australia.
	Catholic schools--Australia.
	Religious education--Australia.
	Catholic Church--Doctrines.
Notes	Includes index.
Series	The Broken Bay Institute mission and education series

Open minds, devoted hearts: portraits of adult religious educators

LCCN	2015473064
Type of material	Book
Personal name	Tauber, Sarah M., author.

Main title	Open minds, devoted hearts: portraits of adult religious educators / Sarah M. Tauber.
Published/Produced	Eugene, Oregon: Pickwick Publications, [2015] ©2015
Description	xvi, 168 pages; 23 cm.
ISBN	9781498218764
LC classification	BM70 .T38 2015
Subjects	Jewish religious education of adults.
Notes	"Horizons in religious education, the Religious Education Association"--Cover.
	Includes bibliographical references (pages 163-168).
Series	Horizon in religious education; 2

Parenting beyond belief: on raising ethical, caring kids without religion

LCCN	2016031076
Type of material	Book
Main title	Parenting beyond belief: on raising ethical, caring kids without religion / [edited by] Dale McGowan; with contributions by Richard Dawkins, Julia Sweeney, Dr. Phil Zuckerman, and more.
Edition	2nd Edition.
Published/Produced	New York: Amacom, 2016.
Description	xvi, 301 pages; 22 cm
ISBN	9780814437414 (pbk.)
	9780814474266 (previous edition)
LC classification	BL2777.R4 P37 2016
Related names	McGowan, Dale, editor.
Subjects	Parenting--Religious aspects.
	Religious education of children.
	Free thought.

Parenting without God: how to raise moral, ethical, and intelligent children, free from religious dogma

LCCN	2015015105
Type of material	Book
Personal name	Arel, Dan.
Main title	Parenting without God: how to raise moral, ethical, and intelligent children, free from religious dogma / Dan Arel; foreword by Peter Boghossian.
Published/Produced	Durham, North Carolina: Pitchstone Publishing, 2015.
Description	viii, 184 pages; 22 cm
ISBN	9781634310444 (pbk.: alk. paper)
LC classification	BL2777.R4 A74 2015
Subjects	Parenting--Religious aspects.
	Religious education of children.
	Atheism.
Notes	Includes bibliographical references.

Performance, Memory, and Processions in Ancient Rome: The Pompa Circensis from the late Republic to late Antiquity

LCCN	2016015481
Type of material	Book
Personal name	Latham, Jacob A., 1974- author.
Main title	Performance, Memory, and Processions in Ancient Rome: The Pompa Circensis from the late Republic to late Antiquity / Jacob A. Latham, University of Tennessee, Knoxville.
Published/Produced	New York, NY: Cambridge University Press, 2016.
Description	xxii, 345 pages: illustrations, maps; 26 cm
ISBN	9781107130715 (hardback)
LC classification	DG81 .L29 2016

Summary	"The pompa circensis, the procession which preceded the chariot races in the arena, was both a prominent political pageant and a hallowed religious ritual. Traversing a landscape of memory, the procession wove together spaces and institutions, monuments and performers, gods and humans into an image of the city, whose contours shifted as Rome changed. In the late Republic, the parade produced an image of Rome as the senate and the people with their gods - a deeply traditional symbol of the city which was transformed during the empire when an imperial image was built on top of the republican one. In late antiquity, the procession fashioned a multiplicity of Romes: imperial, traditional, and Christian. In this book, Jacob A. Latham explores the webs of symbolic meanings in the play between performance and itinerary, tracing the transformations of the circus procession from the late Republic to late antiquity"-- Provided by publisher.
Contents	Dedication; Acknowledgements; List of illustrations; Abbreviations; Introduction: 1. History in the subjunctive; 2. Idioms of spectacle between Hellenism and Imperialism; 3. Ritual rhythms of the pompa circensis; Part I. An Ideal-type between the Republic and Memories of the Republic: 1. Pompa hominum: gravity and levity, resonance and wonder, ritual failure; 1.1 'Rituals in ink': Dionysius of Halicarnassus; 1.2 Gravity, levity, and ritual resonance in the pompa hominum; 1.2.1 'Those holding the greatest authority'; 1.2.2 '[Roman] sons on the verge of manhood'; 1.2.3 'The charioteers followed'; 1.2.4

'Numerous companies of dancers'; 1.2.5 'Bands of dancers playing satyrs'; 1.2.6 'Censers in which incense and frankincense were burned'; 1.3 Wonder: spectacle and the pompa circensis; 1.4 Ritual failure in the pompa hominum; 2. Pompa deorum: performing theology, performing the gods; 2.1 Religious education and performed 'theology'; 2.2 Performing the gods; 2.2.1 Fercula and simulacra; 2.2.2 Exuviae and tensae; 2.2.3 Folkloric figures; 2.3 Regulations, risks, and ritual failure in the pompa deorum; 3. Iter pompae circensis: memory, resonance, the image of the city; 3.1 An itinerary of collective memory; 3.2 Resonance and repetition; 3.2.1 Capitolium: 'the citadel and Capitolium, the seat of the gods, the senate, and the head of public judgment'; 3.3.2 Forum Romanum: 'wider intercolumniations should be distributed around the spectacles... and in balconies should be placed in the upper stories'; 3.2.3 Velabrum: 'the vile throng of the vicus Tuscus'; 3.2.4 Aedes Cereris; 3.2.5 Circus Maximus: 'they come to see, they come that they may be seen'; 3.3 Imaging Rome on the ground and in the imagination; 3.3.1 Way-finding in Republican Rome; 3.3.2 Symbolic cityscapes: Senatus populusque Romanus et dei and Aurea Roma; 3.4 An ideal-type between the Republic and memories of the Republic; Part II. The Pompa Circensis from Julius Caesar to Late Antiquity: 4. 'Honors greater than human': Imperial cult and the pompa circensis; 4.1 Imperial gods in the pompa circensis: from Caesar to the Severans; 4.1.1 Dynastic beginnings: Caesar to Augustus; 4.1.2 The Augustan settlement: honoring divus

Augustus; 4.1.3 Innovation into tradition: the Julio-Claudians; 4.1.4 Divi, divae, and the imperial family from the Flavians to the Severans; 4.1.5 The traditional gods; 4.2 An imperial palimpsest: the itinerary from Augustus to Septimius Severus; 4.2.1 Restoring cultural memory in Imperial Rome; 4.2.2 Deus Praesens: Imperial cult temples and triumphal arches; 5. Behind 'the Veil of power': ritual failure, ordinary humans, and Ludic processions during the High Empire; 5.1 Imperial ritual failure; 5.2 'Ordinary' humans in the pompa circensis; 5.3 The pompa circensis outside Rome and the pompa (amphi-)theatralis; 5.3.1 The pompa circensis outside Rome; 5.3.2 The pompa (amphi-)theatralis; 5.4 'The horses, fleet as the wind, will contend for the first palm'; 6. The pompa circensis in Late Antiquity: imperialization, Christianization, restoration; 6.1 Pompa diaboli: Christian rhetoric and the pompa circensis; 6.2 Voluptates: imperial law and the 'secularization' of the ludi; 6.3 Emperors and victory: the pompa circensis in Late Antiquity; 6.4 The sub-imperial pompa circensis in Late Antiquity; 6.5 Restoring the 'Republic': the Late Antique itinerary; Conclusion; Bibliography; Index.

Subjects   Politics and culture--Rome.
Processions--Rome.
History / Ancient / General.

Notes   Includes bibliographical references (pages 297-334) and index.

Prisms of faith: perspectives on religious education and the cultivation of catholic identity

LCCN	2016295605
Type of material	Book
Main title	Prisms of faith: perspectives on religious education and the cultivation of catholic identity / edited by Robert E. Alvis & Ryan LaMothe.
Published/Created	Eugene, Oregon: Pickwick Publications, [2016]
Description	x, 150 pages; 23 cm
ISBN	9781498229906 (pbk.)
Related names	Alvis, Robert E., editor.
	LaMothe, Ryan, 1955- editor.
Contents	Introduction / Ryan LaMothe -- Use of the Apostolic Fathers in the Catechism of the Catholic Church / Clayton N. Jefford -- "The mystery meaning you": Augustine's mystagogical preaching on the church as the body of Christ / Kimberly F. Baker -- Catholic identity and religious education in modern Poland / Robert E. Alvis -- Christian education: rights and obligations in light of the 1983 Code of Canon Law / Fr. Patrick Cooney, OSB -- Liturgical catechesis and Catholic identity / Diana Dudoit Raiche -- Catholic identity and adult moral formation / Fr. Mark O'Keefe, OSB -- Religious education that promotes Catholic identity: a review and assessment of approaches / Michael P. Horan.
Notes	Includes bibliographical references.

Public theology, religious diversity, and interreligious learning

LCCN	2018018250
Type of material	Book

Main title	Public theology, religious diversity, and interreligious learning / by Manfred L. Pirner, Johannes Lähnemann, Werner Haussmann, and Susanne Schwarz.
Published/Produced	New York: Routledge, [2018]
ISBN	9781138583924 (hardback)
LC classification	BT83.63 .P86 2018
Related names	Pirner, Manfred L., editor.
	Lähnemann, Johannes, editor.
	Haussmann, Werner, 1960-, editor.
	Schwarz, Susanne, Dr. phil., editor.
Contents	Introduction -- Part A: public theology from diverse religious and non-religious perspectives -- Contributions of religions to the common good in pluralistic societies from a Christian perspective?: some critical remarks -- The contribution of religions to the common good in pluralistic societies: a Jewish perspective, exemplified by the concept of Tikkun Olam -- The contribution of religions to the common good in pluralistic societies: an Islamic perspective -- Islamic contributions to the universal conception of the common good in multi-confessional societies: hermeneutical foundations -- Towards enlightenment: Buddhism's contribution to common good through establishing contemplative culture -- The contributions of religions to the common good: philosophical perspectives -- Contributions of religions to the common good in a pluralistic society: an empirical answer from a sociological perspective -- Monotheism, curse or blessing? -- Part B. the challenge of interreligious dialogue and learning -- Public theology and interreligious dialogue -- Public theology or

religious studies?: deliberations on the basis of multifaith religious education -- Public religious pedagogy and interreligious learning -- The public church and public religious education as forms of 'Protestant presence': confessional and interreligious perspectives -- Islamic education in Europe: an opportunity for equal rights or a way to control Islam? -- The contribution of public religious education to promoting peace: perspectives from Israel -- The contribution of interreligious NGOs and interfaith initiatives to public education -- The spirituality of mindfulness: a religious contribution to public education.

Subjects Public theology.
Common good.
Education--Religious aspects.

Series Routledge research in religion and education; 9

Quranic schools in northern Nigeria: everyday experiences of youth, faith, and poverty

LCCN 2017277456
Type of material Book
Personal name Hoechner, Hannah, 1985- author.
Main title Quranic schools in northern Nigeria: everyday experiences of youth, faith, and poverty / Hannah Hoechner.
Published/Produced London: International African Institute; Cambridge, United Kingdom; New York, NY, USA: Cambridge University Press, 2018.
©2018
Description xix, 267 pages: illustrations, maps; 24 cm.
ISBN 9781108425292 hardcover
LC classification LC911.N6 H64 2018

Summary

In a global context of widespread fears over Islamic radicalisation and militancy, poor Muslim youth, especially those socialised in religious seminaries, have attracted overwhelmingly negative attention. In northern Nigeria, male Qur'anic students have garnered a reputation of resorting to violence in order to claim their share of highly unequally distributed resources. Drawing on material from long-term ethnographic and participatory fieldwork among Qur'anic students and their communities, this book offers an alternative perspective on youth, faith, and poverty.

Contents

Porridge, piety, and patience: Qur'anic schooling in northern Nigeria -- Fair game for unfair accusations? Discourses about Qur'anic students -- 'Secular schooling is schooling for the rich!': inequality and educational change in northern Nigeria -- Peasants, privations, and piousness: how boys become Qur'anic students -- Inequality at close range: domestic service for the better-off -- Concealment, asceticism, and cunning Americans: how to deal with being poor -- Mango medicine and morality: pursuing a respectable position within society -- Spiritual security services in an insecure setting: Kano's 'prayer economy' -- Roles, risks, and reproduction: what almajiri education implies for society and for the future -- Annex: Synopsis of 'Duniya Juyi Juyi-- How Life Goes'.

Subjects

Islamic religious education of children--Nigeria.
Islamic religious education--Nigeria.
Education--Nigeria.
Koranschule

	Islamische Erziehung
	Nigeria
Notes	Includes bibliographical references (pages 235-260) and index.
Additional formats	Online version: Hoechner, Hannah, 1985- Quranic schools in northern Nigeria. London: International African Institute; Cambridge, United Kingdom: Cambridge University Press, 2018 9781108694322 (OCoLC)1030605465
Series	The international African library; 54
	International African library; 54.

Rabbi Scherman on chinuch: practical, perceptive answers to contemporary questions

LCCN	2018421486
Type of material	Book
Personal name	Scherman, Nosson, author.
Main title	Rabbi Scherman on chinuch: practical, perceptive answers to contemporary questions / Rabbi Nosson Scherman.
Edition	First edition.
Published/Produced	Brooklyn, N.Y.: ArtScroll/Mesorah Publications Ltd, June 2017.
Description	488 pages; 24 cm
ISBN	9781422619117
	1422619117
LC classification	BM103 .S255 2017
Subjects	Jewish religious education--Philosophy.
	Child rearing--Religious aspects--Judaism.
Series	ArtScroll series

Rappaport 55: a novel

LCCN	2017275458
Type of material	Book

Personal name	Haller, Dov, author.
Main title	Rappaport 55: a novel / by Dov Haller.
Published/Produced	Brooklyn, NY: Shaar Press, March 2017. ©2017
Description	288 pages; 24 cm
ISBN	9781422618738 1422618730
LC classification	PS3608.A548296 R36 2017
Variant title	Rappaport fifty-five.
Summary	Step into Rappaport 55. The tiny apartments off the narrow alley ways of Meah Shearim are called dirarahs. The heating rarely works, and the water pressure is weak, but the power and potency of life in the dirah is unmatched. Here the young men who've come to learn in Israeli yeshivas sleep and cook and experience a life very different from the one they've known back home, in American or Canada or England or Australia. Rappaport 55 is just one more dirah on streets filled with them - but the people inside will intrigue you. Because you know them. And because real life is happening here, you find yourself totally involved in the challenges and struggles and the big and little successes of this group of young men on the cusp of adulthood.
Subjects	Yeshivas--Jerusalem--Fiction. Foreign study--Jerusalem--Fiction. Ultra-Orthodox Jews--Fiction. Jewish religious education--Israel--Fiction. Me'ah She'arim (Jerusalem)--Fiction.
Form/Genre	Jewish religious fiction.

Reading the way to the netherworld: education and the representations of the beyond in later antiquity

LCCN	2017288319
Type of material	Book
Main title	Reading the way to the netherworld: education and the representations of the beyond in later antiquity / Ilinca Tanaseanu-Döbler, Anna Lefteratou, Gabriela Ryser, Konstantinos Stamatopoulos (eds.).
Published/Produced	Göttingen: Vandenhoeck & Ruprecht, [2017]
Description	550 pages; 24 cm.
ISBN	9783525540305 (hardback: acid-free paper) 3525540302 (hardback)
LC classification	PA3014.F88 R45 2017
Portion of title	Education and the representations of the beyond in later antiquity
Related names	Tanaseanu-Döbler, Ilinca, editor. Lefteratou, Anna, 1980- editor. Ryser, Gabriela, editor. Stamatopoulos, Konstantinos, editor.
Subjects	Future, The, in literature--Congresses. Greek literature--History and criticism--Congresses. Latin literature--History and criticism--Congresses. Christian literature, Early--History and criticism--Congresses. Religious education--Congresses. Christian education--Congresses. Jewish religious education--Congresses.
Form/Genre	Conference papers and proceedings.
Notes	International conference proceedings. Includes bibliographical references and indexes. 14 English, 7 German contributions.

Series	Beiträge zur europäischen Religionsgeschichte (BERG), 2198-1035; volume 4 V&R academic

Re-enchanting education and spiritual wellbeing: fostering belonging and meaning-making for global citizens

LCCN	2017013892
Type of material	Book
Main title	Re-enchanting education and spiritual wellbeing: fostering belonging and meaning-making for global citizens / edited by Marian de Souza and Anna Halafoff.
Published/Produced	London; New York, NY: Routledge, 2018.
Description	vi, 219 pages; 24 cm.
ISBN	9781138095670 (hardback) 9781138095687 (pbk.)
LC classification	LB1027.2 .R46 2018
Related names	De Souza, Marian, editor. Halafoff, Anna, editor.
Contents	Spiritual wellbeing in education / Marian de Souza and Anna Halafof -- Beyond faith?: recent trends in religion and spirituality among teenagers / Andrew Singleton -- Spirituality in Australian education: a legacy of confusion, omission and obstruction / Terence Lovat -- Building the foundations of global citizenship in young children / Tony Eaude -- Worldview education as a viable perspective for educating global citizens / Dzintra Ilisko -- The significance of media culture for spiritual well-being: a challenge for public education / Manfred L. Pirner -- Being spiritually educated / R. Scott Webster -- Life-education and religious education in national, prefectural and other public schools in Japan /

Fumiaki Iwata -- Music and spirit: exploring a creative spiritual pedagogy / Ruth Wills -- Seeing what is true and holy in others / John Dupuch -- Childhoods past and present: a reflexive approach to enhancing children's spiritual wellbeing / Kate Adam -- Educational reforms in Japan: are they contributing to a sense of wellbeing and happiness among young people? / Dorothea Filus -- Reflections on gender discrimination in the spiritual life of a Muslim community: gender in elementary and middle school religion textbooks in Turkey / Mualla Yildiz -- Yingadi Aboriginal immersion: a program to nurture spirituality / Olga Buttigieg -- Spiritual wellbeing and the national schools chaplaincy program in Australia / Avril Howard -- Fostering a sense of belonging and identity through sound and spirituality / Dawn Joseph -- Nurturing the spiritual child: recognising, addressing and nurturing spirituality in early years' classrooms through a dispositional framework / Brendan Hyde.

Subjects   Education--Religious aspects.
Education--Psychological aspects.
Education and globalization.
World citizenship.

Notes   Includes bibliographical references.

Regulating religion in Asia: norms, modes, and challenges
LCCN   2018039861
Type of material   Book
Main title   Regulating religion in Asia: norms, modes, and challenges / edited by Jaclyn L. Neo, Arif A. Jamal, Daniel P.S. Goh.
Published/Produced   New York: Cambridge University Press, 2019.

ISBN	9781108416177
LC classification	BL1035 .R35 2019
Related names	Neo, Jaclyn L., editor.
	Jamal, Arif A., editor.
	Goh, Pei Siong Daniel, editor.
Contents	Regulatory markers / Arif A. Jamal -- Conceptualizing the regulation of religion / Jaclyn L. Neo -- The role of authority and sanctity in state-religion conflicts / Shai Wozner & Gilad Abiri -- Jurisdictional vs. official control: regulating the Buddhist sangha in South and Southeast Asia / Ben Schontal -- Defining and regulating religion in early independent Indonesia / Kevin Fogg -- Principled pluralism, relational constitutionalism and regulating religion within Singapore's secular democratic model / Thio Li-Ann -- Legal regulation of religion in Vietnam / Bui Ngoc Son -- Regulating Buddhism in Myanmar: the case of deviant Buddhist sects / Nyi Nyi Kyaw -- The bureaucratization of religious education in the Islamic Republic of Iran / Mirjam Kunkler -- Managing religious competition in China: case study of regulating social & charitable service provisions by religious organizations / Jianlin Chen & Loveday J. Liu -- Regulating religion through administrative law: religious conversion in Malaysia beyond fundamental rights / Matthew Nelson and Dian Shah -- Legal pluralism, patronage secularism and the challenge of prophetic Christianity in Singapore / Daniel Goh -- Equality in secularism: contemporary debates on social stratification and the Indian constitution / Mohsin Alam -- Regulating the state

	and the hawz a: legal pluralism and the ironies of Shi'i law / Haider Hamoudi.
Subjects	Religion and state--Asia--Congresses.
	Religious law and legislation--Asia--Congresses.
	Asia--Religion--21st century--Congresses.
Notes	"Most of the chapters in this volume were presented at a conference entitled "Regulating Religion: Normativity and Change at the Intersection of Law and Religion" which was held at the Faculty of Law of the National University of Singapore (NUS Law) on 14 and 15 December 2015"--Acknowledgements.
	Includes bibliographical references and index.

Relax, it's just God: how and why to talk to your kids about religion when you're not religious

LCCN	2014955707
Type of material	Book
Personal name	Russell, Wendy Thomas, author.
Main title	Relax, it's just God: how and why to talk to your kids about religion when you're not religious / Wendy Thomas Russell.
Edition	First edition.
Published/Produced	Long Beach, California: Brown Paper Press, [2015]
Description	xii, 179 pages; 21 cm
ISBN	9781941932001
	1941932002
LC classification	BV1475.3 .R88 2015
Portion of title	How and why to talk to your kids about religion when you're not religious
Summary	A rapidly growing demographic cohort in America, non-religious parents are at the forefront of a major and unprecedented cultural shift.

	Unable to fall back on what they were taught as children, many of these parents are struggling--or simply failing--to address complicated religious questions and issues with their children in ways that promote curiosity, kindness, and independence. Author Wendy Thomas Russell sifts through hard data--including the results of her own survey of 1,000 nonreligious parents--and delivers gentle but straightforward advice to this often-overlooked segment of the American population. With a thoughtful voice infused with humor, Russell seamlessly merges scientific thought, scholarly research, and everyday experience with respect for a full range of ways to view the world.
Contents	Part one: O we of little faith -- Part two: A new direction -- Part three: Dealing with sticky issues.
Subjects	Religious education of children.
	Parenting--Religious aspects.
	Free thought.
Notes	Includes bibliographical references.

Relics for the present: contemporary reflections on the Talmud: Berakhot II

LCCN	2017303595
Type of material	Book
Personal name	Cooper, Levi, author.
Main title	Relics for the present: contemporary reflections on the Talmud: Berakhot II / Levi Cooper.
Edition	First edition.
Published/Produced	New Milford, CT: Maggid Books, 2015.
Description	xii, 301; 21 cm
ISBN	9781592644421 (hardcover)
	1592644422 (hardcover)

LC classification	BM723 .C666 2015
Summary	Why is wine so central to Jewish rituals? Is talmudic medical advice binding today? What is the connection between long meals and long life? And when is it appropriate to apply a humra? In this page-by-page companion to Berakhot, the first tractate of the Talmud, popular teacher and community leader Rabbi Levi Cooper explores the wisdom of the Jewish sages, transforming their ancient teachings into lessons for everyday life.
Subjects	Talmud--Criticism, interpretation, etc.
	Benedictions.
	Talmud.
	Jewish way of life.
	Jewish religious education.
Form/Genre	Criticism, interpretation, etc.

Religion and education

LCCN	2018300537
Type of material	Book
Main title	Religion and education / Jan De Groof and Gracienne Lauwers (eds.).
Published/Produced	Oisterwijk, The Netherlands: Wolf Legal Publishers, [2015]
Description	578pages: charts; 24 cm.
ISBN	9789462401310
LC classification	MLCM 2018/44921 (B)
Related names	Groof, Jan de, editor.
Subjects	Cultural pluralism--Congresses.
	Multicultural education--Congresses.
	Religious education--Congresses.
Notes	Minimal Level Cataloging Plus.
	Includes bibliographical references.

Series Studies in human rights and education

Religion and nationhood: insider and outsider perspectives on religious education in England
LCCN 2016509338
Type of material Book
Main title Religion and nationhood: insider and outsider perspectives on religious education in England / edited by Brian Gates.
Published/Produced Tübingen: Mohr Siebeck, [2016]
Description viii, 512 pages; 24 cm.
ISBN 9783161547294 (pbk.)
LC classification BV1470.G7 R45 2016
Portion of title Insider and outsider perspectives on religious education in England
Related names Gates, Brian E. (Brian Edward), editor.
Subjects Religious education--England.
Christianity and other religions--England.
Notes Includes bibliographical references (pages 467-490) and indexes.
Series Praktische Theologie in Geschichte und Gegenwart, 1862-8958; 21

Religion and the American constitutional experiment
LCCN 2015035938
Type of material Book
Personal name Witte, John, 1959- author.
Main title Religion and the American constitutional experiment / John Witte, Jr. and Joel A. Nichols.
Edition 4th edition.
Published/Produced New York, NY: Oxford University Press, [2016]
Description xiv, 403 pages; 24 cm
ISBN 9780190459420 (paperback)
LC classification KF4783 .W58 2016

Related names
Summary

Nichols, Joel A., 1972- author.

"This new edition of a classic textbook provides a comprehensive, interdisciplinary overview of the history, theology, and law of American religious liberty. The authors offer a balanced and accessible analysis of First Amendment cases and controversies, and compare them to both the original teachings of the American founders and current international norms of religious liberty"-- Provided by publisher.

"This accessible introduction tells the American story of religious liberty from its colonial beginnings to the latest Supreme Court cases. The authors provide extensive analysis of the formation of the First Amendment religion clauses and the plausible original intent or understanding of the founders. They describe the enduring principles of American religious freedom--liberty of conscience, free exercise of religion, religious equality, religious pluralism, separation of church and state, and no establishment of religion--as those principles were developed by the founders and applied by the Supreme Court. Successive chapters analyze the two hundred plus Supreme Court cases on religious freedom--on the free exercise of religion, the roles of government and religion in education, the place of religion in public life, and the interaction of religious organizations and the state. A final chapter shows how favorably American religious freedom compares with international human rights norms and European Court of Human Rights case law. Lucid, comprehensive, multidisciplinary, and balanced,

Bibliography 181

Contents

this volume is an ideal classroom text and armchair paperback. Detailed appendices offer drafts of each of the religion clauses debated in 1788 and 1789, a table of all state constitutional laws on religious freedom, and a summary of every Supreme Court case on religious liberty from 1815 to 2015. Throughout the volume, the authors address frankly and fully the hot button issues of our day: religious freedom versus sexual liberty, freedom of conscience and its limitations, religious group rights and the worries about abuse, faith-based legal systems and their place in liberal democracies, and the fresh rise of anti-Semitism, Islamophobia, and anti-Christianity in America and abroad. For this new edition, the authors have updated each chapter in light of new scholarship and new Supreme Court case law (through the 2015 term) and have added an appendix mapping some of the cutting edge issues of religious liberty and church-state relations"-- Provided by publisher.

The American Experiment in Historical Context -- The Theology and Politics of the Religion Clauses -- The Essential Rights and Liberties of Religion -- Forging the First Amendment Religion Clauses -- Religious Liberty in the States and Nation Before 1947 -- The Free Exercise of Religion: Mapping the Doctrinal Terrain -- The Free Exercise of Religion, Free Religious Speech, and Religious Freedom Statutes -- Modern Establishment Law: Mapping the Doctrinal Terrain -- Religion and Public Education: No Establishment of Religion, But Equal Access for Religion -- Government and Religious Education:

	Accommodation, Separation, and Equal Treatment -- Religion and Public Life -- Religious Organizations and the Law -- The American Law of Religious Freedom in Comparative Perspective -- Concluding Reflections -- Appendix 1: Drafts of Federal Religion Clauses (1787-1789) -- Appendix 2: State Constitutional Provisions on Religion (as of 1947) -- Appendix 3: United States Supreme Court Decisions Relating to Religious Liberty.
Subjects	United States. Constitution. 1st Amendment.
	Freedom of religion--United States.
	Church and state--United States.
	Religion / Religion, Politics & State.
	Law / Constitutional.
	Political Science / Government / Judicial Branch.
Notes	Includes bibliographical references (pages 339-385) and index.
Other edition	Revision of: Witte, John, 1959- Religion and the American constitutional experiment. 3rd ed. Boulder, CO: Westview Press, 2011. (DLC) 2010003209. 9780813344751.

Religion and violence: Muslim and Christian theological and pedagogical reflections

LCCN	2017457565
Type of material	Book
Main title	Religion and violence: Muslim and Christian theological and pedagogical reflections / Ednan Aslan, Marcia Hermansen (eds.).
Published/Produced	Wiesbaden, Germany: Springer VS, [2017]
Description	vi, 269 pages; 21 cm
ISBN	9783658183011 (pbk.)
	3658183012 (pbk.)

LC classification	BP190.5.V56 R45 2017
Related names	Aslan, Ednan, 1959- editor.
	Hermansen, Marcia K., 1951- editor.
Contents	Preface: Islam and violence / Ednan Aslan -- Religion and violence: Christian and Muslim theological and pedagogical reflections. volume introduction / Marcia Hermansen -- The drama triangle of religion and violence / R. Ruard Ganzevoort -- Violence vs. religion / Ferid Muhic -- Violence and religion: a complex relationship / Wolfgang Palaver -- The integration of Muslims and the Charlie Hebdo attacks. cleavages and convergences between religious denominations in France / Claude Dargent -- Eastern Orthodox perspectives on violence / Emil Bjørn Hilton Saggau -- Embracing the other: lessons from history and contemporary Christian thought / Kostake Milkov -- The theological background of violence in Islam / Ednan Aslan -- Civil disobedience in Islamic politico-legal theory: a challenging balance between justice and stability / Osman Tartan -- Muslim theologians of nonviolence / Marcia Hermansen -- The Sunna of fighting: background, dimensions, scope, and consequences / Ulvi Karagedik -- Women's entitlement to autonomy in Islam and related controversies surrounding verse 4:34 / Ranja Ebrahim -- Responding to the Marrakesh declaration with a United States declaration. a call to preserve and protect Muslim civil rights / Jason Renken -- Against religiously motivated violence. religious education's contribution to peaceful relationships between different religions - what should it entail and how can it be evaluated? /

	Friedrich Schweitzer -- Violence as a challenge for religious education: psychological, theological, and educational perspectives / Martin Rothgangel -- Journeying into a peaceful Islam: a worldview framework approach / John Valk and Mualla Selçuk.
Subjects	Violence--Religious aspects.
	Violence--Religious aspects--Islam.
Notes	Includes bibliographical references.
Series	Wiener Beiträge zur Islamforschung

Religion in the classroom: dilemmas for democratic education

LCCN	2014022806
Type of material	Book
Personal name	James, Jennifer Hauver.
Main title	Religion in the classroom: dilemmas for democratic education / Jennifer Hauver James with Simone Schweber, Robert Kunzman, Keith C. Barton, Kimberly Logan.
Published/Produced	New York: Routledge, 2015.
Description	xviii, 101 pages; 23 cm
ISBN	9780415832960 (hardback)
	9780415832977 (pbk.)
	9780203507445 (e-book)
LC classification	LC107 .J36 2015
Related names	Barton, Keith C.
Contents	On religion -- Toward democratic living and learning -- Navigating the legal and ethical dimensions of our work -- The not-so-hidden curriculum of religion in public schools -- Unpacking narratives of calling and purpose in teaching / Kimberly Logan -- Fishing below the surface: understanding the role of religion in student learning / Simone Schweber --

	reconsidering religion in the curriculum / Keith C. Barton -- Talking with students who already know the answer: navigating ethical certainty in democratic dialogue / Robert Kunzman -- Continuing the conversation.
Subjects	Religion in the public schools.
	Religious education.
Notes	Includes bibliographical references and index.

Religion in the primary school: ethos, diversity, citizenship

LCCN	2014037785
Type of material	Book
Personal name	Hemming, Peter J.
Main title	Religion in the primary school: ethos, diversity, citizenship / Peter J. Hemming.
Published/Produced	London; New York: Routledge, 2015.
Description	150 pages; 24 cm.
ISBN	9780415714877 (hardback)
LC classification	LC116.G7 H46 2015
Contents	Introduction -- Religion, citizenship and society -- Education, religion and ethnography -- School ethos and religion -- Post-secular values -- Meaningful encounters -- Cohesive communities -- Religious difference and citizenship -- Conclusion.
Subjects	Religion in the public schools--Great Britain.
	Catholic elementary schools--Great Britain.
	Education, Primary--Great Britain.
	Religious education of children--Great Britain.
Notes	Includes bibliographical references (pages 127-145) and index.
Series	Foundations and futures of education.

Religion, law, and education: tensions and perspectives

LCCN	2017471542
Type of material	Book
Main title	Religion, law, and education: tensions and perspectives / edited by Jan de Groof, Georgia du Plessis, and Maria Smirnova.
Published/Produced	Oisterwijk, The Netherlands: Wolf Legal Publishers, [2017] ©2017
Description	280 pages; 24 cm
ISBN	9789462404113 (pbk.) 9462404119 (pbk.)
LC classification	BV1471.3 .R3783 2017
Related names	Groof, Jan de, editor, contributor. du Plessis, Georgia, editor, contributor. Smirnova, Maria, editor, contributor. Glenn, Charles Leslie, 1938- contributor. Kodelja, Zdenko, contributor. Martínez López-Muñiz, José Luis, contributor. Sheridan, Sean O., contributor. Garvey, John H., 1948- contributor. Moschella, Melissa, 1979- contributor. Ponikowska, Marta, contributor. Panaretos, John, contributor. Gerencsér, Balázs Szabolcs, Dr., contributor. Dronkers, J., contributor. Jeynes, William, contributor. Matveev, Vitaly, contributor. Rozhkov, Artemy, contributor. Kiviorg, Merilin, 1973- contributor. Ginter, Juri, contributor. Sarv, Ene-Silvia, contributor. Ranieri, Nina, contributor. Limongi, Angela, contributor.

Rossi, Danilo, contributor.
Lucena, Elisa, contributor.
Souza, Meire Cristina, contributor.
Lutaif, Michel K., contributor.
Beçak, Rubens, contributor.
Cirino, Luis Felipe, contributor.
Beckmann, J. L., contributor.
Varnham, Sally, 1950- contributor.

Summary
This book provides an encompassing analysis of the position of religion in education in several countries across the globe. It first analyses the wider issues and complexities surrounding the position of freedom of religion or belief in education systems and the need to respect, protect and promote the religious or (non-religious) beliefs of all those involved and participating in education. Various specific themes are constantly at the foreground, namely: the religious distinctiveness of private schools, the protection of religious and belief diversity in education, the protection of parental rights and religious freedoms, the protection of children's rights and religious freedoms and managing the dissemination of religious knowledge in public schools. Secondly, this book provides important case studies explaining the various approaches pertaining to the reconciliation of law and state, religion and education and secularism and diversity that exist in the world. A more encyclopedic approach is followed and provides insights, through the country case studies, into the contemporary issues surrounding religious and non-religious schools in these selected jurisdictions.

Contents

Preface / Jan de Groof; Georgia du Plessis; Maria Smirnova -- School religious distinctiveness: the consequences for parents, pupils and teachers / Charles L. Glenn -- Religious freedom and free choice of schools / Zdenko Kodelja -- Religious education versus secularism?: the context of private and public schools / José Luis Martínez López-Muñiz -- The United States national agenda on challeneges/conflicts of Catholic schools vis-à-vis the state / Sean O. Sheridan -- The place of faith in Catholic higher education in the United States of America / John Garvey -- Parental rights in education from the American and European case law perspective / Melissa Moschella; Marta Ponikowska -- Education, religion and politics: the case of Greece / John Panaretos -- State and church: education in Hungary (the content of a human right and the role of external instruments) / Balázs Szabolcs Gerencsér -- Islamic primary schools in the Netherlands / Jaap Dronkers -- Recommendations for maintaining the Christian identity of Christian schools in the European Union / William Jeynes -- Religious rights as an element of school choice in Russia: contemporary contours of law, policy and court practice / Maria Smirnova -- The relationship between different religious confessions and public schools in Russia: equality or inequality? / Vitaly Matveev; Artemy Rozhkov -- Freedom of religion or belief in education in Estonia / Merilin Kiviorg; Jüri Ginter; Ene-Silvia Sarv -- Religious education and the secular state: an overview of Latin America / Nina Ranieri; Angela Limongi; Danilo Rossi; Elisa Lucena;

	Meire Cristina Souza; Michel K. Lutaif -- Home schooling Brazil: a new judicial outlook and tradition / Rubens Beçak; Luis Felipe Cirino -- Religion and education in South Africa: an introduction / Johan Beckmann -- The dissemination of religious knowledge in South African public schools / Georgia Alida du Plessis -- The role of Catholic schools in Australia in educating for human rights and social justice: an overview / Sally Varnahm -- The school: a most challenging domain in the complex partnership between religion, education and the law - a few reflections / Jan de Groof.
Subjects	Religious education.
	Religion and law.
Notes	Includes bibliographical references.

Religions and education in antiquity: studies in honour of Michel Desjardins

LCCN	2018039898
Type of material	Book
Main title	Religions and education in antiquity: studies in honour of Michel Desjardins / edited by Alex Damm.
Published/Produced	Leiden; Boston: Brill, [2018]
Description	1 online resource.
ISBN	9789004384613 (E-book)
LC classification	BL42
Related names	Damm, Alex, editor.
	Desjardins, Michel R. (Michel Robert), 1951- honouree.
Summary	"Religions and Education in Antiquity gathers ten essays on teaching and learning in the contexts of ancient Western religions, including Judaism,

early Christianity and Gnostic Christian traditions. Beginning with an overview of religious education in the ancient Near Eastern and Mediterranean worlds, editor Alex Damm and the contributors together demonstrate the mutual influence of religion and education on each other; the relevance of educational traditions in addressing (for instance) historical or exegetical issues; and the thoroughgoing importance of education to religious life across time and space in antiquity. Highly useful to scholars of religion, theology, classics and education, this volume affords a state of the art study on pedagogy and learning in ancient religious contexts"-- Provided by publisher.

Contents Religions and education in antiquity: an introduction / Alex Damm -- Wisdom from the wise: pedagogical principles from proverbs / John L. McLaughlin -- Education in the sacrospace of Qumran Judaism / Wayne O. McCready -- Late Second Temple Judaism: a reconstruction and re-description as a religio-cultural system / Jack N. Lightstone -- Techne in Plato and the New Testament / Joseph A. Novak -- Why not to pity Rome: Revelation 18:22-23a in its ancient educational context / Alex Damm -- Those who hear: the power of learners in 1 Timothy / Mona Tokarek LaFosse -- Translation matters: the Coptic translation of Thomas / John Horman -- Pedagogy, text and the solitary self in the Gospel of Thomas / William Arnal -- Praises and rebukes in the gnostic revelation dialogues / Michael Kaler.

Subjects Desjardins, Michel R. (Michel Robert), 1951-

	Religious education--History.
	Education, Ancient.
Form/Genre	Festschriften.
Notes	Includes bibliographical references and index.
Additional formats	Print version: Religions and education in antiquity Leiden; Boston: Brill, [2018] 9789004384439 (DLC) 2018033943
Series	Numen book series. Studies in the history of religions, 0169-8834; volume 160

Religions and education in antiquity: studies in honour of Michel Desjardins

LCCN	2018033943
Type of material	Book
Main title	Religions and education in antiquity: studies in honour of Michel Desjardins / edited by Alex Damm.
Published/Produced	Leiden; Boston: Brill, [2018]
ISBN	9789004384439 (hardback: alk. paper)
	(e-book)
LC classification	BL42 .R437 2018
Related names	Damm, Alex, editor.
	Desjardins, Michel R. (Michel Robert), 1951- honouree.
Summary	"Religions and Education in Antiquity gathers ten essays on teaching and learning in the contexts of ancient Western religions, including Judaism, early Christianity and Gnostic Christian traditions. Beginning with an overview of religious education in the ancient Near Eastern and Mediterranean worlds, editor Alex Damm and the contributors together demonstrate the mutual influence of religion and education on each other; the relevance of educational traditions in

	addressing (for instance) historical or exegetical issues; and the thoroughgoing importance of education to religious life across time and space in antiquity. Highly useful to scholars of religion, theology, classics and education, this volume affords a state of the art study on pedagogy and learning in ancient religious contexts"-- Provided by publisher.
Contents	Religions and education in antiquity: an introduction / Alex Damm -- Wisdom from the wise: pedagogical principles from proverbs / John L. McLaughlin -- Education in the sacrospace of Qumran Judaism / Wayne O. McCready -- Late Second Temple Judaism: a reconstruction and re-description as a religio-cultural system / Jack N. Lightstone -- Techne in Plato and the New Testament / Joseph A. Novak -- Why not to pity Rome: Revelation 18:22-23a in its ancient educational context / Alex Damm -- Those who hear: the power of learners in 1 Timothy / Mona Tokarek LaFosse -- Translation matters: the Coptic translation of Thomas / John Horman -- Pedagogy, text and the solitary self in the Gospel of Thomas / William Arnal -- Praises and rebukes in the gnostic revelation dialogues / Michael Kaler.
Subjects	Desjardins, Michel R. (Michel Robert), 1951- Religious education--History. Education, Ancient.
Form/Genre	Festschriften.
Notes	Includes bibliographical references and index.
Additional formats	Online version: Religions and education in antiquity Leiden; Boston: Brill, [2018] 9789004384613 (DLC) 2018039898

Series Numen book series. Studies in the history of religions, 0169-8834; volume 160

Religious education: educating for diversity
LCCN 2015015288
Type of material Book
Personal name Barnes, Philip (L. Philip)
Main title Religious education: educating for diversity / L. Philip Barnes and Andrew Davis; edited by J. Mark Halstead.
Published/Produced London; New York: Bloomsbury Academic, 2015.
Description ix, 146 pages; 22 cm
Links Cover image http://www.netread.com/jcusers2/bk1388/069/9781472571069/image/lgcover.9781472571069.jpg
ISBN 9781472571069 (paperback)
LC classification BV1471.3 .B374 2015
Related names Davis, Andrew, 1948-
Halstead, J. Mark.
Summary "Religious Education: Educating for Diversity raises issues that are central to the theory and practice of education, and in particular religious education, in modern liberal democracies characterized by diversity in its different forms. What kind of religious education is best equipped both to challenge prejudice and intolerance in society and to develop responsible and respectful relationships between people from different communities or with different commitments? Two eminent educators address this question and propose contrasting answers. Attention is given to the aims of education and the contribution of religious education to the curriculum; historical

	forms of religious education; the nature of diversity in society; the roots of prejudice; different methodologies in religious education and their philosophical and religious commitments; and to positive strategies to enable religious education to realise its potential and contribute to the social and moral aims of liberal education"-- Provided by publisher.
Contents	Notes on Contributors -- Series Editor's Preface -- Foreword, J. Mark Halstead -- Part I - Religious Education: Taking Religious Difference Seriously, L. Philip Barnes -- Part II - Religious Education: A Pluralist Apporoach, Andrew Davis -- Afterword, J. Mark Halstead -- Bibliography -- Index.
Subjects	Religious education--Philosophy.
	Religious education--Social aspects.
	Education--Religious aspects.
	Education, Humanistic.
	Democracy and education.
	Education / Educational Policy & Reform / General.
	Religion / Education.
Notes	Includes bibliographical references and index.
Series	Key debates in educational policy

Religious education and critical realism: knowledge, reality and religious literacy

LCCN	2015021307
Type of material	Book
Personal name	Wright, Andrew, 1958- author.
Main title	Religious education and critical realism: knowledge, reality and religious literacy / Andrew Wright.

Published/Produced	London; New York: Routledge, Taylor & Francis Group, 2016.
Description	viii, 266 pages; 24 cm.
ISBN	9780415559874 (hbk: alk. paper)
LC classification	BV1464 .W75 2016
Subjects	Religious education--Philosophy. Critical realism.
Notes	Includes bibliographical references (pages 239-252) and index.
Series	New studies in critical realism and spirituality

Religious education and the public sphere

LCCN	2018020300
Type of material	Book
Personal name	Hannam, Patricia, author.
Main title	Religious education and the public sphere / Patricia Hannam.
Published/Produced	London; New York, NY: Routledge is an imprint of the Taylor & Francis Group, an Informa Business, 2019.
Description	vii, 157 pages; 24 cm.
ISBN	9780815354659 (hbk)
LC classification	LC107 .H28 2019
Contents	An historical analysis of religious education in the public sphere -- The root of the problem -- Influential theoretical positions -- Some contemporary responses to old problems -- Addressing assumptions -- Reconceptualising education -- What does it mean to be religious? -- New possibilities for religious education? -- What should religious education aim to achieve in the public sphere? -- Practical considerations: what might this mean for the teacher? -- Epilogue and

	some practical considerations: what might this mean for a religious education curriculum?
Subjects	Arendt, Hannah, 1906-1975.
	Weil, Simone, 1909-1943.
	Religion in the public schools.
Notes	Includes bibliographical references and index.
Additional formats	Online version: Hannam, Patricia, author. Religious education and the public sphere Abingdon, Oxon; New York, NY: Routledge is an imprint of the Taylor & Francis Group, an Informa Business, 2019 9781351132237 (DLC) 2018031074
Series	Theorizing education series

Religious education and the public sphere

LCCN	2018031074
Type of material	Book
Personal name	Hannam, Patricia, author.
Main title	Religious education and the public sphere / Patricia Hannam.
Published/Produced	Abingdon, Oxon; New York, NY: Routledge is an imprint of the Taylor & Francis Group, an Informa Business, 2019.
Description	1 online resource.
ISBN	9781351132237 (E-book)
LC classification	LC107
Contents	An historical analysis of religious education in the public sphere -- The root of the problem -- Influential theoretical positions -- Some contemporary responses to old problems -- Addressing assumptions -- Reconceptualising education -- What does it mean to be religious? -- New possibilities for religious education? -- What should religious education aim to achieve in the

	public sphere? -- Practical considerations: what might this mean for the teacher? -- Epilogue and some practical considerations: what might this mean for a religious education curriculum?
Subjects	Arendt, Hannah, 1906-1975.
	Weil, Simone, 1909-1943.
	Religion in the public schools.
Notes	Includes bibliographical references and index.
Additional formats	Print version: Hannam, Patricia, author. Religious education and the public sphere Abingdon, Oxon; New York, NY: Routledge is an imprint of the Taylor & Francis Group, an Informa Business, 2019 9780815354659 (DLC) 2018020300
Series	Theorizing education series

Religious education as a dialogue with difference: fostering democratic citizenship through the study of religions in schools

LCCN	2018056762
Type of material	Book
Personal name	O'Grady, Kevin, author.
Main title	Religious education as a dialogue with difference: fostering democratic citizenship through the study of religions in schools / by Kevin O'Grady.
Published/Produced	New York: Routledge, 2019.
ISBN	9781138479920 (hardback)
	9781351064385 (ebk)
LC classification	LC331 .O43 2019
Contents	Motivation in RE: beginnings -- RE, adolescence and creativity -- Action research, ethnography, epistemology and ethics -- RE as a dialogue with difference -- Democratic citizenship or religious literacy?: aims and values for RE -- Dialogue and conflict in RE -- Democratic citizenship and RE revisited -- Does RE work? -- Review,

	recommendations, questions for the future and final remarks.
Subjects	Religious education.
	Religions--Study and teaching (Secondary)
	Citizenship--Study and teaching (Secondary)
	Democracy and education.
	Religion in the public schools.
Notes	Includes index.
Series	Routledge research in religion and education; 10

Religious education for plural societies: the selected works of Robert Jackson

LCCN	2018027749
Type of material	Book
Personal name	Jackson, Robert, 1945- author.
Uniform title	Works. Selections
Main title	Religious education for plural societies: the selected works of Robert Jackson / Robert Jackson.
Published/Produced	Abingdon, Oxon; New York, NY: Routledge, 2019.
ISBN	9781138550674 (hardback)
LC classification	BL42 .J334 2019
Contents	Religious education and the arts of interpretation revisited -- Studying British Hindu children and representing them in school texts -- The diversity of experience in the religious upbringing of children from Christian families in Britain -- The "young people's attitudes to religious diversity" project in the context of Warwick Religions and Education Research Unit (WRERU) research -- Studying religious diversity in public education: an interpretive approach to religious and intercultural understanding -- The representation

	of religions -- Implications of an interpretive approach -- Contextual religious education and the interpretive approach -- Religious education in the context of plurality -- Religious education's contribution to intercultural education, citizenship education and values education -- Towards a pluralistic religious education -- Dialogical liberalism: a human rights rationale for "education about religions and beliefs" -- Inclusive study of religions and world views in schools: signposts from the council of Europe -- The politicisation and securitisation of religious education?: a rejoinder.
Subjects	Religious education.
	Religious pluralism.
	Education--Religious aspects.
	Religious education--Great Britain.
	Religious pluralism--Great Britain.
	Education--Religious aspects--Great Britain.
Notes	Includes bibliographical references.

Religious education from a critical realist perspective: Sensus fidei and critical thinking

LCCN	2018042242
Type of material	Book
Personal name	Go, Johnny C., author.
Main title	Religious education from a critical realist perspective: Sensus fidei and critical thinking / Johnny C. Go.
Published/Produced	New York: Routledge, 2019.
ISBN	9781138498242 (hbk)
LC classification	BX926.3 .G6 2019
Contents	Critical thinking in Catholic religious education -- Critical realism and Catholic Christianity -- A

	critical realist account of critical thinking -- An empirical investigation of teacher epistemologies -- A case for a critical realist Catholic religious epistemology -- Catholic religious critical thinking as the exercise of Sensus fidei.
Subjects	Catholic Church--Education--Philippines. Christian education. Faith and reason. Critical thinking. Sensus fidelium.
Notes	Includes bibliographical references and index.
Additional formats	Online version: Go, Johnny C., author. Religious education from a critical realist perspective New York: Routledge, 2019 9781351016636 (DLC) 2018055645
Series	Routledge studies in critical realism

Religious education from a critical realist perspective: Sensus fidei and critical thinking

LCCN	2018055645
Type of material	Book
Personal name	Go, Johnny C., author.
Main title	Religious education from a critical realist perspective: Sensus fidei and critical thinking / Johnny C. Go.
Published/Produced	New York: Routledge, 2019.
Description	1 online resource.
ISBN	9781351016636 (ebk) 9781351016629 (web pdf) 9781351016612 (epub) 9781351016605 (mobi/kindle)
LC classification	BX926.3
Contents	Critical thinking in Catholic religious education -- Critical realism and Catholic Christianity -- A

	critical realist account of critical thinking -- An empirical investigation of teacher epistemologies -- A case for a critical realist Catholic religious epistemology -- Catholic religious critical thinking as the exercise of Sensus fidei.
Subjects	Catholic Church--Education--Philippines. Christian education. Faith and reason. Critical thinking. Sensus fidelium.
Notes	Includes bibliographical references and index.
Additional formats	Print version: Go, Johnny C., author. Religious education from a critical realist perspective New York: Routledge, 2019 9781138498242 (DLC) 2018042242
Series	Routledge studies in critical realism

Religious education in a global-local world

LCCN	2016945969
Type of material	Book
Personal name	Berglund, Jenny.
Main title	Religious education in a global-local world / Jenny Berglund.
Published/Produced	New York, NY: Springer Berlin Heidelberg, 2016.
Links	Contributor biographical information https://www.loc.gov/catdir/enhancements/fy1620/2016945969-b.html
	Publisher description https://www.loc.gov/catdir/enhancements/fy1620/2016945969-d.html
	Table of contents only https://www.loc.gov/catdir/enhancements/fy1620/2016945969-t.html
ISBN	9783319322872

Religious education in Catholic schools: perspectives from Ireland and the UK

LCCN	2018002490
Type of material	Book
Main title	Religious education in Catholic schools: perspectives from Ireland and the UK / Sean Whittle (ed.)
Published/Produced	Oxford: Peter Lang AG, International Academic Publishers, [2018]
Description	x, 260 pages; 24 cm
ISBN	9781787079823 (alk. paper)
LC classification	LC506.I7 .R44 2018
Related names	Whittle, Sean, editor.
Summary	"This volume draws together researchers from Ireland and the UK in order to bring into focus the complex range of issues around the teaching of Religious Education in Catholic schools within a pluralist society" -- Provided by publisher.
Contents	Introduction by Sean Whittle -- The Role of RE Teachers: Between Pedagogy and Ecclesiology / John Sullivan -- The context of Religious Education in Catholic schools in Ireland / Dr. Gareth Byrne (Mater Dei, Dublin) -- Educators, Ethos and Catholic primary schools in Ireland / Dr. Fiona Dineen (Limerick diocese) -- The role of God parents: what does the choice of God parents suggest about education attitudes / Dr. Bernie Sweetman -- Will we have teachers for Catholic primary schools in Ireland? / Daniel O'Connell -- Religious Education: The Irish Secondary / Brendan P. Carmody SJ -- Giving voice to children's experience in RE / Dr. Cora O'Farral -- RE in English and Welsh Catholic school / Dr. Sean Whittle, (Heythrop College) --

	Reaffirming the place of scripture in RE / Professor Stephen McKinney -- Realising the relevance of Intertestamental studies for contemporary RE / Professor Susan Doherty -- Using scripture with SEND pupils reflections from a practitioner / Mr. David Purcell -- Scripture, RE and the demands of our pluralist society / Mr. John Stoer -- Is it time for non-confessional RE in Catholic schools / Dr. Sean Whittle (Heythrop College) -- Conclusion: RE in Catholic schools: Setting the agenda for future research.
Subjects	Catholic Church--Education--Ireland.
	Catholic Church--Education--Great Britain.
	Catholic schools--Ireland.
	Catholic schools--Great Britain.
	Religious education--Ireland.
	Religious education--Great Britain.
Notes	Includes bibliographical references and index.

Religious education in Indonesia: an empirical study of religious education models in Islamic, Christian and Hindu affiliated schools

LCCN	2016427341
Type of material	Book
Personal name	Yusuf, Mohamad, author.
Main title	Religious education in Indonesia: an empirical study of religious education models in Islamic, Christian and Hindu affiliated schools / Mohamad Yusuf.
Published/Produced	Zürich: Lit, [2016]
	©2016
Description	xi, 237 pages: illustrations; 24 cm.
ISBN	9783643907134 (pbk.)
	3643907133 (pbk.)

LC classification	BL42.5.I5 Y87 2016
Subjects	Religious education--Indonesia.
	Religious education--Comparative studies.
	Religious education.
	Indonesia.
Form/Genre	Comparative studies.
Notes	Author's doctoral thesis.
	Includes bibliographical references (pages 221-231).
	In English; summary in Dutch.
Series	Interreligious studies; Volume 10

Religious education in the secondary school: an introduction to teaching, learning and the world religions

LCCN	2014019984
Type of material	Book
Personal name	Holt, James.
Main title	Religious education in the secondary school: an introduction to teaching, learning and the world religions / James D. Holt.
Published/Produced	London; New York: Routledge, 2015.
Description	x, 230 pages; 26 cm.
ISBN	9781138018990 (hardback)
	9781138019003 (paperback)
LC classification	LC331 .H65 2015
Summary	"Religious Education in the Secondary School is a comprehensive, straightforward introduction to the effective teaching of Religious Education in the secondary classroom. Acknowledging the highly valuable yet often misunderstood contribution of RE, this text shows how the subject can be taught in a way that explores the impact of religion on the lives of people and society, engaging pupils and preparing them to

become individuals who celebrate and respect diversity. It is illustrated throughout with ideas for teaching at different key stages and offers expert chapters introducing you to both the World Religions and the core aspects of effective teaching and learning. With an emphasis on developing an understanding of the importance - and different ways - of meeting the learning needs of all pupils, key chapters cover:-Understanding different pedagogies of RE -Spirituality and RE- Tips on effective planning and assessment -An approach to teaching across the Key Stages-Core subject knowledge in Buddhism, Christianity, Hinduism, Islam, Judaism and Sikhism. Written by an experienced teacher, teacher educator and examiner, Religious Education in the Secondary School is a succinct compendium and has a real classroom applicability offering all trainee RE teachers, as well as those teaching Religious Education as specialists or non-specialists a wealth of support and inspiration"-- Provided by publisher.

Subjects   Religious education.
Religions--Study and teaching (Secondary)
Religion in the public schools.
Education / General.
Education / Secondary.

Notes   Includes bibliographical references and index.

Religious education in Thirteenth-Century England: the creed and articles of faith

LCCN   2015009782
Type of material   Book
Personal name   Reeves, Andrew (History Professor)

Main title	Religious education in Thirteenth-Century England: the creed and articles of faith / by Andrew Reeves.
Published/Produced	Leiden; Boston: Brill, [2015]
Description	xiv, 218 pages; 25 cm.
ISBN	9789004294431 (hardback: alk. paper)
LC classification	BR750 .R44 2015
Subjects	Religious education--England--History. Creeds--History and criticism. England--Church history--1066-1485.
Notes	Includes bibliographical references and indexes.
Series	Education and society in the Middle Ages and Renaissance, 0926-6070; VOLUME 50

Religious education.

LCCN	2018946694
Type of material	Book
Main title	Religious education.
Published/Produced	New York, NY: Springer Berlin Heidelberg, 2018.
ISBN	9783658216764

Schooling indifference: re-imagining RE in multi-cultural and gendered spaces

LCCN	2017005847
Type of material	Book
Personal name	I'Anson, John, author.
Main title	Schooling indifference: re-imagining RE in multi-cultural and gendered spaces / John I'Anson and Alison Jasper.
Published/Produced	New York: Routledge/Taylor & Francis Group, 2017.
Description	vii, 179 pages; 24 cm.
ISBN	9781138184695 (hbk: alk. paper)

LC classification	BL42.5.G7 L36 2017
Related names	Jasper, Alison E. author.
Subjects	Religious education--Great Britain.
	Religious education--Philosophy.
Notes	Includes bibliographical references and index.
Series	Gender, theology and spirituality; 19

Schools and the politics of religion and diversity in the Republic of Ireland: separate but equal?

LCCN	2016285354
Type of material	Book
Personal name	Fischer, Karin, 1972- author.
Main title	Schools and the politics of religion and diversity in the Republic of Ireland: separate but equal? / Karin Fischer.
Published/Produced	Manchester: Manchester University Press, 2016. ©2016
Description	x, 237 pages; 24 cm
ISBN	9780719091964 (hardback)
	0719091969 (hardback)
LC classification	LC116.I7 F57 2016
Subjects	Religious education--Ireland.
	Education and state--Ireland.
	Religious education.
	Ireland.
Notes	Includes bibliographical references (pages 215-230) and index.

Second Temple Jewish paideia in context

LCCN	2017030317
Type of material	Book
Main title	Second Temple Jewish paideia in context / edited by Jason M. Zurawski and Gabriele Boccaccini.
Edition	Edition 1.

Published/Produced	Berlin; Boston: De Gruyter, [2017]
Description	vi, 308 pages; 24 cm.
ISBN	9783110546064 (hardcover)
LC classification	LA47 .S43 2017
Related names	Zurawski, Jason, editor.
	Boccaccini, Gabriele, 1958- editor.
Abstract	"The subject of this volume, Jewish paideia or education during the Second Temple period, had long received little attention. Yet these fourteen essays demonstrate the fundamental importance of the topic for understanding the history of the period. They also represent the broad array of approaches required to comprehend this multi-faceted subject. The papers were first offered at the 5th Nangeroni Meeting (Naples, Italy, July 2015)"--Provided by publisher.
Contents	Introduction: perspectives on Second Temple Jewish Paideia from the Fifth Nangeroni meeting / Jason M. Zurawski and Gabriele Boccaccini -- Scribal education in ancient Israel and Judah into the Persian period / William M. Schniedewind -- Jewish education in Ben Sira / Frank Ueberschaer -- Reassessing the exclusivism of Ben Sira's Jewish Paideia / Samuel L. Adams -- The formation of a sage according to Ben Sira / Elisa Uusimäki -- Students of God in the house of Torah: education in the Dead Sea Scrolls / Matthew Goff -- Greek paideia and the Jewish community of Alexandria in the letter of Aristeas / Benjamin G. Wright -- The Testament of Orpheus, Aristobulus, and the Derveni papyrus: between didactic hymnography and Alexandrian exegesis / Luca Arcari -- Discipline, transmission, and writing: notes on education in the Testaments

of the Twelve Patriarchs / Patrick Pouchelle -- The School of Moses in Alexandria: an attempt to reconstruct the School of Philo / Gregory E. Sterling -- Philo's questions and the adaptation of Greek philosophical curriculum / Sean A. Adams -- Dissolving the philosophy-religion dichotomy in the context of Jewish Paideia: Wisdom of Solomon, 4 Maccabees, and Philo / Anders Klostergaard Petersen -- The author of 4 Maccabees and Greek paideia: facets of the formation of a Hellenistic Jewish rhetor / David A. deSilva -- Embodying the ways in Christ: Paul's teaching of the nations / Kathy Ehrensperger -- Christians, pagans, and the politics of paideia in Late Antiquity / Jason von Ehrenkrook -- Jewish education and identity: towards an understanding of Second Temple Paideia / Jason M. Zurawski.

Subjects   Jews--Education--History--To 1500.
Judaism--History--Post-exilic period, 586 B.C.-210 A.D.
Jewish religious education.
Education, Ancient.

Notes   Includes bibliographical references and index.

Series   Beihefte zur Zeitschrift für die neutestamentliche Wissenschaft; Volume 228

Secular conversions: political institutions and religious education in the United States and Australia, 1800-2000

LCCN   2016014634
Type of material   Book
Personal name   Mayrl, Damon, 1977- author.
Main title   Secular conversions: political institutions and religious education in the United States and

	Australia, 1800-2000 / Damon Mayrl, Universidad Carlos III de Madrid.
Published/Produced	Cambridge, United Kingdom; New York: Cambridge University Press, 2016.
Description	xii, 286 pages; 24 cm
ISBN	9781107103719 (hardback: alk. paper)
	9781107503236 (pbk.: alk. paper)
LC classification	BL2525 .M385 2016
Subjects	Secularism--United States.
	Secularization.
	Religion and politics--United States.
	Religious education--United States.
	Secularism--Australia.
	Religion and politics--Australia.
	Religious education--Australia.
	United States--Religion.
	Australia--Religion.
Notes	Includes bibliographical references and index.

Secularism, decolonisation, and the Cold War in South and Southeast Asia

LCCN	2017011570
Type of material	Book
Personal name	Six, Clemens, 1975- author.
Main title	Secularism, decolonisation, and the Cold War in South and Southeast Asia / Clemens Six.
Published/Produced	London; New York: Routledge, Taylor & Francis Group, 2018.
Description	xii, 305 pages; 25 cm.
ISBN	9781138052024 (hbk)
	(ebk)
LC classification	BL2765.S64 S59 2018
Summary	"The intensifying conflicts between religious communities in contemporary South and

Southeast Asia signify the importance of gaining a clearer understanding of how societies have historically organised and mastered their religious diversity. Based on extensive archival research in Asia, Europe, and the United States this book suggests a new approach to interpreting and explaining secularism not as a Western concept but as a distinct form of practice in 20th century global history. In six case studies on the contemporary history of India, Indonesia, Malaysia, and Singapore it analyses secularism as a project to create a high degree of distance between the state and religion during the era of decolonisation and the emerging Cold War between 1945 and 1970. To demonstrate the interplay between local and transnational dynamics, the case studies look at patterns of urban planning, the struggle against religious nationalism, conflicts around religious education, and (anti)communism as a dispute over secularism and social reform. The book emphasises in particular the role of non-state actors as key supporters of secular statehood--a role that has thus far not received sufficient attention. A novel approach to studying secularism in Asia, the book discusses the different ways that global transformations such as decolonisation and the Cold War interacted with local relations to re-shape and re-locate religion in society"-- Provided by publisher.

Subjects   Secularism--South Asia.
Secularism--Southeast Asia.
Decolonization--South Asia.
Decolonization--Southeast Asia.

Religion and politics--South Asia.
Religion and politics--Southeast Asia.
Religion and sociology--South Asia.
Religion and sociology--Southeast Asia.
Cold War.
South Asia--Religion--20th century.
Southeast Asia--Religion--20th century.

Notes   Includes bibliographical references (pages 259-297) and index.
Series   Routledge studies in the modern history of Asia; 126

Sex and Religion: Two Texts of Early Feminist Psychoanalysis

LCCN   2015004389
Type of material   Book
Personal name   Andreas-Salomé, Lou, 1861-1937, author.
Uniform title   Works. Selections. English
Main title   Sex and Religion: Two Texts of Early Feminist Psychoanalysis / Lou Andreas-Salomé; with an introduction by Matthew Del Nevo and Gary Winship; translated by Maike Oergel and Kristine Jennings.
Published/Produced   New Brunswick, New Jersey: Transaction Publishers, [2016]
Description   xxiv, 93 pages; 24 cm
ISBN   9781412856966 (acid-free paper)
LC classification   PT2601.N4 A2 2016
Related names   Del Nevo, Matthew, writer of introduction.
Winship, Gary, writer of introduction.
Oergel, Maike, 1964- translator.
Jennings, Kristine, translator.
Andreas-Salomé, Lou, 1861-1937. Drei Briefe an einen Knaben. English.

	Andreas-Salomé, Lou, 1861-1937. Teufel und seine Grossmutter. English.
Scope and content	Drei Breife an einen Knaben (Three Letters to a Young Boy) and Der Teufel und Seine Grossmutter (The Devil & His Grandmother) are texts that explore sexuality across the lifespan with some unexpected twists and turns. The Devil & His Grandmother treats the collision of sexuality and religion, and therefore religious education indirectly. The Three Letters was originally authored in 1912 with two letters addressed to Helene Klinenberg's son and a third added in 1913. The Three Letters were edited, appended and finally published in 1917 by Kurt Wolff's Verlag in Leipzig. -- Provided by publisher.
Subjects	Andreas-Salomé, Lou, 1861-1937--Translations into English.
	Sex instruction for boys.
	Sex (Psychology)--Drama.
	Religion--Drama.
Notes	The Devil & His Grandmother is a play.
	Includes bibliographical references.

Spirituality in education in a global, pluralised world

LCCN	2015033276
Type of material	Book
Personal name	De Souza, Marian, author.
Main title	Spirituality in education in a global, pluralised world / Marian de Souza.
Published/Produced	London; New York Routledge [2016]
Description	170 pages; 24 cm
ISBN	9781138804746 (hbk; alk. paper)
LC classification	BL42 .D47 2016

Subjects	Religious education--Study and teaching.
	Religious education--Teaching methods.
Notes	Includes bibliographical references (pages 152 165) and index.

Spirituals: a multidisciplinary bibliography for research and performance

LCCN	2018560122
Type of material	Book
Personal name	Abromeit, Kathleen A., 1962- author.
Main title	Spirituals: a multidisciplinary bibliography for research and performance / by Kathleen A. Abromeit.
Published/Produced	Middleton, Wisconsin: Co-published by Music Library Association and A-R Editions, Inc., [2015]
	©2015
Description	xiv, 301 pages; 24 cm.
	24 cm.
ISBN	9780895797995 (paperback)
	0895797992 (paperback)
LC classification	ML128.S4 A29 2015
Related names	Music Library Association, publisher.
Summary	Spirituals originated among enslaved Africans in America during the colonial era. They resonate throughout African American history from that time to the civil rights movement, from the cotton fields to the concert stage, and influenced everything from gospel music to blues and rap. They have offered solace in times of suffering, served as clandestine signals on the Underground Railroad, and been a source of celebration and religious inspiration. Spirituals are born from the womb of African American experience, yet they

transcend national, disciplinary, and linguistic boundaries as they connect music, theology, literature and poetry, history, society, and education. In doing so, they reach every aspect of human experience. To make sense of the immense impact spirituals have made on music, culture, and society, this bibliography cites writings from a multidisciplinary perspective. This annotated bibliography documents articles, books, and dissertations published since 1902. Of those, 150 are books; 80 are chapters within books; 615 are journal articles, and 150 are dissertations, along with a selection of highly significant items published before 1920. The most recent publications included date from early 2014. Disciplines researched include music, literature and poetry, American history, religion, and African American Studies. Items included in the annotated bibliography are limited to English-language sources that were published in the United States and focus on African American spirituals in the United States, but there are a few select citations that focus on spirituals outside of the United States. Of the one thousand annotations, they are divided, roughly evenly, between: general studies and geographical studies; information about early spirituals; use of spirituals in art music, church music, and popular music; composers who based music on spirituals; performers of spirituals (ensembles and individuals); Bible, theology, and religious education; literature and poetry; pedagogical considerations, including the teaching of spirituals as well as prominent educators;

reference works and a list of resources that were unavailable for review but are potentially useful. This book also offers considerable depth on particular topics such as the Fisk Jubilee Singers and William Grant Still with over thirty citations devoted to each. At the same time, materials included are quite diverse, with topics such as spirituals in Zora Neale Hurston's novels; bible studies based on spirituals; enriching the teaching of geography through spirituals; Marian Anderson's historic concert at the Lincoln Memorial; spiritual roots of rap; teaching dialect to singers; expressing African American religion in spirituals; Samuel Coleridge-Taylor's music; slave tradition of singing among the Gullah. The book contains indices by author, subject, and spiritual title. Additionally, an appendix of spirituals by biblical reference, listing both spiritual title to scriptural reference as well as scripture to spiritual title is included. T. L. Collins, Christian educator, compiled the appendix [Publisher description]

Contents Reference works: Bibliographies and catalogs; Dictionaries and encyclopedias; Discographies and filmographies; Indexes; Lyrics -- Early spirituals: Histories of early spirituals; Origins; Slave religion and culture; Religious music -- Historical studies and surveys: Histories; Society and culture; Theory, aesthetics, and philosophy -- Use of spirituals in other types of music: Art music; Church music; Popular music -- Composers who based music on spirituals: Survey studies of composers using spirituals; Individual composers -- Performers of spirituals: Ensembles;

	Individual performers -- Geographical studies: Cross-cultural influences; International; United States -- Bible, theology, and religious education: African American churches and the use of scripture; Experience and identity; Social unity and politics; Theological interpretations; Miscellaneous -- Spirituals in literature: Fiction; Poetry; Literary criticism; First-person accounts; Individual authors -- Education and teaching: Teaching the singing of spirituals; Classroom instruction; Educators -- Anthologies containing historical information -- Items not available for review -- Indexes consulted -- Appendix: Scriptural references.
Subjects	Spirituals (Songs)--Bibliography.
	Gospel music--Bibliography.
	African Americans--Music--Bibliography.
	Negrospiritual.
	African Americans.
	Gospel music.
	Spirituals (Songs)
Form/Genre	Bibliographies.
Notes	Includes bibliographical references and indexes.
	Text in English.
Series	Music Library Association index and bibliography series; volume 38
	MLA index and bibliography series; 38.

St. Ignatius Church at Chapel Point: sharing God's word since 1641
LCCN	2016903939
Type of material	Book
Main title	St. Ignatius Church at Chapel Point: sharing God's word since 1641 / St. Ignatius Church.

Published/Produced	Port Tobacco, Maryland: St. Ignatius Church at Chapel Point, [2016]
Description	142 pages: illustrations (some color); 23 x 29 cm
ISBN	9780692654286 (library binding)
LC classification	BX4603.P643 S75 2016
Variant title	Saint Ignatius Church at Chapel Point
Summary	A history of St. Ignatius Church in Port Tobacco, Maryland, the oldest continuously operating Catholic parish in the United States.
Contents	Introduction -- From our pastor -- The Jesuit mission in colonial Maryland -- The journey to Maryland begins: Fr. Andrew White -- Our Piscataway heritage -- Relic of the true cross -- The Carmelite nuns -- Ignatius and the early society -- Jesuit suppression and restoration -- The legacy of education -- Mission churches and home chapels -- Fr. Bernadine Wiget's letter, 1875 -- The buildings at St. Thomas Manor -- War at Chapel Point -- Civil War -- The plantation, grain mill and trade -- Slavery -- Tunnel lore -- The fire of 1866 -- Cemetery -- Chapel Point, the town that never was -- Chapel Point Park -- Segregation -- Pew Rents -- Parish life 1900-1930s -- Stained glass windows -- Needlepoint kneelers -- List of pastors: 1662 to present -- History timeline -- Liturgy through the years -- Religious education: CCD -- Fraternal and religious organizations -- Devotions --Summer festivals -- Parish mission revivals -- Gardiner Award recipients -- Loyola retreat house -- Religious freedom national scenic byway -- Governor Hogan's visit -- Event photos -- Appendices -- The Woodstock letters.
Subjects	Catholic church buildings--Maryland. Catholic church buildings.

	Manners and customs.
	Port Tobacco (Md.)--Church history.
	Port Tobacco (Md.)--History.
	Port Tobacco (Md.)--Social life and customs.
	Maryland.
	Maryland--Port Tobacco.
Form/Genre	Church history.
	History.
Notes	Cover title.

State and religion in Israel: a philosophical-legal inquiry

LCCN	2018027885
Type of material	Book
Personal name	Sapir, Gideon, author.
Main title	State and religion in Israel: a philosophical-legal inquiry / Gideon Sapir, Daniel Statman.
Edition	First edition.
Published/Produced	New York: Cambridge University Press, [2018] ©2018
ISBN	9781107150829 (hardback: alk. paper)
	9781316605455 (pbk.: alk. paper)
LC classification	BM538.S7 S27 2018
Related names	Statman, Daniel, author.
Summary	"State and Religion in Israel begins with a philosophical analysis of the two main questions regarding the role of religion in liberal states: should such states institute a 'Wall of Separation' between state and religion? Should they offer religious practices and religious communities special protection?"-- Provided by publisher.
Contents	Part 1: Theory -- 1. Liberalism and neutrality (1): Arguments against support -- 2. Liberalism and neutrality (2): Arguments against preference -- 3. The assumed dangers of religion -- 4. Religious

	reasons for separation -- 5. Freedom of religion -- 6. Protection of religious feelings -- 7. Freedom from religion -- 8. Religious coercion: the place of religious arguments in the public sphere -- Part 2: From theory to practice -- 9. Marriage and divorce -- 10. Religious education -- 11. Serving religious needs -- 12. Drafting yeshiva students into the army -- 13. The Sabbath in a Jewish State -- 14. The supreme court on the protection of and from religion -- 15. Minority religions in Israel.
Subjects	Judaism and state--Israel--Philosophy.
	Religion and state--Israel--Philosophy.
	Democracy--Religious aspects--Judaism.
	Jewish philosophy--Israel--History--21st century.
	Israel--Politics and government.
Notes	Includes bibliographical references.

State religious education and the state of religious life

LCCN	2018303049
Type of material	Book
Personal name	Gearon, Liam, author.
Main title	State religious education and the state of religious life / Liam Gearon and Joseph Prud'homme.
Published/Produced	Eugene, Oregon: Pickwick Publications, [2018] ©2018
Description	viii, 210 pages; 23 cm.
ISBN	9781625647269
	1625647263
LC classification	LC111 .G43 2018
Related names	Prud'homme, Joseph Gilbert, 1971- author.
Subjects	Bible--Study and teaching--United States.
	Religion in the public schools--United States.
	Religious education--United States.
	Religion and state--United States.

Notes	Religion and civil society. Includes bibliographical references (pages 163-183) and index.

Strength through adversity: when bad things happen to good people

LCCN	2015431659
Type of material	Book
Personal name	Top, Brent L., author.
Uniform title	Strength to endure
Main title	Strength through adversity: when bad things happen to good people / Brent L. Top.
Published/Produced	American Fork, Utah: Covenant Communications, Inc., [2015] ©2015
Description	136 pages; 23 cm
ISBN	9781621089001 1621089002
LC classification	BX8643.S93 T67 2015
Variant title	Subtitle appears on cover as: Why bad things happen to good people
Summary	BYU Dean of Religious Education Brent L. Top explores the healing principles that God has given to help us understand and endure adversity.
Subjects	Suffering--Religious aspects--Church of Jesus Christ of Latter-day Saints. Suffering--Religious aspects--Mormon Church.
Notes	Includes bibliographical references (pages 133-136).

Teaching civic engagement

LCCN	2015016792
Type of material	Book
Main title	Teaching civic engagement / edited by Forrest Clingerman and Reid B. Locklin.

Published/Produced	New York, NY: Oxford University Press, [2016]
Description	xxiv, 308 pages; 24 cm
ISBN	9780190250508 (cloth: alk. paper)
LC classification	LC220.5 .T38 2016
Related names	Clingerman, Forrest.
	Locklin, Reid B.
Contents	Discourse, Democracy, and the Many Faces of Civic Engagement: Four Guiding Objectives for the University Classroom / Reid B. Locklin, with Ellen Posman -- Sacred Sites and Staging Grounds: The Four Guiding Objectives of Civic Engagement in the Religion Classroom / Ellen Posman, with Reid B. Locklin -- Teaching for Civic Engagement: Insights from a Two-Year Workshop / Melissa Stewart -- Giving and Receiving Hospitality during Community Engagement Courses / Marianne Delaporte -- Civic Engagement in the Heart of the City / Rebekka King -- Engaging Media and Messages in the Religion Classroom / Hans Wiersma -- Service and Community-Based Learning: A Pedagogy for Civic Engagement and Critical Thinking / Phil Wingeier-Rayo -- Religious Diversity, Civic Engagement and Community-Engaged Pedagogy: Forging Bonds of Solidarity through Interfaith Dialogue / Nicholas Rademacher -- Stopping the Zombie Apocalypse: Ascetic Withdrawal as a Form of Civic Learning / Elizabeth W. Corrie -- Thinking about the "Civic" in Civic Engagement and Its Deployment in the Religion Classroom / Carolyn M. Jones Medine -- More than Global Citizenship: How Religious Studies Expands Participation in Global Communities / Karen Derris and Erin Runions --

	Political Involvement, the Advocacy of Process, and the Religion Classroom / Forrest Clingerman and Swasti Bhattacharyya -- The Difference between Religious Studies and Theology in the Teaching of Civic Engagement / Tom Pearson -- Dreams of Democracy / Tina Pippen.
Subjects	Service learning--Study and teaching. Social justice--Study and teaching. Religious education--Social aspects.
Notes	Includes bibliographical references (pages 267-290) and index.

Teaching for a multifaith world

LCCN	2017303044
Type of material	Book
Main title	Teaching for a multifaith world / edited by Eleazar S. Fernandez.
Published/Produced	Eugene, Oregon: Pickwick Publications, [2017] ©2017
Description	xxviii, 219 pages: illustrations; 23 cm
ISBN	9781498239745 (paperback) 1498239749 (paperback) 9781498239769 (hardcover) 1498239765 (hardcover) (ebook)
LC classification	BV1471.3 .T43 2017
Related names	Fernandez, Eleazar S., editor.
Summary	"When religious diversity is our reality, radical hospitality to people of other faiths is not a luxury but a necessity. More than necessary for our survival, radical hospitality to religious diversity is necessary if we are to thrive as a global society. By no means does the practice of hospitality in a multifaith world require that we be oblivious of

our differences. On the contrary, it demands a respectful embrace of our differences because that's who we are. Neither does radical hospitality require that we water down our commitment, because faithfulness and openness are not contradictory. We must be able to say with burning passion that we are open to the claims of other faiths because we are faithful to our religious heritage. The essays in this book do not offer simply theological exhortations; they offer specific ways of how we can become religiously competent citizens in a multifaith world. Let's take the bold steps of radical openness with this book on our side!" -- Publisher's description.

Contents

Introduction: Multifaith education matters -- Our journey in multifaith education / Robert Hunt -- Multifaith context and competencies / Eleazar S. Fernandez -- Designing curricular approaches for interfaith competency or Why does learning how to live in a "community of communities" matter? / Mary E. Hess -- Religious self, religious other: coformation as a model for interreligious education / Jennifer Peace -- Beyond world religions: pedagogical principles and practices for the encouragement of interfaith hospitality and collaboration / Lucinda Mosher -- Pursuing and teaching justice in multifaith contexts / Justus Baird -- Spiritual formation in a multifaith world / Ruben L.F. Habito -- Pastoral and spiritual care in multifaith contexts / Daniel S. Schipani -- Chaplaincy education meets multireligious literacy development: strategies for teaching models and methods of spiritual caregiving in multifaith contexts / Lucinda Mosher -- Public

	ministry in a world of many faiths / Shanta Premawardhana -- Letting the arts lead: the role of the arts in interfaith dialogue / Cindi Beth Johnson, with Jann Cather Weaver -- "The sacrament of human life": cultivating intentional interreligious learning in congregations / Sheryl A. Kujawa-Holbrook -- Appendix. Reflective matrix: spectrum of reflective practice in seminary teaching.
Subjects	Multiculturalism--Religious aspects.
	Religious education.
Notes	Includes bibliographical references.

Teaching religion using technology in higher education

LCCN	2018010273
Type of material	Book
Personal name	Hilton, John, III, author.
Main title	Teaching religion using technology in higher education / edited by John Hilton III.
Published/Produced	New York, NY: Routledge, 2018.
ISBN	9781138087224 (hbkk)
LC classification	BL41 .H47 2018
Contents	Third-screen teaching: enhancing classroom learning with mobile devices / Richard Newton -- Student-created podcasts as a means of knowledge assessment / David Kniep -- Who do you vote that I am?: using student response systems in religion courses / Renate Hood -- Teaching religion with clickers / Kristy L. Slominski -- "Seeing" the sacred landscape: a digital geographies approach to contextualizing ancient sites in religious education / Kyle M. Oliver -- If you'll tweet along with me: effectively using social media in religious education / Rob

O'Lynn -- Social media in higher-ed religion studies / Brooke Lester -- Blended learning in religious education: what, why, and how / Anthony Sweat -- Character-izing gameful learning: using student-guided narratives to motivate, engage, and inform learners / Christopher Heard, Steven V. Rouse -- Technology twist on the visiting professor / Gerald L. Stevens -- Taming the MOOS: massive online open seminars in religion / Phyllis Zagano -- Welcoming the stranger to the conversation / Charlotte Heeg -- Comparing spiritual outcomes in face-to-face versus online delivery of a religion course / John Hilton III, Kenneth Plummer, Ben Fryar, & Ryan Gardner.

Subjects   Religion--Study and teaching (Higher)
Educational technology.
Notes   Includes bibliographical references.
Series   Routledge research in religion and education; 8

Teaching religious education: researchers in the classroom
LCCN   2017042710
Type of material   Book
Personal name   Stern, Julian. author
Main title   Teaching religious education: researchers in the classroom / Julian Stern.
Edition   Second edition.
Published/Produced   London; New York: Bloomsbury, Academic, an imprint of Bloomsbury Publishing Plc, 2018.
Description   vii, 199 pages; 26 cm
ISBN   9781350037106 (Hb)
9781350037090 (pb)
LC classification   BL42.5.G7 S74 2018

Subjects	Religious education--Study and teaching--Great Britain.
Notes	Includes bibliographical references [pages172-190] and index.
Additional formats	Online version: Stern, Julian. Teaching religious education Second edition. London, UK; New York, NY: Bloomsbury Academic, 2019 9781350037120 (DLC) 2017058978

Teaching religious education: researchers in the classroom

LCCN	2017058978
Type of material	Book
Personal name	Stern, Julian.
Main title	Teaching religious education: researchers in the classroom / Julian Stern.
Edition	Second edition.
Published/Produced	London, UK; New York, NY: Bloomsbury Academic, 2019.
Description	1 online resource.
ISBN	9781350037120 (PDF eBook)
	9781350037113 (EPUB eBook)
LC classification	BL42.5.G7
Contents	Preface to the second edition -- Introduction: inclusive research -- Dialogue within and between -- The real lives of teachers and pupils in religious education -- Re around the world -- Understanding pedagogy in religious education -- Inclusion, diversity and religious education -- Working with sacred texts -- Spirituality -- Ethnographic research in communities -- Thinking about philosophy, truth, and religious education -- Ethics, rights, morality and virtues -- Creativity and RE -- The future of Research.

Subjects	Religious education--Study and teaching--Great Britain.
Notes	Includes bibliographical references and index.
Additional formats	Print version: Stern, Julian. Teaching religious education Second edition. London, UK; New York, NY: Bloomsbury Academic, 2019 9781350037106 (DLC) 2017042710

Teaching religious education creatively

LCCN	2014025138
Type of material	Book
Main title	Teaching religious education creatively / edited by Sally Elton-Chalcraft.
Published/Produced	Milton Park, Abingdon, Oxon; New York, NY: Routledge, 2015.
Description	xiii, 180 pages; 26 cm.
ISBN	9780415742573 (hbk)
	9780415742580 (pbk)
LC classification	BV1471.3 .T38 2015
Related names	Elton-Chalcraft, Sally.
Summary	"Teaching Religious Education Creatively offers a brand new approach for the primary classroom and is crammed full of innovative ideas for bringing the teaching of RE to life. It helps teachers understand what constitutes a healthy curriculum that will encourage children to appreciate and understand different belief systems. Perhaps most importantly, it also challenges teachers to understand RE as a transformatory subject that offers children the tools to be discerning, to work out their own beliefs and answer puzzling questions. Underpinned by the latest research and theory and with contemporary, cutting-edge practice at the

forefront, expert authors emphasise creative thinking strategies and teaching creatively. Key topics explored include: What is creative teaching and learning? Why is it important to teach creatively and teach for creativity? What is Religious Education? Why is it important for children to learn 'about' and 'from' religion? How can you teach non-biased RE creatively as a discrete subject and integrate it with other curriculum areas? Teaching Religious Education Creatively is for all teachers who want to learn more about innovative teaching and learning in RE in order to improve understanding and enjoyment and transform their own as well as their pupil's lives"-- Provided by publisher.

Subjects Religious education.
Education / General.
Education / Elementary.
Notes Includes bibliographical references and index.
Series Learning to teach in the primary school series

Teaching religious literacy: a guide to religious and spiritual diversity in higher education

LCCN 2016056752
Type of material Book
Personal name Ennis, Ariel, author.
Main title Teaching religious literacy: a guide to religious and spiritual diversity in higher education / Ariel Ennis.
Published/Produced New York: Routledge, 2017.
Description xvii, [91] pages; 21 cm
ISBN 9781138635852 (Hardback)
LC classification BL42 .E56 2017
Subjects Religious education.

Education, Higher.
Religious pluralism.
Religions--Study and teaching.

The Bible in music: a dictionary of songs, works, and more

LCCN	2015012867
Type of material	Book
Personal name	Long, Siobhan.
Main title	The Bible in music: a dictionary of songs, works, and more / Siobhán Dowling Long, John F. A. Sawyer.
Published/Produced	Lanham, Maryland: Rowman & Littlefield, [2015] ©2015
Description	xxxi, 339 pages; 24 cm
ISBN	9780810884519 (hardcover alkaline paper) 9780810884526 (ebook)
LC classification	ML102.C5 L66 2015
Related names	Sawyer, John F. A., author.
Summary	There have been numerous publications over the last several decades on the Bible in literature, film, and art. But until now, no reference work has appeared on the Bible as depicted in Western music. In The Bible in Music: A Dictionary of Songs, Works, and More, scholars Siobhâan Dowling Long and John F.A. Sawyer correct this gap in Biblical reference literature, providing a convenient guide to musical interpretations of the Bible. As well as providing examples of classical music from the Middle Ages through modern times, Dowling Long and Sawyer also examine the Bible's impact on popular culture with numerous entries on hymns, spirituals, musicals, film music, and contemporary popular music.

	Each entry contains essential information about the original context of the work (date, composer, etc.) and, where relevant, its afterlife in literature, film, politics, and liturgy. The book also includes an index of biblical references; an index of biblical names; a detailed timeline that places key events, works, and publications in their historical context; a bibliography; and a glossary of technical terms. The Bible in Music will fascinate anyone familiar with the Bible, but it is also designed to encourage choirs, musicians, musicologists, lecturers, teachers, and students of music and religious education to discover and perform lesser-known pieces, as well as helping them to listen to familiar music with a fresh perspective. - Back cover.
Contents	Acronymns and abbreviations -- Chronology -- Introduction -- The Dictionary -- Glossary of technical terms -- Bibliography -- List of authors, composers, and musicians -- Index of biblical names and subjects -- Index of biblical references -- About the authors.
Subjects	Bible--Songs and music--Dictionaries. Bible in music--Dictionaries.
Notes	Includes bibliographical references (pages 287-294) and index.

The Bloomsbury reader in religion and childhood

LCCN	2016037876
Type of material	Book
Main title	The Bloomsbury reader in religion and childhood / edited by Anna Strhan, Stephen G. Parker and Susan B. Ridgely.

Published/Produced	London; New York: Bloomsbury Academic, an imprint of Bloomsbury Publishing Plc, 2017.
Description	xi, 393 pages; 26 cm
ISBN	9781474251105 (hb)
LC classification	BL85 .B56 2017
Related names	Strhan, Anna, editor.
Subjects	Religions.
	Children--Religious aspects.
	Children--Religious life.
	Religious education of children.
Notes	Includes bibliographical references and indexes.

The contested place of religion in family law

LCCN	2017043605
Type of material	Book
Main title	The contested place of religion in family law / edited by Robin Fretwell Wilson, University of Illinois College of Law.
Published/Produced	Cambridge, United Kingdom; New York, NY, USA: Cambridge University Press, 2018.
Description	xxv, 717 pages: illustrations; 24 cm
ISBN	9781108417600 (hardback)
LC classification	KF505 .C657 2018
Related names	Wilson, Robin Fretwell, editor.
Summary	"Like many beliefs, religious views matter across an individual's life and the life cycle of a family - from birth to marriage, through child-rearing, and, eventually, death. This volume examines clashes over religious liberty within the personal realm of the family. Against swirling religious beliefs, secular values, and legal regulation, this volume offers a forward-looking examination of tensions between religious freedom and the state's protective function. Contributors unpack some of

the Court's recent decisions and explain how they set the stage for ongoing disputes. They evaluate religious claims around birth control, circumcision, modesty, religious education, marriage, polygamy, shared parenting, corporal punishment, faith healing, divorce, and the end of life. Authors span legislators, attorneys, academics, journalists, ministers, physicians, child advocates, and representatives of minority faiths. The Contested Place of Religion in Family Law begins an overdue conversation on questions dividing the nation"-- Provided by publisher.

"This volume comes at an important moment. In the space of three years, the United States Supreme Court decided cases about marriage equality, the government's ability to require contraceptives as part of employer health policies, and the ability of religious actors to step aside from duties that otherwise apply. The cases ranked among the most closely watched of each term. Two of them captured the nation's attention and highlighted the sharp divide on the Court-and among Americans-as to these issues"-- Provided by publisher.

Contents Foreword Senator Orrin Hatch; Introduction Robin Fretwell Wilson; Part I. The Foundations and Boundaries of Religious Liberty: The Risky Business of RFRAs after Hobby Lobby Elizabeth Sepper; Religion and the Family in the Wake of Hobby Lobby Michael A. Helfand; Part II. Religious Claims at Birth: Religious Exceptionalism and Religiously Motivated Harm Michele Bratcher Goodwin; Contraceptive Access and Religious Liberty: Can We Afford to

Protect Both? Mark L. Rienzi; The Contraceptive-Coverage Cases and the Problem of Politicized Free-Exercise Lawsuits Gregory M. Lipper; The Substantial Burden Question: Secular Tools for Secular Courts Michael A. Helfand; Coming Soon to a Court Near You: Male Circumcision in Religious Families in Europe and the United States Eric Rassbach; Part III. Religious Claims in Childrearing: The Easiest Accommodation: Abandoning Other People's Children to Their Parents' Religious Views James G. Dwyer; Marriage Agreements and Religious Family Life Brian H. Bix; Religious Parents Who Divorce Margaret F. Brinig; Regulating the Relationship between Parents: Moving Beyond Marriage and Custody Law Merle H. Weiner; Bad Faith: When Religious Beliefs Imperil Children Dr. Paul A. Offit; By Faith Alone: When Religious Beliefs and Child Welfare Collide Robin Fretwell Wilson and Shaakirrah Sanders; Part IV. Rethinking Marriage After Obergefell: After Obergefell: Locating the Contemporary State Interest in Marriage Kari E. Hong; Transformational Marriage: How to End the Culture Wars over Same-Sex Marriage Robin B. Kar; Divorcing Marriage and the State Post-Obergefell Robin Fretwell Wilson; Why No Polygamy John Witte, Jr.; Scrutinizing Polygamy Under Religious Freedom Restoration Acts Maura Irene Strassberg; Part V. Religious Claims at End of Life: Religion and Advance Medical Directives: Formulation and Enforcement Implications Richard L. Kaplan; Personal Religious Identity at the End of Life Naomi Cahn and Reverend Amy

Ziettlow; Part VI. Shaping the Legal Culture of the Family: Taking Colliding Trains Off a Collision Path: Lessons from the Utah Compromise for Civil Society J. Stuart Adams; Family Law and Civil Rights Movements: Examining the Influence of Courts and Legislatures on Racial and Sexual Orientation Equality Anthony Michael Kreis; Latter-Day Constitutionalism: Sexuality, Gender, and Mormons William N. Eskridge, Jr.; Part VII. International Perspectives: The Future of Marriage in Secular Societies Patrick M. Parkinson; A Tale of Fragmentation and Intertwinement: The Sacred and the Secular Systems for Forming and Dissolving Marriages in Israel Karin Carmit Yefet and Arianne Renan Barzilay; Religious Modesty for Women and Girls: A Comparative Analysis of Legal Protections in France and the United States Asma T. Uddin.

Subjects   Domestic relations--United States.
Freedom of religion--United States.
Religious minorities--Legal status, laws, etc.--United States.
Law / Family Law / General.

Notes   Includes bibliographical references and index.

The curious case of Kiryas Joel: the rise of a village theocracy and the battle to defend the separation of church and state

LCCN   2015048056
Type of material   Book
Personal name   Grumet, Louis, author.
Main title   The curious case of Kiryas Joel: the rise of a village theocracy and the battle to defend the

	separation of church and state / Louis Grumet, John M. Caher; foreword by Judith S. Kaye.
Published/Produced	Chicago, Illinois: Chicago Review Press, [2016]
Description	xii, 286 pages; 24 cm
ISBN	9781613735008 (hardback)
LC classification	KF228.K565 G78 2016
Related names	Caher, John M., author.
Summary	"Twenty years ago, on the last day of session, the New York State Legislature created a publicly funded school district to cater to the interests of a religious sect called Kiryas Joel, an extremely insular group of Hasidic Jews. The sect had bought land in upstate New York, populated it solely with members of its faction, and created a village that exerted extraordinary political pressure over both political parties in the Legislature. Marking the first time in American history that a governmental unit was established for a religious group, the Legislature's action prompted years of litigation that eventually went to the Supreme Court. The 1994 case, The Board of Education of the Village of Kiryas Joel v. Grumet, stands as the most important legal precedent in the fight to uphold the separation of church and state. In The Curious Case of Kiryas Joel, plaintiff Louis Grumet opens a window onto the Satmar Hasidic community and details the inside story of his fight for the First Amendment. Informed by numerous interviews, media accounts, court transcripts, and more, The Curious Case of Kiryas Joel tantalizes with a peek at cynical power politics driven by votes. This story--a blend of politics, religion, cultural clashes, and constitutional tension--is an object lesson in the

ongoing debate over freedom of vs. freedom from religion"-- Provided by publisher.

"The 1994 US Supreme Court case Board of Education of Kiryas Joel Village School District v. Grumet stands as the most important legal precedent in the fight to uphold the separation of church and state. In this book, plaintiff Louis Grumet opens a window onto the insular sect of Hasidic Jews at the center of the case, and details the inside story of his fight for the First Amendment and against New York's most powerful politicians"-- Provided by publisher.

Contents Prologue: "curious" Joel -- A new homeland -- Who moves in? -- Who governs? -- Who educates? -- Who is worshipped? -- Who litigates? -- Who is our adversary? -- Here comes the judge -- Establishment -- Reviewing the decision -- Does it pass the test? -- Would the Supreme Court care? -- The Supreme Court opens the door -- Strange bedfellows -- May it please the court -- Judicial deliberations -- Supremely decided -- Déjà Vu -- Epilogue.

Subjects Kiryas Joel Union Free School District (Monroe, N.Y.)--Trials, litigation, etc.

Satmar Hasidim--New York (State)--Kiryas Joel--Trials, litigation, etc.

Satmar Hasidim--Legal status, laws, etc.--New York (State)--Kiryas Joel.

Religion in the public schools--Law and legislation--New York (State)

Jewish religious education of children with disabilities--New York (State)--Kiryas Joel.

Jewish religious schools--New York (State)--Kiryas Joel.

	Freedom of religion--United States.
	Church and state--United States.
	Law / Constitutional.
	Law / Legal History.
	History / United States / 21st Century.
	History / United States / State & Local / Middle Atlantic (DC, DE, MD, NJ, NY, PA).
	Political Science / Government / Judicial Branch.
	Religion / Judaism / Conservative.
Notes	Includes bibliographical references (pages 269-276) and index.
Additional formats	Online version: Grumet, Louis, author. Curious case of Kiryas Joel Chicago: Chicago Review Press, 2016 9781613735015 (DLC) 2015048469

The Deoband madrassah movement: countercultural trends and tendencies

LCCN	2014046372
Type of material	Book
Personal name	Moj, Muhammad, author.
Main title	The Deoband madrassah movement: countercultural trends and tendencies / Muhammad Moj.
Published/Produced	London: Anthem Press, 2015. ©2015
ISBN	9781783083886 (hardcover: alkaline paper) 9781783083893 (papercover: alkaline paper)
LC classification	BP166.14.D4 M65 2015
Contents	The Deoband madrassah movement (DMM): research context -- Origin of the DMM: seeds of a counterculture -- The DMM in united India: activist countercultural trends -- The DMM in Pakistan: countercultural politics and extremism -- Deobandi Islam: countering folk Islam and

	popular custom -- The DMM versus mainstream society: viewpoints of Deobandi journals and students.
Subjects	Deoband School (Islam)
	Islam and politics--Pakistan.
	Islamic religious education--Pakistan.
	Islamic fundamentalism--Pakistan.
Notes	Includes bibliographical references and index.
Series	Diversity and plurality in South Asia

The economics of religion in India

LCCN	2018002799
Type of material	Book
Personal name	Iyer, Sriya, author.
Main title	The economics of religion in India / Sriya Iyer.
Published/Produced	Cambridge, Massachusetts: The Belknap Press of Harvard University Press, 2018.
ISBN	9780674979642 (alk. paper)
LC classification	HB72 .I945 2018
Summary	Based on research conducted in India for over a decade, The Economics of Religion in India outlines the historical growth of religion and contemporary attitudes towards it in the country. The study of religion is related to broader themes of religious conflict and extremism, especially Hindu-Muslim riots since 1950. The book contributes to the economics of religion by discussing how religion relates to growing inequality in India, changes in demography, socio-economic status, and religious competition. The author presents original research findings from a survey of 600 Hindu, Muslim, Christian, Jain and Sikh religious organizations across seven Indian states with respect to their religious and

	nonreligious provision of such services as health and education. In addition, she discusses the introduction of mathematics, science, English, and computers into traditional religious curricula; and explores the marketing, communication, and branding of religion in India. Ultimately, the book aims to inform economic and social policy in countries with religiously pluralistic populations.-- Provided by publisher
Contents	What is religion and how do economists think about it? -- Religion and religious conflict in Indian life -- The survey of religious organizations -- Temples and economists: religious services -- Faith and the faithful: non-religious services -- Inequality, demography, and socio-economic status -- The modern madrasa: a cast study of religious education in India -- Religious competition and religious marketing.
Subjects	Religion and sociology--India.
	Social conflict--India--Religious aspects.
	India--Religion--Economic aspects.
Notes	Includes bibliographical references and index.

The empirical science of religious education

LCCN	2015031453
Type of material	Book
Main title	The empirical science of religious education / edited by Mandy Robbins and Leslie J. Francis.
Published/Produced	London; New York: Routledge, Taylor & Francis Group, 2016.
Description	xxxii, 290 pages; 24 cm
ISBN	9781138929852 (hardback)
LC classification	BV1471.3 .E528 2016
Related titles	British journal of religious education.

Related names	Robbins, Mandy, editor of compilation.
	Francis, Leslie J., editor of compilation.
Subjects	Religious education--Cross-cultural studies.
Notes	Articles originally published in the British journal of religious education.
	Includes bibliographical references and indexes.

The future of publicly funded faith schools: a critical perspective

LCCN	2017054390
Type of material	Book
Personal name	Pring, Richard, author.
Main title	The future of publicly funded faith schools: a critical perspective / Richard Pring.
Published/Produced	London; New York: Routledge, Taylor & Francis Group, 2018.
Description	x, 182 pages; 24 cm
ISBN	9781138569676 (hardback)
	9781138569683 (pbk.)
LC classification	LC116.G7 P75 2018
Summary	"The Future of Publicly Funded Faith Schools addresses and critically examines the arguments both for and against the continued maintenance of faith-based schools within a publicly funded state system. Addressing the issue systemically, first grounding the discussion in the practical world of education before raising the central philosophical issues stemming from faith-based education, it provides a balanced synthesis of the different arguments surrounding faith schools. The book expounds upon the different threats facing faith-based schools, including their perceived potential to undermine social cohesion within a multicultural society, and the questioning of their right to receive public funding, and examines

what these mean for their future. Examining these threats, it questions: - What it means for a school to be 'faith-based' - The nature of religious education both within and without a faith-based school environment - The ethical, epistemological and political issues arising from faith-based education - The concepts of the common good and social cohesion - Whether there is possible reconciliation between opposing parties The Future of Publicly Funded Faith Schools makes a unique contribution to the literature in this area and is crucial reading for anyone interested in what the future holds for publicly funded faith schools including academics, researchers and postgraduate students in the fields of education, religious studies, policy and politics of education, sociology and philosophy"-- Provided by publisher.

Contents Contemporary political and cultural context -- Historical background and the current position -- Making sense of facts and figures -- International perspective -- Three traditions -- Response to the secular age -- Religious education: an extended vision -- Service to society -- Ethics: education and its aims -- Espitemology: knowledge, truth and reason in religious education -- Civic society: common good and social pluralism -- For or against faith schools? Finding an answer.

Subjects Religion in the public schools--Great Britain. Church and education--Great Britain.

Notes Includes bibliographical references and indexes.

The grace of playing: pedagogies for learning into God's new creation
LCCN 2016301880

Type of material	Book
Personal name	Goto, Courtney T. author
Main title	The grace of playing: pedagogies for learning into God's new creation / Courtney T. Goto.
Published/Produced	Eugene, Oregon: Pickwick Publications, [2016] ©2016
Description	xxi, 149 pages: illustrations; 23 cm.
ISBN	9781498233002
	1498233007
LC classification	BV1464 .G68 2016
Subjects	Teaching--Religious aspects--Christianity.
	Play--Religious aspects--Christianity.
	Christian education--Philosophy.
Notes	Includes bibliographical reference (pages 139-149)
Series	Horizons in religious education

The jarring road to democratic inclusion

LCCN	2016029375
Type of material	Book
Main title	The jarring road to democratic inclusion / edited by Aviad Rubin and Yusuf Sarfati.
Published/Produced	Lanham: Lexington Books, [2016]
Description	ix, 254 pages: illustrations; 24 cm
ISBN	9781498525077 (cloth: alk. paper)
	(ebook)
LC classification	DS119.8.T9 J37 2016
Cover title	The jarring road to democratic inclusion: a comparative assessment of state-society engagements in Israel and Turkey
Related names	Rubin, Aviad, editor.
	Sarfati, Yusuf, 1977- editor.
Summary	This edited volume brings together chapters that offer theoretically pertinent comparisons between

various dimensions of Israeli and Turkish politics. Each chapter covers a different aspect of state-society interactions in both countries from a comparative perspective, including the public role of religion, political culture, women rights movements, religious education, religious movements, marriage regulation, labor market inclusion, and ethnic minorities.

Contents Introduction: Israel and Turkey in comparative perspective / Yusuf Sarfati and Aviad Rubin -- Contesting the religious in a (secular) democracy: a comparative assessment of the theoretical, judicial, and political approaches to the public role of religion / Sultan Tepe -- Political mobilization through religious schooling: a comparison of Ma'ayan schools in Israel and Imam Hatip schools in Turkey / Yusuf Sarfati -- Challenges to the religious-political establishment: the cases of anticapitalist Muslims in Turkey and women of the wall in Israel / Gözde Erdeniz -- Comparative trajectories of the women's movement in Israel and Turkey: transforming policy and agendas in divided societies / Canan Aslan Akman -- Dominant vs. hegemonic tendencies as critical features in Israel's and Turkey's political cultures / Aviad Rubin -- Elections 2015: Israel and Turkey-the joint list and the HDP / Louis Fishman -- Marriage regulation in Israel and Turkey: the interplay between institutional dynamics and public preferences / Niva Golan-Nadir -- On the margins of social citizenship: Turkish women in Germany and Palestinian women in Israel / Inna Michaeli.

Subjects Israel--Foreign relations--Turkey.

	Turkey--Foreign relations--Israel.
	Israel--Politics and government.
	Turkey--Politics and government.
Notes	Includes bibliographical references and index.
Additional formats	Online version: Jarring road to democratic inclusion Lanham: Lexington Books, [2016] 9781498525084 (DLC) 2016031871

The Jewish educator's companion: practical tools and inspirational ideas

LCCN	2017012315
Type of material	Book
Personal name	Frankel, Batsheva, author.
Main title	The Jewish educator's companion: practical tools and inspirational ideas / Batsheva Frankel.
Published/Produced	Springfield, NJ: Behrman House, Inc., [2017] ©2017
Description	197 pages; 28 cm
ISBN	9780874419948 (pbk.)
LC classification	BM727 .F65 2017
Subjects	Jewish students--Religious life--Handbooks, manuals, etc.
	Jewish religious education--Activity programs.

The ministry of religious education

LCCN	2015947049
Type of material	Book
Personal name	Sallwasser, Carrie, author.
Main title	The ministry of religious education / Carrie Sallwasser.
Published/Produced	Collegeville, Minnesota: Liturgical Press, [2016] ©2016
Description	xi, 76 pages; 21 cm.

Links	Contributor biographical information https://www.loc.gov/catdir/enhancements/fy1614/2015947049-b.html
	Publisher description https://www.loc.gov/catdir/enhancements/fy1614/2015947049-d.html
ISBN	0814649521
	9780814649527
LC classification	BX1918 .S34 2016
Summary	"Ministering as a catechist is one of the highest callings within the church. Your 'yes' to this calling, for whatever reason, needs to be affirmed and supported by an understanding of the ministry of catechesis, your role as minister, the audience to whom you are ministering, and the art of this ministry. Carrie Sallwasser offers an overview of the ministry of religious education for novice and veteran catechists alike that will aid in their on-going formation as catechists in the ministry of forming disciples."--Publisher description.
Contents	Preface: the Good Samaritan catechist -- Introduction: what have I done? -- The ministry, or What and Why? -- The minister, or It's all about me -- The ministered of catechesis, or Who do I teach? -- The art of religious education, or What and how do I teach? -- Beatitudes for catechists.
Subjects	Catechists--Catholic Church.
	Religious education--Teacher training.
Notes	Includes bibliographical references (page 75).
Series	Collegeville ministry series

The Oxford handbook of religion and American education

LCCN	2017052755
Type of material	Book

Main title	The Oxford handbook of religion and American education / edited by Michael D. Waggoner and Nathan C. Walker; foreword by Martin E Marty.
Published/Produced	New York, NY: Oxford University Press, [2018]
Description	xxvi, 493 pages; 26 cm.
ISBN	9780199386819 (cloth)
LC classification	BL42.5.U5 O95 2018
Related names	Waggoner, Michael, editor.
Subjects	Religious education--United States.
Notes	Includes bibliographical references (pages 464-465) and index.
Additional formats	Online version: Oxford handbook of religion and American education New York: Oxford University Press, 2018 9780199386826 (DLC) 2018026651
Series	Oxford handbooks

The Oxford handbook of religion and American education

LCCN	2018026651
Type of material	Book
Main title	The Oxford handbook of religion and American education / edited by Michael D. Waggoner and Nathan C. Walker.
Published/Produced	New York: Oxford University Press, 2018.
Description	1 online resource.
ISBN	9780199386826 (updf)
	9780199386833 (online content)
LC classification	BL42.5.U5
Related names	Waggoner, Michael, editor.
Subjects	Religious education--United States.
Notes	Includes bibliographical references and index.
Additional formats	Print version: Oxford handbook of religion and American education New York: Oxford

	University Press, 2018 9780199386819 (DLC) 2017052755
Series	Oxford handbooks

The purposeful graduate: why colleges must talk to students about vocation

LCCN	2014033596
Type of material	Book
Personal name	Clydesdale, Timothy T. (Timothy Thomas), 1965- author.
Main title	The purposeful graduate: why colleges must talk to students about vocation / Tim Clydesdale.
Published/Produced	Chicago; London: The University of Chicago Press, [2015]
Description	xxiii, 334 pages; 24 cm
ISBN	9780226236346 (cloth: alk. paper) 9780226236483 (e-book)
LC classification	LC1037.5 .C594 2015
Contents	Purposeful paths -- Contexts -- Matters of design -- Students -- Faculty and staff -- Strategies and ecologies -- Larger lessons -- Appendix 1: list of participating institutions in the Lilly Endowment Inc.'s programs for the theological exploration of vocation initiative, 2000-2009 -- Appendix 2: methodology -- Appendix 3: interview and survey questions -- Appendix 4: visited campuses, program participation, and post award continuation -- Appendix 5: resources for purpose exploration programming.
Subjects	Career education--United States. Religious education--United States. College students--Recruiting--United States.
Notes	Includes bibliographical references and index.

The religious men in Jebel Marra: the process of learning and the performance of Islamic rituals and practices

LCCN	2017449211
Type of material	Book
Personal name	Mohammed, Bakheit M. Nur, author.
Main title	The religious men in Jebel Marra: the process of learning and the performance of Islamic rituals and practices / Bakheit M. Nur Mohammed.
Published/Produced	Berlin: Lit Verlag, [2017] ©2017
Description	404 pages: illustrations (some color), map; 23 cm.
ISBN	9783643909169 (pbk.) 3643909160 (pbk.) (online)
LC classification	BP43.S73 M632 2017
Summary	"The study investigates how Muslim religious specialists (fuqarâ, sing. fakî) acquire Qur'anic knowledge in the context of the 'communities of practice'. It contextualises the Qur'anic schools of Jebel Marra in the Sudan arguing that the fuqarâ increase their access to knowledge of the Qur'an by socially interacting with each other. The book is grounded in a[n] ethnographic study of Qur'anic memorisation and activities that the fuqarâ perform after graduation from Qur'anic schools. It thus provides a fresh perspective to Islamic learning and epistemology. 'The great value of the study lies in the author's reconstruction of the practices and techniques, cognitive and corporeal, which are systematically employed to memorise the whole of the Qur'an"-- Page 4 of cover.
Contents	Introduction -- Islam among the Fur -- The Qur'anic schools: their spatial and social organisations -- Learning stages: the acquisition

	of knowledge in a social context -- The impact of the Darfur conflict on Qur'anic schools and traditional Islamic culture -- The graduates of Qur'anic schools and the interconnection between knowledge and work -- Activities of the prominent fuqarâ: the teaching, writing, and performance of the communal rituals -- Activities of the ordinary fuqarâ: performance of the individual rituals -- Conclusion: the fuqarâ, their learning style and activities.
Subjects	Qur'an--Study and teaching--Sudan--Marra Mountains.
	Islamic religious education--Sudan--Marra Mountains.
	Muslim scholars--Sudan--Marra Mountains.
	Muslim men--Religious life--Sudan--Marra Mountains.
	Islam--Sudan--Marra Mountains--Customs and practices.
	Islam--Sudan--Marra Mountains--Rituals.
	Fur (African people)--Religion.
	Anthropology of religion--Sudan--Marra Mountains.
Notes	Includes bibliographical references (pages 387-403).
Dissertation note	Originally presented as the author's thesis (doctoral)--BIGSAS, Universität Bayreuth, 2016.
Additional formats	(GyWOH)har175018895
Series	Beiträge zur Afrikaforschung, 0938-7285; Band 81
	Beiträge zur Afrikaforschung; Bd. 81. 0938-7285

The resilience of religion in American higher education
LCCN 2018007019

Type of material	Book
Personal name	Schmalzbauer, John Arnold, 1968- author.
Main title	The resilience of religion in American higher education / John Schmalzbauer and Kathleen A. Mahoney.
Published/Produced	Waco, Texas: Baylor University Press, [2018]
Description	283 pages; 24 cm
ISBN	9781481308717 (hardback: alk. paper)
LC classification	BL42.5.U5 S36 2018
Related names	Mahoney, Kathleen A., 1957- author.
Subjects	Religion--Study and teaching (Higher)--United States.
	Religious education--United States.
	Universities and colleges--Curricula--United States.
	Education, Higher.
Notes	Includes bibliographical references and index.
Additional formats	Online version: Schmalzbauer, John Arnold, 1968- author. Resilience of religion in American higher education Waco, Texas: Baylor University Press, [2018] 9781481308885 (DLC) 2018039644

The resilience of religion in American higher education

LCCN	2018039644
Type of material	Book
Personal name	Schmalzbauer, John Arnold, 1968- author.
Main title	The resilience of religion in American higher education / John Schmalzbauer and Kathleen A. Mahoney.
Published/Produced	Waco, Texas: Baylor University Press, [2018]
Description	1 online resource.
ISBN	9781481308885 (Web PDF)
	9781481308878 (ebook-Mobi/Kindle)

	9781481308731 (ePub)
LC classification	BL42.5.U5
Related names	Mahoney, Kathleen A., 1957- author.
Subjects	Religion--Study and teaching (Higher)--United States.
	Religious education--United States.
	Universities and colleges--Curricula--United States.
	Education, Higher.
Notes	Includes bibliographical references and index.
Additional formats	Print version: Schmalzbauer, John Arnold, 1968- author. Resilience of religion in American higher education Waco, Texas: Baylor University Press, [2018] 9781481308717 (DLC) 2018007019

The role of madrasas: assessing parental choice, financial pipelines and recent developments in religious education in Pakistan & Afghanistan

LCCN	2018322317
Type of material	Book
Main title	The role of madrasas: assessing parental choice, financial pipelines and recent developments in religious education in Pakistan & Afghanistan / edited by David Vestenskov.
Published/Produced	Copenhagen: Royal Danish Defence College, 2017.
Description	153 pages: Illustrations; 28 cm
ISBN	9788771472134
LC classification	BP43.P18 .R65 2017
Related names	Vestenskov, David, editor.
	Center for Global & Strategic Studies.
Subjects	Islamic religious education--Pakistan.
	Islamic religious education--Afghanistan.
	Madrasahs--Pakistan.

	Madrasahs--Afghanistan.
	Terrorism--Religious aspects--Islam.
	Islamic fundamentalism--Pakistan.
	Islamic fundamentalism--Afghanistan.
Notes	Includes bibliographical references.

The Routledge handbook of Turkish politics

LCCN	2018049246
Type of material	Book
Main title	The Routledge handbook of Turkish politics / edited by Alpaslan Özerdem and Matthew Whiting.
Published/Produced	Milton Park, Abingdon, Oxon; New York, NY: Routledge, 2019.
ISBN	9781138500556 (hardback) (ebook)
LC classification	DR576 .R68 2019
Portion of title	Handbook of Turkish politics
Related names	Özerdem, Alpaslan, editor.
	Whiting, Matthew. editor.
Summary	Turkey is going through possibly the most turbulent period in its history, with major consequences both nationally and internationally. The country today looks dramatically different from the Republic founded by Atatürk in 1923 on values including republicanism and laicism. The pace of change has been rapid and fundamental, with core interlinked changes in ruling institutions, political culture, political economy, and society. Divided into six main parts, this Handbook provides a single-source overview of Turkish politics: - Part I: History and the making of Contemporary Turkey - Part II: Politics and Institutions - Part III: The Economy, Environment

Contents

and Development - Part IV: The Kurdish Insurgency and Security - Part V: State, Society and Rights - Part VI: External Relations This comprehensive Handbook is an essential resource for students of Politics, International Relations, International/Security Studies with an interest on contemporary Turkey.

History and the making of contemporary Turkey -- Turkish politics: structures and dynamics / Samim Akgönul & Baskin Oran -- Turkey's never ending search for democracy / Ilter Turan -- Turkish secularism: looking forward and beyond the west / Murat Somer -- Political Islam / Kristin Fabbe & Efe Murat Balikçioglu -- The politics of Turkish nationalism: continuity and change / Durukan Kuzu -- Politics and institutions -- Elections, parties and the party system / Ersin Kalaycioglu -- The presidency: from independence to the AKP / Menderes Çinar & Nalan Soyarik Sentürk -- Civil military relations / Metin Heper -- NGOs and civil society / Markus Ketola -- The media and media policy / Eylm Yanardagoglu -- The economy, environment and development -- Political economy / Ali Burak Güven -- Energy security and policy: between bandwagoning and hedging / H. Akin Ünver -- The politics of environment and climate change / Ümit Sahin -- The economic role of cities / Stephen Karam -- Governing the diaspora(s) and the limits of diaspora diplomacy / Bahar Baser -- Disaster management policy and governance / Helena Hermansson & Naim Kapucu -- The Kurdish insurgency and security -- The Kurdish question / Zeynep N. Kaya & Matthew Whiting -

-- The Kurdish insurgency / David Romano -- The perennial Kurdish question and failed peace processes / Cengiz Çandar -- Terrorism, counter-insurgency and societal relations / Gareth Jenkins -- The village guard system: counter-insurgency and local collaboration / Evren Balta -- The 15 July 2016 failed coup and the security sector / Yaprak Gürsoy -- State, society and rights -- Human rights / Zehra F. Kabasakal Arat -- Politics and the women's movement / Sevgi Adak -- Religious minorities / Samim Akgönül -- Religious education / Bekir S. Gür -- The transformation of health and healthcare / Enis Baris -- External relations -- Foreign policy, 1923-2018 / Mustafa Aydin -- Resetting foreign policy in a time of global turmoil / E. Fuat Keyman -- Turkey and its neighbours in the Middle East: Iran, Iraq and Syria / Behlül Özkan -- US-Turkish relations in turmoil / Kemal Kirisci -- Turkey and Russia / Pavel K. Baev -- Forgotten promises and the possibilities for reviving relations between Turkey and the EU / Füsun Özerdem -- Turkey's Cyprus policy in transition / Birol A. Yesilada -- Turkey-NATO relations: strategic imperatives, identity-building and predicaments / Müge Kinacioglu -- Turkey and UN peace keeping missions / Haluk Karadag -- Turkey as an emerging global humanitarian and peacebuilding actor / Alpaslan Özerdem.

Subjects   Kurds--Turkey--Politics and government--20th century.

Kurds--Turkey--Politics and government--21st century.

Turkey--Politics and government--20th century.

	Turkey--Politics and government--21st century.
	Turkey--Economic conditions.
	Turkey--Economic policy.
	Turkey--Foreign relations.
Notes	Non-Latin script record
	Includes bibliographical references and index.
Additional formats	Online version: Routledge handbook of Turkish politics Milton Park, Abingdon, Oxon; New York, NY: Routledge, 2019 9781315143842 (DLC) 2018051152

The Routledge handbook of Turkish politics

LCCN	2018051152
Type of material	Book
Main title	The Routledge handbook of Turkish politics / edited by Alpaslan Özerdem and Matthew Whiting.
Published/Produced	Milton Park, Abingdon, Oxon; New York, NY: Routledge, 2019.
Description	1 online resource.
ISBN	9781315143842 (master)
	9781351387477 (Adobe Reader)
	9781351387460 (Epub)
	9781351387453 (Mobipocket)
LC classification	DR576
Portion of title	Handbook of Turkish politics
Related names	Özerdem, Alpaslan, editor.
	Whiting, Matthew. editor.
Summary	Turkey is going through possibly the most turbulent period in its history, with major consequences both nationally and internationally. The country today looks dramatically different from the Republic founded by Atatürk in 1923 on values including republicanism and laicism. The

pace of change has been rapid and fundamental, with core interlinked changes in ruling institutions, political culture, political economy, and society. Divided into six main parts, this Handbook provides a single-source overview of Turkish politics: - Part I: History and the making of Contemporary Turkey - Part II: Politics and Institutions - Part III: The Economy, Environment and Development - Part IV: The Kurdish Insurgency and Security - Part V: State, Society and Rights - Part VI: External Relations This comprehensive Handbook is an essential resource for students of Politics, International Relations, International/Security Studies with an interest on contemporary Turkey.

Contents

History and the making of contemporary Turkey -- Turkish politics: structures and dynamics / Samim Akgönul & Baskin Oran -- Turkey's never ending search for democracy / Ilter Turan -- Turkish secularism: looking forward and beyond the west / Murat Somer -- Political Islam / Kristin Fabbe & Efe Murat Balikçioglu -- The politics of Turkish nationalism: continuity and change / Durukan Kuzu -- Politics and institutions -- Elections, parties and the party system / Ersin Kalaycioglu -- The presidency: from independence to the AKP / Menderes Çinar & Nalan Soyarik Sentürk -- Civil military relations / Metin Heper -- NGOs and civil society / Markus Ketola -- The media and media policy / Eylm Yanardagoglu -- The economy, environment and development -- Political economy / Ali Burak Güven -- Energy security and policy: between bandwagoning and hedging / H. Akin Ünver --

The politics of environment and climate change / Ümit Sahin -- The economic role of cities / Stephen Karam -- Governing the diaspora(s) and the limits of diaspora diplomacy / Bahar Baser -- Disaster management policy and governance / Helena Hermansson & Naim Kapucu -- The Kurdish insurgency and security -- The Kurdish question / Zeynep N. Kaya & Matthew Whiting -- The Kurdish insurgency / David Romano -- The perennial Kurdish question and failed peace processes / Cengiz Çandar -- Terrorism, counter-insurgency and societal relations / Gareth Jenkins -- The village guard system: counter-insurgency and local collaboration / Evren Balta -- The 15 July 2016 failed coup and the security sector / Yaprak Gürsoy -- State, society and rights -- Human rights / Zehra F. Kabasakal Arat -- Politics and the women's movement / Sevgi Adak -- Religious minorities / Samim Akgönül -- Religious education / Bekir S. Gür -- The transformation of health and healthcare / Enis Baris -- External relations -- Foreign policy, 1923-2018 / Mustafa Aydin -- Resetting foreign policy in a time of global turmoil / E. Fuat Keyman -- Turkey and its neighbours in the Middle East: Iran, Iraq and Syria / Behlül Özkan -- US-Turkish relations in turmoil / Kemal Kirisci -- Turkey and Russia / Pavel K. Baev -- Forgotten promises and the possibilities for reviving relations between Turkey and the EU / Füsun Özerdem -- Turkey's Cyprus policy in transition / Birol A. Yesilada -- Turkey-NATO relations: strategic imperatives, identity-building and predicaments / Müge Kinacioglu -- Turkey and UN peace keeping

	missions / Haluk Karadag -- Turkey as an emerging global humanitarian and peacebuilding actor / Alpaslan Özerdem.
Subjects	Kurds--Turkey--Politics and government--20th century.
	Kurds--Turkey--Politics and government--21st century.
	Turkey--Politics and government--20th century.
	Turkey--Politics and government--21st century.
	Turkey--Economic conditions.
	Turkey--Economic policy.
	Turkey--Foreign relations.
Notes	Non-Latin script record
	Includes bibliographical references and index.
Additional formats	Print version: Routledge handbook of Turkish politics Milton Park, Abingdon, Oxon; New York, NY: Routledge, 2019 9781138500556 (DLC) 2018049246

The SAGE handbook of curriculum, pedagogy and assessment

LCCN	2015941576
Type of material	Book
Main title	The SAGE handbook of curriculum, pedagogy and assessment / edited by Dominic Wyse, Louise Hayward and Jessica Pandya.
Published/Produced	Los Angeles: SAGE reference, [2016]
	©2016
Description	2 volumes (xxx, ix, 1063 pages): illustrations; 26 cm
ISBN	9781446297025 (set; hbk.)
	1446297020 (set; hbk.)
	(set; ebook)
Portion of title	Curriculum, pedagogy and assessment
Related names	Wyse, Dominic, 1964- editor.

Contents

Hayward, Louise (E. Louise), editor.
Pandya, Jessica Zacher, editor.

Gender and the curriculum / Jannette Elwood -- Children's rights and student voice: their intersections and the implications for curriculum and pedagogy / Laura Lundy and Alison Cook-Sather -- Alongside virtual youth using the internet: creating and researching learning interactions / Vic Lally -- Curriculum and teacher development / Jerry Rosiek and D. Jean Clandinin -- Curriculum and pedagogy: the future of teacher professional learning and the development of adaptive expertise / Deidre Le Fevre, Helen Timperley and Fiona Ell -- Pedagogy and curriculum - teachers as learners / Kay Livingston -- Visual art / Richard Hickman and Rebecca Heaton -- The performing arts in learning, curriculum and culture / Anton Franks -- The 'value' of computers and computing: toward a new axiology of educational technology / Mark Evan Nelson -- Geography / David Lambert -- History curriculum: a transatlantic analysis / Tim Keirn -- World languages curriculum Amalia Llombart-Huesca -- Physical education / Mike Jess and Malcolm Thorburn -- Religious education / Leonard Franchi, James Conroy and Stephen McKinney -- Science education and economic growth: some implications for curriculum, pedagogy and assessment / Derek Bell and Petra Skiebe-Corrette -- Assessing pre-college engineering education curricula: a holistic and practice-oriented perspective / James Teslow, Yan Sun and Johannes Strobel -- Environmental and Sustainability education: a fragile history of the present / Margaret Somerville -- Assessment for learning: a pedagogical tool / Kari Smith -- Implementing assessment for learning in a Confucius context: the case of Hong Kong 2004-14 / Ricky Lam -- Assessment for learning community: learners, teachers and policymakers / Mary F. Hill -- Curriculum reform in testing and accountability contexts / Val Klenowski and Merilyn Carter -- Professional standards and the assessment work of teachers / Claire Maree Wyatt-Smith and Anne Looney -- Curriculum in the twenty-first century and the future of examinations / Jo-Anne Baird and Therese N. Hopfenbeck -- Student assessment and its relationship with curriculum, teaching and learning in the twenty-first century / Deborah Nusche -- National assessment and intelligent accountability / Sandra Johnson -- Economic impact of education: evidence and relevance / Kristinn Hermannsson -- Public and private boundaries in curriculum and educational policy / Vera Peroni -- International assessments of student learning outcomes / Andreas Schleicher -- Comparison and countries / Esther Care and Bruce Beswick -- Effects of globalized assessment on local curricula: what Japanese teachers face and how they challenge it / Shinya Takekawa -- The ebb and flow of curricular autonomy: balance between local freedom and national prescription in curricula / Claire Sinnema -- National standards in policy and practice / Michael Moore, Don Zancanella and JuliAnna Avila -- Curriculum development and school

	leadership: unattainable responsibility or realistic ambition? / Ciaran Sugrue -- Teacher education - making connections with curriculum, pedagogy and assessment / Ian Menter.
Subjects	Education--Curricula.
	Curriculum-based assessment.
	Curriculum-based assessment.
	Education--Curricula.
Notes	Includes bibliographical references and index.

The scriptural universe of ancient Christianity

LCCN	2016015530
Type of material	Book
Personal name	Stroumsa, Guy G., author.
Main title	The scriptural universe of ancient Christianity / Guy G. Stroumsa.
Published/Produced	Cambridge, Massachusetts: Harvard University Press, 2016.
Description	184 pages; 25 cm
ISBN	9780674545137 (cloth)
LC classification	BL71 .S77 2016
Summary	Late antiquity saw a revolution in literate culture the consequences of which, for more than a millennium, were no less dramatic than those of the invention of the movable type in early modernity. Both the transformation of the physical support of the books (from scroll to codex) and also, more importantly, the redaction of foundational texts of new religions, permitted the birth and growth of new, world religions, such as Christianity, Manichaeism, and then Islam. Within and without the borders of the Roman Empire, it was often in translation that those texts circulated, and that commentaries were

elaborated, usually in writing but also orally. But the status of books underwent in the Roman world even more radical changes, which have to do with their central role in religion and religious education. Books, including sacred books, had of course existed in archaic and ancient societies, but they were now invested with a new status as they were taking the place previously held by sacrifice at the very core of ritual.-- Provided by publisher

Subjects Sacred books--History and criticism.
Church history--Primitive and early church, ca. 30-600.
Christianity and other religions.
Books--Religious aspects--Christianity.
Notes Includes index.

The Unitarian Universalist pocket guide
LCCN 2018052452
Type of material Book
Main title The Unitarian Universalist pocket guide / edited by Rev. Susan Frederick-Gray.
Edition Sixth edition.
Published/Produced Boston: Skinner House Books, [2019]
ISBN 9781558968264 (pbk.)
LC classification BX9841.3 .U55 2019
Related names Frederick-Gray, Susan, 1975- editor.
Summary "Now in its 6th edition, The Unitarian Universalist Pocket Guide is one of the most complete introductions to Unitarian Universalism available, covering ministry, worship, religious education, social justice, and history"-- Provided by publisher.
Contents Our faith / Rosemary Bray McNatt -- Bringing my whole self / Takiyah Amin -- Saving our lives /

Roberta Finkelstein -- A search for truth and meaning / Aneesa Shaikh -- The playground atheist gets saved / Jake Morrill -- Not the last to need saving / Megan Dowdell -- Our ministry / Cheryl Walker -- A minister's testimony / Nic Cable -- Our worship / Erika Hewitt -- A worship associate's testimony / Karen Valbuena -- Our religious education / Jessica York -- A religious educator's testimony / Joy Berry -- Our work for social justice / Elizabeth Nguyen -- Activists' testimony / Susan and Mac Goekler -- Our justice communities / Aisha Hauser -- A lay leader's testimony / Karla Baehr -- Our roots / Dan McKanan.

Subjects   Unitarian Universalist Association.
Notes   Includes bibliographical references.

Theology at the crossroads of university, church and society: dialogue, difference and Catholic identity

LCCN   2017275277
Type of material   Book
Personal name   Boeve, L. (Lieven), author.
Uniform title   Theologie in dialoog. English
Main title   Theology at the crossroads of university, church and society: dialogue, difference and Catholic identity / Lieven Boeve.
Published/Produced   London; New York, NY: Bloomsbury T & T Clark, an imprint of Bloomsbury Publishing Plc, 2016.
Description   vii, 239 pages; 24 cm
ISBN   9780567672209 (hardback)
0567672204 (hardback)
(ePDF)
(ePub)

LC classification   BX1753 .B6413 2016

Summary   Lieven Boeve examines the place of theology in the university, the church and society. He emphasizes that theology certainly belongs to all of these three domains as it belongs to the nature of theology to involve itself in all three spheres, especially at the crossroads where they overlap. Boeve discusses the recent document Theology Today from the International Theological Commission which circumscribes theology's place and task in the Catholic Church. Boeve discusses how the difficult relation between theology and philosophy is typical for a Church which has difficulty with the dialogue in today's world; as well as examines the relation between theology and religious studies. Going further, Boeve offers a reflection on Catholic identity today, focusing more specifically on education. He presents four models for considering the identity of Catholic schools in the light of the changed society and argues that dialogue in a context of plurality and difference can lead to new, fruitful ways to shape even the Catholic identity. Boeve concludes his discussion with a short assessment of Pope Benedict's papacy and emphasizes the need for the Catholic Church to convert itself before it can call the world to do the same.

Contents   Introduction: In the margin and at the crossroads. Part 1: Foundation, horizon and location. Foundation: revelation as God's dialogue with people and history; Horizon: the challenge of plurality and difference; Location: from the margins and at the crossroads of the university, church and society -- Part 2. At the crossroads of University and church. More room for theology in the church? A critical-empathetic reading of Theology Today; The swan or the dove? On the difficult dialoque between theology and philosophy; Mutual interruption: towards a productive tension between theology and religious studies -- Part 3. Theology and society: the issue of Catholic identity. Catholic identity in a post-Christian and post-secular society: four models and a roadmap; Qualitative pluralism as a hallmark of the Catholic dialogue school; Catholic religious education: still plausible today?

Subjects   Catholic Church--Theology.
Theology--21st century.
Dialogue--Religious aspects--Catholic Church.
Education, Higher--Religious aspects--Catholic Church.
Christianity and culture.
Catholics--Religious identity.
Church renewal--Catholic Church.

Notes   "This book is a slightly modified English translation of Theologie in dialoog: op het kruitspunt van universiteit, kerk en samenleving: over dialoog, verschil en katholieke identiteit (Kalmthout: Pelckmans, 2014)"--Page [235].
Translated from the Dutch.
Includes bibliographical references and index.

Theology Made In Dignity: on the precarious role of theology in religious education.
LCCN   2017301399
Type of material   Book
Personal name   ROEBBEN, B.

Main title	THEOLOGY MADE IN DIGNITY: on the precarious role of theology in religious education.
Published/Created	[Place of publication not identified]: PEETERS Publishers, 2016.
Description	p. cm.
ISBN	9042934166 9789042934160
Summary	In a post-secular society contemporaries are challenged to raise and face existential questions in the midst of a plurality of (religious and non-religious) worldviews. Children, adolescents and young adults are especially eager for orientation in negotiating this plurality. Religious Education in European schools can provide them with solid insights and a safe space to accept this challenge. In this book the narrative, communicative and spiritual dimensions of religious education are discussed. In the act of theologizing with children, adolescents and young adults, "in each other?s presence" and with a view to wisdom traditions, they are empowered to patiently engage in new ways. Alternative patterns of framing identity and community, experience and interpretation, transcendence and immanence, can then emerge. The book is rooted in the teaching praxis of the author and reaches out to the centers of initial teacher education, where future leaders learn to discover the theological dignity of religious education.
Subjects	Religious education--Europe. Religious pluralism--Europe.

Values, human rights and religious education: contested grounds
LCCN	2018941687

Type of material	Book
Personal name	Astley, Jeff.
Main title	Values, human rights and religious education: contested grounds / Jeff Astley, Leslie Francis, David Lankshear.
Published/Produced	New York, NY: Peter Lang, 2018.
ISBN	9781788745253 (alk. paper)
Series	Religion, education and values; 14

Waiting here for you: an Advent journey of hope

LCCN	2016301898
Type of material	Book
Personal name	Giglio, Louie.
Main title	Waiting here for you: an Advent journey of hope / Louis Giglio.
Published/Produced	Atlanta, GA: Passion Publishing: Thomas Nelson, [2015] ©2014
Description	111 pages: illustrations; 18 cm
Links	Publisher description https://www.loc.gov/catdir/enhancements/fy1614/2016301898-d.html
ISBN	9780718085087 (softcover) 0718085086
LC classification	BV40 .G53 2015
Variant title	Advent journey of hope
Summary	Advent is a season of expectant waiting and preparation, but to many people it is a season of dread: presents to buy, family gatherings to endure. Giglio takes you on an Advent journey to discover that waiting is not wasting when you're waiting on the Lord. Discover how to find peace for your soul as anticipation leads toward celebration!
Subjects	Advent.

	Advent--Prayers and devotions.
	Worship.
	Religious education.
	Advent.
	Religious education.
	Worship.
Form/Genre	Prayers and devotions.

We need to talk about religious education: manifestos for the future of RE

LCCN	2017022503
Type of material	Book
Main title	We need to talk about religious education: manifestos for the future of RE / edited by Mike Castelli, Mark Chater.
Published/Produced	London; Philadelphia: Jessica Kingsley Publishers, 2018.
Description	264 pages; 23 cm
ISBN	9781785922695
LC classification	BL42.5.G7 W4 2018
Variant title	We need to talk about Religious Education
Related names	Mike Castelli, editor.
Subjects	Religious education--Great Britain.
Notes	Includes bibliographical references and indexes.

What is a madrasa?

LCCN	2014034904
Type of material	Book
Personal name	Moosa, Ebrahim.
Main title	What is a madrasa? / Ebrahim Moosa.
Published/Produced	Chapel Hill: The University of North Carolina Press, [2015]
Description	290 pages: illustrations; 25 cm.
ISBN	9781469620138 (cloth: alk. paper)

	9781469620145 (ebook)
LC classification	LC904 .M66 2015
Subjects	Madrasahs.
	Islamic education.
	Islamic religious education.
Notes	Includes bibliographical references and index.
Series	Islamic civilization and Muslim networks

RELATED NOVA PUBLICATIONS

THE IMPACT OF CULTURE ON PALLIATIVE CARE PRACTICE AND APPLICATION: RELIGIOUS BELIEFS, EDUCATION AND SOCIOECONOMIC STATUS[*]

Esmat A Hassan[†], *PhD*

Division of Agric. & Biological Research, National Research Centre,
Dokki, Giza, Egypt

A preliminary study on palliative care practice and application was carried out in Egypt. The study depended on an on the spot direct contact and discussion with the individual patients who faced dealing with cancer, their families and social surroundings. By questioning palliative care acceptance, availability and needs, the study aimed at reaching significant

---

[*] The full version of this chapter can be found in *Palliative Care: Volume 2, The Role and Importance of Research in Promoting Palliative Care Practice: Methods and Outcomes*, edited by Michael Silbermann, published by Nova Science Publishers, Inc, New York, 2019.
[†] Corresponding Author's E-mail: esmat_hassan@yahoo.com.

conclusions thereby suggesting recommendations. The study revealed the following observations:

The service provided would be regardless of the level of education, economic status, deep rooted beliefs or inherited traditions which govern and control behavior toward palliative care..

1. When it appeared that an acceptance of the service would be made possible, the gender of the person performing the service was questioned. Also the cost of the service was a constant factor.
2. The younger individuals, though belonging to very conservative families, were more open to receiving such a service.

From the study, it appears that palliative care offered to adults, either in hospital, or at home, is absent. From the observations it was concluded that certain recommendations were made to assist families subjected to facing cancer and to answer the questions raised briefly as to: How, Where Who and the Cost of undergoing the treatment.

RELIGIOUS EDUCATION AT PUBLIC SCHOOLS IN GEORGIA[*]

Levan Mateshvili[†], PhD
Professor at GTU, Tbilisi, Georgia

Religious education at public schools in Georgia is discussed in this work. Current condition of religious education in Georgia is described and

---

[*] The full version of this chapter can be found in *Information and Computer Technology, Modeling and Control: Proceedings of the International Scientific Conference Devoted to the 85th Anniversary of Academician I. V. Prangishvili*, edited by Ivane Gorgidze, Tamar Lominadze, Maka Khartishvili and Ketevan Makhashvili, published by Nova Science Publishers, Inc, New York, 2017.
[†] Corresponding Author's E-mail: mamalevani@bk.ru.

analyzed including its juridical aspect. The issues of religious education in European countries are also described.

New demands and responsibilities arose from the point of view of creating democratic institutions and respecting the principles of human rights.

In parallel to developments, integration of religious education in school curricular became a topical, but at the same time a disputable and acute issue. In the view of above, it would be reasonable and valuable to make brief analysis of this issue and bring comparison of attitudes, principles and practice in European countries.

We should not forget historical past of the Georgian nation famous for its tolerance towards other religions and in confirmation to this bring an example that Orthodox Christians, Monophysites, Muslims and Jews have been living side by side for many centuries in the territory of Georgia.

CHALLENGES AND PERSPECTIVES OF TEACHING MUSLIM RELIGIOUS EDUCATION IN THE 21ST CENTURY[*]

Adil Mamodaly
Montreal, Canada

As political and religious tensions continue to rise globally, and the frequency and scale of terrorism proliferates, incendiary defamations about Islam and Muslims further deepen the divide between the Muslim and Judeo-Christian worlds. Arguably, it can be said that acts of violence are not representative of any religious tradition and are instead politically and economically motivated. Nevertheless, they continue to be portrayed

---

[*] The full version of this chapter can be found in *Islam: Global Issues, Challenges and Perspectives of the 21st Century*, edited by Doreen Peters, published by Nova Science Publishers, Inc, New York, 2016.

through a religious rhetoric. One might wonder, therefore, how religious educators, and Muslim educators in particular, address these issues in their classrooms. Are they prepared to engage with such topics? What are their challenges? Can a prodigious religious education be the panacea for the violence taking place in numerous countries? As religious educators, what might be our end goal and how are we to achieve it? The term religious education itself can be defined broadly and at times contentiously. For example, whether students should learn about or from religion, or both. Equally important, is to consider pedagogical approaches to teaching Muslim religious education and whether nurturing a 'sense of belonging' can have a greater impact on developing students' identity. To teach religion in the 21st century is by no means an easy feat and one which requires greater dialogue amongst all educators be they public school teachers, community based religious educators or curriculum writers.

This small scale qualitative study is approached through the methodology of narrative inquiry with a phenomenological orientation. Ten Muslim educators across Canada, France, UK and the USA participated in the study. The chapter will analyse and discuss the challenges and perspectives of teaching Muslim religious education in 21st century western contexts through teacher narratives. Emergent themes from their narratives have been structured as such: (1) Teachers and Students: A Glimpse into Life World and Lived Experience (2) The Influence of Media on Teachers and Students (3) Perspectives on (Muslim) Religious Education (4) Pedagogical Approaches and Teacher Preparedness (5) Creating a Sense of Belonging through Spaces of Contemplation. Through this study we aim to have a better understanding of the complexities associated with teaching Muslim religious education and offer key considerations. Implicitly, the chapter will engage in a discussion of the current socio-political landscape to situate the context in which this study has taken place. The author will conclude with recommendations for further research and possibilities for teacher education programs.

INDEX

#

20th century, 5, 83, 143, 152, 153, 211, 212, 255, 258, 259
21st century, 59, 81, 82, 98, 126, 147, 175, 220, 255, 259, 266, 274

A

academic tasks, 68
acquisition of knowledge, 249
action research, 13, 68
adolescents, 9, 267
adulthood, 171
adults, 161, 267, 272
age, 13, 34, 105, 127, 152, 242
assessment, 90, 103, 106, 113, 166, 205, 225, 243, 244, 259, 260, 261, 262, 265
attitudes, vii, 1, 61, 198, 202, 239, 273
autonomy, viii, 20, 22, 24, 44, 45, 97, 105, 183, 261

B

Balkan territories, 145
Balkans, 132, 143, 144
belief systems, 140, 142, 228
Bible, 121, 136, 137, 138, 139, 141, 142, 158, 159, 215, 217, 220, 229, 230, 231
Britain, 133, 134, 158, 185, 198, 203, 242
Buddhism, 110, 140, 141, 142, 167, 175, 205
bureaucratization, 175
business ethics, 74
businesses, 59, 68

C

Catholic Church, 57, 99, 116, 160, 166, 200, 201, 203, 246, 265, 266
Catholic school, 160, 188, 201, 202, 203, 265
Catholics, 266
challenges, ix, 3, 55, 67, 71, 86, 87, 88, 154, 171, 174, 228, 274
child development, 6
childhood, 112, 231
children, vii, viii, 3, 12, 19, 22, 24, 27, 29, 30, 32, 33, 34, 35, 36, 37, 38, 39, 40, 41, 77, 78, 82, 83, 100, 128, 129, 131, 137, 139, 141, 143, 148, 150, 151, 154, 155,

159, 161, 162, 169, 173, 176, 177, 185, 187, 198, 202, 228, 232, 237, 267
Christian spirituality, v, vii, ix, 55, 56, 57, 60, 61, 62, 63, 64, 65, 66, 70, 71, 72, 74, 75
Christianity, 57, 64, 73, 74, 85, 86, 122, 126, 129, 130, 140, 141, 142, 146, 148, 151, 154, 175, 179, 181, 189, 191, 199, 200, 205, 243, 262, 263, 266
Christians, 73, 209, 273
citizens, 23, 134, 173, 224
citizenship, 83, 88, 130, 132, 173, 174, 185, 197, 199, 244
civil rights, 183, 214
civil society, 132, 220, 254, 257
classroom, 6, 24, 44, 90, 102, 103, 113, 180, 184, 204, 225, 226, 227, 228
classroom management, 6
colleges, 120, 121, 122, 247, 248, 251, 252
community, vii, viii, 7, 12, 13, 19, 20, 21, 23, 25, 27, 28, 31, 35, 37, 38, 41, 42, 43, 45, 51, 53, 65, 71, 84, 85, 91, 93, 101, 128, 137, 152, 174, 178, 208, 224, 236, 261, 267, 274
community identity, viii, 19, 20, 25, 43, 46
conception, viii, 2, 3, 4, 5, 6, 11, 13, 15, 167
conflict, 23, 45, 95, 99, 105, 197, 239, 240, 249
cooperation, 37, 42, 104, 130, 154
creative teaching, 228
creative thinking, 228
creativity, 11, 197, 228
critical analysis, 134
critical thinking, 59, 199, 200
criticism, 172, 206, 217, 263
cultural clash, 236
cultural heritage, 106, 126
cultural influence, 216
cultural memory, 165
cultural transformation, 65

culture, 21, 25, 51, 58, 67, 94, 105, 120, 121, 126, 165, 167, 173, 215, 216, 230, 243, 249, 253, 256, 260, 262, 266
curricula, 22, 45, 239, 260, 261
curriculum, viii, 2, 3, 8, 9, 11, 12, 23, 37, 45, 58, 70, 90, 118, 119, 144, 184, 193, 195, 196, 209, 228, 259, 261, 274
curriculum development, viii, 2

D

delegitimization, 29
democracy, 123, 244, 254, 257
distance learning, 159
diversity, 42, 56, 65, 68, 105, 111, 166, 185, 187, 193, 198, 204, 207, 211, 223, 227, 229

E

ecological edge, 20, 21, 28, 42, 45
ecological systems, viii, 19, 53
Ecological Systems' Theory, 24
economic growth, 260
economic status, 239, 240, 272
educational institutions, 67
educational opportunities, 112
educational policy, 194, 261
educational process, vii, viii, 19, 24
educational research, 9
educational system, viii, 20, 22, 23, 27, 34, 41, 43, 45, 53, 143
educators, 2, 3, 9, 34, 73, 160, 161, 193, 215, 274
elementary school, 185
England, 89, 129, 171, 178, 179, 205, 206
environment, 20, 23, 24, 25, 26, 28, 30, 32, 33, 41, 43, 112, 241, 254, 257
epistemology, 197, 200, 201, 249
equality, 38, 180, 188, 233

ethics, 98, 103, 113, 136, 137, 138, 139, 197
ethnicity, 126
ethnographic approach, 25
ethnographic study, vii, viii, 19, 249
Europe, 57, 73, 83, 103, 104, 106, 115, 131, 144, 150, 151, 152, 157, 168, 199, 211, 234, 267
European Union, 105, 155, 188
exclusion, viii, 20, 30, 31, 39, 42, 43, 44, 80

F

faith, viii, 2, 7, 40, 56, 57, 65, 67, 71, 73, 87, 88, 101, 119, 120, 123, 128, 134, 136, 137, 139, 158, 159, 165, 166, 168, 169, 173, 177, 181, 188, 205, 232, 241, 242, 263
families, vii, viii, 19, 22, 23, 39, 40, 151, 198, 271, 272
family life, 91, 93, 150
financial, 59, 145, 146, 252
foreign affairs, 97
foreign policy, 95, 255, 258
formal reasoning, 8
formation, ix, 2, 20, 21, 28, 59, 126, 166, 180, 208, 224, 246
foundations, 67, 70, 117, 119, 167, 173
France, 151, 183, 235, 274
freedom, 105, 120, 154, 180, 187, 188, 218, 232, 236, 261
friendship, 63, 70

G

Georgia, 186, 187, 272, 273
Germany, 83, 132, 151, 182, 244
glorification, viii, 20, 31, 42, 43, 44
God, 7, 8, 9, 14, 60, 61, 62, 63, 64, 65, 67, 68, 69, 71, 72, 116, 139, 145, 162, 176, 202, 208, 217, 221, 242, 265

Great Britain, 90, 103, 114, 135, 147, 158, 185, 199, 203, 206, 226, 227, 242, 269

H

Halachah, 21, 29, 30, 31, 33, 40, 42, 47, 52
health, 233, 239, 255, 258
hegemony, 20, 28, 29, 30, 31, 38, 42, 46
higher education, 18, 56, 58, 60, 67, 69, 71, 72, 73, 74, 75, 76, 119, 120, 135, 188, 225, 229, 250, 251, 252
history, 7, 11, 20, 57, 88, 92, 93, 95, 97, 107, 109, 120, 126, 127, 129, 143, 159, 179, 183, 191, 192, 206, 208, 211, 212, 214, 218, 219, 236, 253, 256, 260, 263, 265
human, 4, 56, 59, 60, 61, 62, 63, 67, 68, 86, 96, 104, 105, 107, 164, 178, 180, 188, 199, 215, 225, 267, 273
human existence, 61
human experience, 67, 215
human right, 104, 105, 107, 178, 180, 188, 199, 267, 273

I

identity, viii, 2, 19, 20, 21, 23, 24, 25, 26, 28, 29, 30, 31, 32, 35, 36, 37, 38, 39, 40, 41, 42, 43, 44, 45, 51, 74, 91, 92, 99, 105, 109, 121, 124, 126, 150, 165, 166, 174, 188, 209, 217, 255, 258, 264, 265, 266, 267, 274
illusory multi-identities pattern, 37, 41, 44
India, 211, 238, 239, 240
individuals, 2, 10, 24, 204, 215, 272
Indonesia, 175, 203, 204, 211
inequality, 27, 169, 188, 239
institutions, 22, 42, 43, 44, 56, 58, 68, 96, 105, 109, 120, 121, 144, 145, 163, 209, 248, 253, 254, 256, 257, 273

integration, 23, 42, 62, 71, 112, 183, 273
Iran, 117, 118, 119, 175, 255, 258
Islam, 87, 88, 89, 101, 103, 115, 130, 132, 133, 134, 135, 140, 141, 142, 148, 150, 152, 168, 182, 184, 205, 238, 249, 250, 252, 254, 257, 262, 273
Islamabad, 93, 149
Islamic law, 107
Islamic religious education, 78, 94, 101, 115, 118, 119, 131, 133, 135, 145, 149, 152, 158, 169, 239, 250, 252, 269
Islamophobia, 181
Israel, v, vii, viii, 1, 16, 17, 19, 20, 22, 23, 34, 44, 46, 48, 49, 51, 52, 53, 75, 168, 171, 208, 219, 220, 235, 243, 244

J

Jews, 20, 23, 36, 46, 47, 48, 50, 85, 92, 93, 156, 157, 159, 171, 209, 236, 237, 273

K

kindergarten, v, viii, 19, 20, 24, 25, 26, 28, 29, 30, 31, 32, 33, 34, 35, 36, 37, 38, 39, 40, 41, 42, 43, 44, 45, 48, 50, 51, 52, 53, 155
knowledge, vii, 1, 2, 3, 4, 5, 6, 7, 8, 9, 10, 11, 12, 13, 14, 15, 16, 17, 56, 58, 64, 96, 117, 118, 119, 120, 133, 144, 152, 187, 189, 194, 205, 225, 242, 249

L

leadership, 11, 21, 47, 67, 73, 98, 99, 116, 137, 146, 261
learners, 9, 13, 37, 73, 91, 92, 113, 190, 192, 226, 260, 261
learning, vii, ix, 7, 8, 9, 10, 11, 12, 14, 55, 56, 67, 68, 69, 70, 73, 90, 91, 92, 93, 113, 117, 118, 119, 134, 144, 153, 154, 156, 159, 166, 167, 184, 189, 191, 204, 205, 223, 224, 225, 228, 242, 248, 249, 250, 260
learning activity, 70
learning outcomes, 261
learning styles, 11
lesson plan, 24, 26, 83, 136, 137, 138, 140
level of education, 44, 59, 272
liberal education, 194
liberal states, 219

M

memory, 4, 9, 69, 124, 163, 164
Middle East, 101, 132, 255, 258
minorities, 106, 235, 244, 255, 258
mission, 23, 36, 58, 59, 63, 101, 135, 145, 160, 218
Modern Orthodox, viii, 19, 20, 22, 24, 28, 33, 41
modernity, 87, 88, 152, 262
modernization, 156, 157
Moses, 27, 50, 86, 137, 208
music, 8, 21, 64, 68, 138, 139, 214, 216, 217, 229, 230, 231
Muslims, 87, 88, 131, 132, 133, 134, 149, 150, 158, 183, 244, 273

N

narratives, 70, 134, 184, 226, 274
national identity, 125
natural evolution, 58
Nigeria, 84, 85, 86, 87, 147, 148, 168, 169, 170

O

opportunities, ix, 55, 57, 58, 60

Ottoman period, 145

P

Pakistan, 94, 127, 148, 149, 238, 239, 252
parents, 22, 24, 26, 29, 30, 32, 33, 35, 36, 37, 38, 40, 41, 42, 148, 176, 187, 202
participant observation, 12, 26, 66
participants, 12, 13, 27
pattern of respect, viii, 20, 32, 42, 43
peace, 65, 85, 125, 127, 168, 254, 258, 268
peace process, 254, 258
pedagogy, 11, 15, 17, 24, 29, 32, 38, 51, 53, 103, 154, 168, 173, 190, 192, 202, 222, 227, 259, 260, 261
personal relationship, 63, 64
physical environment, 26
physical structure, 23
pluralism, 41, 44, 45, 73, 127, 135, 175, 178, 180, 199, 229, 242, 266, 267
pluralist society, 202, 203
Polanyi, vii, 1, 2, 3, 4, 5, 6, 8, 9, 10, 13, 16
policy, 44, 105, 111, 112, 188, 242, 244, 254, 255, 257, 259, 261
policymakers, 261
political parties, 96, 236
politics, 95, 101, 104, 120, 152, 156, 188, 207, 209, 210, 211, 217, 230, 236, 238, 242, 243, 253, 254, 256, 257, 259
population, 27, 32, 35, 41, 43, 45, 53, 177
portraits, 79, 160, 161
poverty, 168, 169
practical, viii, 2, 4, 5, 6, 11, 12, 13, 14, 15, 16, 17, 60, 87, 88, 112, 113, 140, 142, 146, 170, 195, 196, 241, 245
practical knowledge, viii, 2, 5, 6, 11, 12, 13
practical wisdom, 146
prayer, 2, 11, 21, 38, 66, 68, 69, 71, 169
primary school, 155, 185, 188, 202, 229
principles, 7, 45, 57, 157, 180, 190, 192, 221, 224, 273

probability sampling, 27
procedural knowledge, vii, 1
professional development, 66, 69
public education, 112, 123, 150, 168, 173, 198
public interest, 58
public life, 56, 180
public schools, 111, 123, 150, 173, 184, 185, 187, 188, 196, 197, 198, 205, 220, 237, 242, 272

Q

qualitative research, 12, 17, 26, 46, 51

R

reading, 38, 67, 94, 242, 265
realism, 87, 88, 89, 194, 195, 199, 200, 201
reality, 6, 15, 23, 24, 39, 41, 44, 58, 60, 61, 194, 223
religious beliefs, 20, 60, 150, 232
religious hegemony, 20, 28, 29, 30, 31, 38
religious identity, viii, 20, 21, 28, 29, 31, 32, 35, 37, 39, 40, 42, 43, 53, 127, 234
religious identity categories, 35, 40
Religious State School Education System (RSES), 20, 22, 23, 24, 25, 26, 27, 28, 31, 34, 35, 36, 37, 39, 41, 42, 43, 44, 45, 48, 49, 50, 51, 52, 53
religious traditions, 56, 65, 71
Religious Zionism, 27, 28, 29, 30, 31, 32, 33, 38, 39, 40, 41, 42, 48, 50, 51, 53
researchers, 3, 6, 12, 13, 143, 202, 226, 227, 242
rights, 41, 78, 82, 97, 105, 107, 112, 166, 168, 175, 181, 187, 188, 227, 243, 255, 258, 259

S

scholarship, 155, 156, 181
school, 11, 17, 22, 23, 25, 36, 44, 57, 78, 79, 80, 108, 112, 120, 123, 139, 146, 147, 150, 155, 156, 157, 158, 168, 170, 174, 187, 188, 197, 198, 202, 203, 204, 236, 237, 241, 242, 244, 249, 261, 266, 267, 273, 274
school culture, 17
schooling, 114, 115, 152, 158, 169, 188, 244
science, 5, 10, 58, 71, 95, 103, 107, 120, 239, 240
scientific knowledge, 13
secular identity, viii, 20, 23, 28, 29, 30, 31, 32, 41, 42, 43, 44
secularism, 108, 175, 187, 188, 211, 254, 257
security, 56, 79, 86, 106, 169, 254, 257
social justice, 2, 64, 189, 263, 264
society, 23, 59, 64, 69, 85, 104, 121, 134, 150, 154, 157, 167, 169, 185, 193, 204, 206, 211, 215, 218, 223, 241, 242, 243, 253, 255, 256, 258, 264, 265, 267
sociology, 95, 212, 240, 242
South Africa, 72, 189
South Asia, 211, 212, 239
Southeast Asia, 144, 175, 210, 211, 212
spiritual, viii, 2, 6, 7, 8, 9, 10, 11, 13, 14, 15, 16, 56, 57, 61, 62, 63, 64, 65, 66, 67, 68, 69, 70, 71, 73, 99, 113, 114, 128, 129, 160, 169, 173, 216, 224, 226, 229, 267
spiritual care, 224
spirituality, vii, ix, 2, 7, 55, 56, 57, 60, 61, 62, 63, 64, 65, 70, 71, 72, 73, 75, 168, 173, 195, 207
state religious education system, vii, viii, 19
state schools, 22
Supreme Court, 180, 182, 233, 236, 237

T

tacit, v, vii, 1, 2, 3, 5, 6, 7, 8, 9, 11, 12, 13, 14, 15, 16
teacher preparation, viii, 2, 11
teacher training, 6, 53
teachers, viii, 2, 3, 4, 5, 6, 8, 9, 10, 11, 12, 13, 14, 17, 20, 22, 26, 28, 30, 31, 33, 34, 44, 59, 65, 67, 69, 70, 71, 78, 88, 112, 114, 140, 142, 187, 202, 205, 227, 228, 231, 260, 261, 274
teaching, vii, viii, 2, 3, 6, 11, 13, 14, 15, 17, 24, 33, 38, 39, 59, 70, 73, 75, 83, 84, 86, 90, 92, 93, 103, 107, 111, 113, 114, 115, 132, 134, 135, 136, 137, 138, 139, 140, 147, 153, 154, 159, 160, 184, 189, 191, 197, 198, 202, 204, 205, 209, 213, 215, 217, 220, 221, 222, 223, 224, 225, 226, 227, 228, 229, 243, 250, 251, 261, 267, 273, 274
Tibet, 109, 110
traditions, 57, 64, 65, 91, 92, 128, 140, 141, 142, 156, 160, 189, 191, 242, 267, 272
transcendence, 62, 63, 66, 71, 267
transformation, 63, 64, 72, 255, 258, 262
transformations, 44, 60, 126, 163, 211
Turkey, 144, 145, 174, 243, 244, 253, 254, 255, 256, 257, 258, 259
turning-a-blind-eye pedagogy, 32

U

United Kingdom, 158, 168, 170, 210, 232
United States, 95, 97, 98, 100, 112, 120, 121, 122, 123, 124, 148, 182, 183, 188, 209, 210, 211, 215, 217, 218, 220, 233, 234, 235, 237, 238, 247, 248, 251, 252
Universal Declaration of Human Rights, 107

universities, ix, 55, 56, 58, 59, 60, 62, 66, 68, 69, 71, 73, 74, 120, 122
university, vii, ix, 1, 3, 13, 14, 16, 17, 20, 46, 47, 48, 50, 52, 55, 56, 57, 58, 59, 60, 63, 65, 66, 67, 68, 69, 70, 71, 72, 73, 74, 75, 94, 100, 101, 109, 110, 111, 120, 123, 125, 131, 132, 133, 149, 152, 153, 162, 168, 170, 174, 176, 179, 207, 210, 219, 221, 222, 232, 239, 246, 247, 248, 251, 252, 262, 264, 265, 269
university education, 66

V

violence, 40, 84, 85, 169, 182, 273

vision, 58, 98, 116, 125, 242
vocational training, 59

W

work environment, 71
workforce, 67
workplace, 73
worldview, 74, 154, 184

Y

young adults, 267
young people, 2, 3, 9, 13, 59, 88, 89, 120, 174, 198